Moral Foundations of Management Knowledge

In Memoriam: Professor Robert C. Solomon

Moral Foundations of Management Knowledge

Edited by

Marie-Laure Djelic and Radu Vranceanu

ESSEC Business School, Cergy, France

Edward Elgar
Cheltenham, UK • Northampton, MA, USA

Published by
Edward Elgar Publishing Limited
Glensanda House
Montpellier Parade
Cheltenham
Glos GL50 1UA
UK

Edward Elgar Publishing, Inc.
William Pratt House
9 Dewey Court
Northampton
Massachusetts 01060
USA

A catalogue record for this book is available from the British Library

Library of Congress Cataloguing in Publication Data
Moral foundations of management knowledge / edited by Marie-Laure Djelic and
Radu Vranceanu.
   p. cm.
  "A selection of the most relevant papers presented at the 'Workshop on
Moral Foundations of Management Knowledge: Opening the Black Box.' This
Workshop was organized in Cergy-Pontoise, France, in October 2006 by EIASM
(European Institute for Advanced Studies in Management) and ESSEC Business
School"—P.   .
  Includes bibliographical references and index.
  1. Management—Philosophy—Congresses. 2. Economics—Moral and ethical
aspects—Congresses. 3. Management—Moral and ethical aspects—Congresses.
4. Leadership—Moral and ethical aspects—Congresses. 5. Business
ethics—Congresses. I. Djelic, Marie-Laure. II. Vranceanu, Radu, 1961–
  HD29.M667 2007
  174'.4—dc22
                       2007029857

ISBN 978 1 84720 477 6 (cased)

Printed and bound in Great Britain by MPG Books Ltd, Bodmin, Cornwall

Contents

Contributors

Antonio Argandoña, Professor, Chair of Economics and Ethics, IESE Business School, University of Navarra, Barcelona, Spain.

Laurent Bibard, Professor, Department of Management, ESSEC Business School, Cergy, France.

Mircea Boari, Researcher, FreeTh&Ent Group, Bucharest, Romania, and Visiting Professor, ESSEC Business School, Cergy, France.

Evandro Bocatto, Professor, University Rovira i Virgili, Tarragona, Spain.

Annick Bourguignon, Professor, Department of Accounting and Management Control, ESSEC Business School, Cergy, France.

Lucia Crevani, Researcher, KTH – Royal Institute of Technology, School of Industrial Engineering and Management, Stockholm, Sweden.

Richard Déry, Professor, Department of Management, HEC Montréal, Montréal, Canada.

Marie-Laure Djelic, Professor, Department of Management, ESSEC Business School, Cergy, France.

Kathryn Gordon, Researcher, OECD, Paris, France.

Monica Lindgren, Researcher, KTH – Royal Institute of Technology, School of Industrial Engineering and Management, Stockholm, Sweden.

Chantale Mailhot, Professor, Department of Management, HEC Montréal, Montreal, Canada.

Mary Miller, Researcher, OCMS, Oxford, United Kingdom.

Sara Louise Muhr, PhD Candidate, University of Southern Denmark, Copenhagen, Denmark.

Johann Packendorff, Researcher, KTH – Royal Institute of Technology, School of Industrial Engineering and Management, Stockholm, Sweden.

Eloisa Perez de Toledo, Professor, University Rovira i Virgili, Tarragona, Spain.

Véronique Schaeffer, Associate Professor, University Louis Pasteur, and Researcher, BETA, Strasbourg, France.

Raymond-Alain Thietart, Professor, Department of Management, ESSEC Business School, Cergy, France, and Emeritus Professor, University Paris-Dauphine, Paris, France.

Radu Vranceanu, Professor, Department of Economics, ESSEC Business School, Cergy, France

Gilles van Wijk, Associate Professor, Department of Management, ESSEC Business School, Cergy, France.

Acknowledgments

The chapters in this book are a selection of the most relevant papers presented at the *Workshop on Moral Foundations of Management Knowledge: Opening the Black Box*. This workshop was organized in Cergy-Pontoise, France, in October 2006 by EIASM (European Institute for Advanced Studies in Management) and ESSEC Business School. Robert C. Solomon, Quincy Lee Centennial Professor of Philosophy and Business at the University of Texas at Austin, had accepted to be the Keynote Speaker at that Workshop. Born in 1942, Professor Solomon was one of the most distinguished American scholars in continental philosophy. His writings on Nietzsche and other Existentialist philosophers were legendary. He also brought a major contribution to the emergence and institutionalization of business ethics as an autonomous field of research. His famous book, *Ethics and Excellence*, published in 1993, has become the major reference for the virtue-based perspective on business ethics. This workshop was probably one of the last scientific events attended by Professor Robert C. Solomon. He passed away in January 2007. We will all remember his kindness, his sharp mind but also his deeply humanist vision on society. We collectively feel very privileged to have had the chance to be exposed to his critical perspective and reading of business ethics. We therefore wish to dedicate this volume to Professor Robert C. Solomon, *in memoriam*.

Many people contributed to the success of the workshop and we would like to thank them all. At ESSEC, Dean Pierre Tapie was from the start extremely supportive of the project – both intellectually and materially. All participants at the meeting, some of whom are contributors to this volume, should be thanked for highly fruitful and enriching debates and discussions in a highly collegial atmosphere. At the EIASM, Professor Bruce Kogut, who was then Director of the Scientific Committee, was an early advocate and endorsed the project rapidly. We want to express our deep gratitude for his support. Also at EIASM, Audrey O'Connor played a key structuring and organizing role. At ESSEC, Odile Sirette and Alison Bougi made sure that nothing was left to chance, logistically speaking. We would finally like to thank the team at Edward Elgar – Francine O'Sullivan, Ben Booth and Jo Betteridge – for their support and diligence as well as three anonymous reviewers for helpful comments and suggestions.

Introduction

Marie-Laure Djelic and Radu Vranceanu

For some time, a complex stream of more or less directly related confidence crises and corporate scandals has been confronting managerial practice. This, naturally, was bound to have a ripple effect on the communities producing and diffusing management knowledge. In particular, the global community of business schools and business academics has had to ponder and confront its role and responsibilities in those scandals and crises.

A first reaction was to develop and generalize the teaching of business ethics in business programmes and business schools. Business ethics courses were built with the objective to apprehend a key question: 'what is good managerial behaviour?' Those modules could go one step further to explore how societies or collectives allow and encourage (or not) the emergence of more sustainable behaviours and systems in particular by deploying adequate norms, incentives and regulative frames.

This, however, is only a beginning. If new generations of leaders are to be trained with a more responsible and sustainable take on their own role and activities, then the preoccupation for ethical questions should not be confined to a small number of specific courses or sets of courses. Rather, ethical preoccupations and a sense of responsibility should infuse the curricula of all business schools and business programmes across the world. This naturally means that, as academics and researchers, we need to take a hard look at the ways in which management knowledge and management research incorporate ethical issues.

Modern management thought is a broad umbrella that encompasses several specialized subfields such as accounting, control, finance, human resources management, organizational behaviour, strategy, marketing, operations management, information systems. Management thought and knowledge in their various expressions build upon and nourish themselves from a number of social sciences – in particular economics, sociology and psychology. The principal goal of this book is to raise the question of ethical or moral foundations. Which ethical and moral principles structure the bodies of knowledge that nourish and/or comprise management thought?

Ethical and moral principles tend to become, through time, deeply embedded if not buried or hidden in intellectual and disciplinary subfields, particularly when the latter vie for scientific status. In the process, they often become invisible or indecipherable both to those who advance and diffuse knowledge and to those who receive, interpret and apply it. We explore a set of related issues in this volume all bearing upon the complex question of ethical and moral foundations. What is (are) the definition(s) of 'good behaviour' – and hence 'bad behaviour' – implicit behind the various subfields of management thought? What are the moral or ethical dilemmas and debates that have historically shaped those intellectual subfields even if they since then have faded or been forgotten? What is the conception of human nature and social reality embedded in modern management thought and theories? How do those implicit and hidden cognitive schemes influence the development of research and knowledge in those various subfields? How do they prevent certain issues from emerging? How do they shape debates, practices and beliefs – leaving little room to approach the world differently and to depart from mainstream perspectives?

By suggesting answers to these questions and paths to explore further, this book makes a valuable contribution to contemporary debates on sustainability and responsibility in management practice and knowledge. In this foreword, we start from a definition of ethical or moral foundations that is quite encompassing. We take the two terms to reflect and point to the same thing – that is the broad principles or standards of right or wrong framing a particular theory and associated practices. Such a broad definition makes it possible to accommodate a fair degree of diversity in the different contributions to this volume. The base is common but the reader will see that contributions differ significantly when it comes to further specification of the definition. In particular, there are quite different views as to the ontological nature of ethical or moral principles – whether they are naturally given or historically constructed, whether they are 'all too human' or suggest a 'divine' spark, whether the focus should be on principles of action per se or their consequences. There are also different perspectives on the phenomenological expression of ethical or moral principles – whether or not they can be changed or influenced through rules or laws, whether education and structural constraints are effective mechanisms or whether one can only rely on human 'character' – and hence on extremely early forms of socialization – to ensure that those principles become appropriated.

In spite of those differences, all the authors who have collaborated on this book are in deep agreement on a fundamental premise – management practice and management knowledge are not ethically or morally neutral. Management thought, as a consequence, cannot abstract from discussions and debates on values, ethical goals and moral principles. In fact, all contributions reflect the belief that management practice and management knowledge are deeply rooted in and build upon ethical and moral frames that we need to rediscover, make explicit, explore, debate and discuss. All authors also agree that, in turn, management thought and practice are having an impact upon and shaping in part the broader set of ethical and moral values within society at large. This is particularly strong and striking today when management is taking over and spreading across so many spheres of our everyday lives.

Thus this book departs from a perspective still broadly shared by managers themselves and by many management commentators or scholars who, according to MacIntyre (1981: 74), 'conceive of themselves as morally neutral characters whose skills enable them to devise the most efficient way of achieving whatever end is proposed'. The unrelenting quest for efficiency and productivity bumps into its own limits. In our complex and open world, value-neutrality is a delusion and a dangerous one at that. Managers have to navigate in a world that is not only economic but also political, cultural, shaped by history, ethical and moral traditions and preoccupations. The decontextualized and 'scientifically neutral' tools generally associated with mainstream management knowledge or practice do not appear to be adequate for that. The deep appropriation of cultural, political, ethical and moral debates and questions is not only a mark of social capital for management practitioners and commentators but also, really, a way to enhance managerial skills and daily operational effectiveness if not efficiency. The role of management education and management thought should be to prepare future practitioners and commentators for that complex and multidimensional odyssey.

The book is organized and articulated around four complementary parts. Part I explores the difficult encounter, broadly speaking, between management knowledge and ethical questions or preoccupations. Part II offers a critical analysis of the moral foundations of economics, one of the intellectual pillars of management thought. Part III investigates the moral foundations behind theories of leadership and team management. Part IV, finally, focuses on management systems and the complex interplay therein with ethical and moral issues.

Part I begins with Chapter 1, where Laurent Bibard argues that management knowledge is in the process of acquiring a high level of self-consciousness. This, he argues, is a welcome development. Current changes in management thought and knowledge are strongly driven by globalization and its associated questions. The expression of that is to be found in the preoccupation for sustainable development, corporate social responsibility and business ethics. In that context, business and management cannot pretend any longer to be and remain separate from society and its evolution. Hence, management knowledge increasingly has to integrate interdisciplinary preoccupations and it has to deploy some foundational questioning on ends as well as means. In particular, management knowledge cannot satisfy itself with the quest for efficiency and productivity; it should address and tackle broader societal tensions and their moral implications.

In Chapter 2, Evandro Bocatto and Eloisa Perez de Toledo argue that ethical and moral discussions are still in a pre-paradigmatic stage. Discussing, thus, is arguing viewpoints and, when arguing, the status of axioms is not made explicit. They address this issue suggesting a method that initially incorporates a variety of viewpoints. Afterwards, it invites the arguer to reflect about the various moral foundations and then to choose the moral approach that seems most adequate. The method suggests a procedure that, from symptomatic data – or morality in action – sufficiently deconstructs the sequence of action in a way that the consequential facts are no longer warranted by previous beliefs, but such beliefs are critically examined instead of just being taken for granted.

Kathryn Gordon and Raymond-Alain Thietart in Chapter 3 take a long-term view of the moral foundations of management and management knowledge, a view that stretches back into the distant past to the time when human beings lived as hunter-gatherers in small, durable groups of closely-related individuals. The value of this long-term perspective is that it permits the development of a micro-analytical 'theory' of moral duty and obligation. It sheds light not only on the source of ethical principles but also on sources of obligation; that is, how ethical principles are made to influence individual behaviour in group settings, including the modern business organization.

Part II considers economics and its moral foundations. In Chapter 4, Antonio Argandoña starts from an understanding of economics as a theory of human action. He remarks that the neoclassical paradigm emphasizes those aspects of action that have most to do with choosing between alternative means for achieving specific ends and with its goal, efficiency. This in turn has led to a development that, to a considerable extent, has followed a separate path from that of ethics. The ethical ends must encompass those of economic action, at least as a part of general human conduct. Accordingly, any reflection on the theory of action should be capable of facilitating the reflection of ethics on human conduct. In the same manner, the contributions of ethics should guide rethinking of the economic paradigm of human action. The purpose of this chapter is, precisely, to develop the different aspects of a theory of action that may help us rewrite the basic principles of economics from an ethical viewpoint, and improve our understanding of the nature of ethics from an economic viewpoint.

In Chapter 5, Marie-Laure Djelic emphasizes that 'marketization' is a distinctive feature of the contemporary period of globalization. The term refers both to market ideologies and market-oriented reforms. This chapter considers the ideological and moral 'ground' on which the marketization trend rests with a particular focus on the 'ethics of competition'. This is an exercise in intellectual genealogy. The current movement towards global marketization has to do, historically, with the development of a particular form of capitalism in the United States. Sustaining and reinforcing those structural developments, we find, since the late nineteenth century, a powerful ideological background. American conservatism was then a surprising mixture of classical economic liberalism, Puritan doctrine and Social Darwinism. Through a summary pathway, Marie-Laure Djelic traces the intellectual lineage of contemporary marketization by considering the ethics of competition as they emerge in turn from Adam Smith and early economic liberalism, the Puritan doctrine and Social Darwinism. The chapter ends with a focus on the more recent neoliberal synthesis, symbolized here by the Chicago School.

Mircea Boari provides a sociobiologic analysis of economic morality in Chapter 6. The chapter demonstrates by deductive reasoning based on sociobiological knowledge that the economic principle of rational maximization is intrinsically axiological and ethical. The paper enforces its conclusions with parallels to the history of philosophy whereby, overwhelmingly, virtue is undissociated from reason. The chapter grounds the philosophical ideal of ethical excellence in its material, biological and economic determinants. Rational maximization of self-interest represents the necessary missing link between the infrastructure of human nature and the normative dimension inherent to ethics. An ethics of rationality thus emerges, having economic action as an essential instrumental component.

In Chapter 7, Radu Vranceanu adopts a virtue-ethics perspective to investigate the moral foundations of contemporary economics. He remarks that while the utilitarian approach to morality seems inadequate to account for appropriate human behaviour given the variety and complexity of real-life situations, economics – defined as the science of efficient resource allocation – is often evaluated in the light of this outdated ethical perspective. Radu Vranceanu argues that the moral foundations of contemporary economics and its recommendations can be fitted into the virtue-based definition of ethics. He submits the idea that the model of man underlying economic analyses can match the virtuous person, and that economics, by advocating reasoned choice and careful resource utilization, brings a positive contribution to the moral development of individuals.

Part III turns to theories of leadership and team management. In Chapter 8, Lucia Crevani, Monica Lindgren and Johann Packendorff argue that, within the leadership field, there is an emergent movement towards viewing leadership as the expression of collaboration between two or more persons. This goes against the mainstream in organization theory, where leadership is still seen as the prerogative of a single individual. The idea of unitary command remains alive and strong. The chapter starts with a discussion of the theoretical and moral assumptions behind the unitary command perspective and their consequences – that is, an excessive focus on individuals and a lack of sustainability. Afterwards, the authors argue that all leadership can be seen as processes of interaction between several individuals – by shifting perspective from viewing leadership as a single-person activity to viewing it as collective construction, we can identify new developments of leadership knowledge emphasizing shared leadership and sustainable leadership forms.

In Chapter 9, Mary Miller examines the underlying psychological dimension of love in order to provide an understanding of the moral foundations that frame the theory of transformational leadership. Psychological theories suggest an appropriate definition of love in the organizational context; to wit, love as the 'choice(s) to will the highest good' being conceptually understood within organizational behaviour as 'empathy with action'. Leaders who choose to use this understanding of love as a basis of power create an organizational environment that is non-abusive in the dyad relationship between leader and others. It is being suggested that this kind of theorizing fits the descriptors of transformational leadership. The non-abusive aspect of love as power within an organizational context is one of the aspects necessary in creating an ethical environment.

In Chapter 10, Sara Louise Muhr aims to create awareness of the Levinasian ethical dimensions presupposing creative teamwork. The main argument is that a creative environment is accomplished in the ethical act of facing the Other. Creativity is based on diversity in a team, however diversity is only fully exploited if team members are capable of opening up and responding to what is different from themselves – the Other. Through the ethical response, prejudices and assumptions can be exposed, and team members make themselves vulnerable to questioning and critique. Only through the 'response-able' ethical encounter with the Other – and with respect for his/her otherness – can we hope to build a context where difference is reflected and respected, and where diverse others can learn from each other. The ethical encounter with the Other holds possibilities of transforming the Self – of bringing new things into thought, and thereby serve as a strong foundation for knowledge.

Part IV, finally, turns to management systems. In Chapter 11, Annick Bourguignon points out that management systems are often considered as powerful instruments for dealing with the complexities of today's organizational life and business. Subsequently a significant part of management knowledge focuses on management systems, which are increasingly found in any management sub-field (management control, HRM, and so on). Drawing on the reification framework, the author argues that management systems contribute to reifying the social world, which ultimately can prove detrimental to persons, so that ethics could be at stake in this confrontation.

Gilles van Wijk remarks in Chapter 12 that with the increasing impact of unethical behaviour on human rights, on working life, on small shareholders, and on environment, ethics has become a serious matter of public concern. There is a broad consensus that ethics needs to be restored in business. In practice, this is done by organizing special training in ethics, developing ethics codes, and introducing more stringent legislation. The paradox is that the more something is being done about ethics, the less actual corporate behaviour seems to be impacted. It is argued that a growing awareness and preoccupation for ethics turn the latter into a means rather than leaving it to be an end in itself. Since there is no way to differentiate between actual ethical behaviour and pretence, and since appearing ethical has a number of desirable features, it is rational to instrumentalize ethics in the pursuit of performance. Solving the paradox may require restoring rules and laws to their controlling functions, while ethics returns to be a part of our cultural heritage and a domain of wisdom rather than knowledge.

In Chapter 13, the last chapter, Richard Déry, Chantale Mailhot and Véronique Schaeffer carry out a detailed exploration of the complex relationship between the MBA education and the morality of management. If we should listen to ever persistent rumours, business schools are seemingly besieged from all sides and the enemy is within their walls. Some professors are even prophesizing joyfully the end of the MBA, the mythical programme which nonetheless made them famous. In this context, several authors have presented ethics as the final shield, the ultimate path to redemption which will bring about the rebirth of the programme whose death was announced prematurely. This chapter departs from this approach to readdress the debate on the relevance of the MBA. By studying 293 articles on the MBA which were published since 2000, it demonstrates that ethics could be one political solution among many others and that the MBA is truly the subject of a war of the political worlds where the definition of common good is at stake.

The project to unveil and explore the ethical and moral foundations of management thought and knowledge is clearly an ambitious one. Naturally, this book can only be an early and limited step. But the question is out now and contributions to this volume suggest the necessity and the importance of an intellectual effort over the long run. Further exploration of those issues is warranted and particularly topical. As already argued above, for too many years now the technocratic vision of management, according to which neutrally ethical managers can and should focus only on efficient decision-making, has dominated the debate on 'good' management. The renewed interest in business ethics during the last few years, mainly after the corporate scandals of the late 1990s, revealed and expressed with strength that the quest for efficiency and productivity cannot be abstracted from a reflexion on human values and ethical preoccupations, without putting us at risk of a major breakdown of our systems and institutions.

Since economic or managerial choices imply redistributional trade-offs, management necessarily carries along significant ethical and moral stakes. The definition of the 'good' manager cannot be reduced only to 'performance'; instead it will depend in part upon the idea of 'excellence'. Solomon (1993: 153) defined 'excellence' as indicating 'a sense of mission, a commitment beyond profit potential and the bottom line. It is a word that suggests "doing well" but also "doing good". It is a word that synthesises the demands of the marketplace and the demands of ethics.' While practitioners nowadays seem to internalize more and more this message, management knowledge still puts a heavy weight on the efficiency and performance goals. This book suggests that it is more than high time for management knowledge and management practice to be candid and curious about their ethical or moral foundations but also about their ethical or moral implications.

REFERENCES

MacIntyre, A., (1981), *After Virtue*, London: Duckworth.
Solomon, R. C., (1993), *Ethics and Excellence*, Oxford and New York: Oxford University Press.

PART I

Management Knowledge and Ethical Issues: A
Difficult Encounter

1. Towards a Phenomenology of Management: From Modelling to Day-to-day Moral Sensemaking Cognition

Laurent Bibard

INTRODUCTION

The world in which management moves, and which in turn is transformed by management, has in the last ten years embarked on a radical attack, both theoretical and practical, against contemporary management's nihilism. One practical expression of managerial nihilism is the 'absence of orientation of action': although it is never acknowledged, just as neo-Taylorism is triumphing and confirming certain validities of Taylorism, the belief that firms exist in order to make profits and only to make profits is more active and adhered to than ever – albeit discreetly. The openly expressed, 'politically correct' creed is now that firms should clearly display civic awareness, that they have as much social responsibility as citizens endowed with identity and political status, and that sustainable development concerns everyone, all against a backdrop of a theoretical and practical appreciation of ethics as a driving theme in management and its theories.

The discourse in favour of ethics is not mere rhetoric. It is partly rhetoric, but not exclusively so: if only through the trick of reasoning asserting that even if firms do not believe in ethics, it not only profitable but necessary for them to claim, announce and defend ethical policies – and maybe even to apply them (Petrick and Quinn, 1997), in order to guarantee continued profitability (Ballot, 2005).

This chapter contributes to the theoretical attack on contemporary nihilism in both the theories and practices of management. The argument on the practical level is as follows. Being interwoven with men and women's everyday lives whether they like it or not, management is playing an increasingly important role: it is through management that firms are, or are not, 'ethical'; it is also through management that good decisions are, or are not, made, and it is through management that what is fair and unfair is decided (d'Iribarne, 1993; Boltanski and Thévenot, 1991). More radically, management has a political role in the noble sense of the term, the sense at the origins of all political thought, which debates the question of how humans can be guaranteed a collectively fair life without damaging the legitimate interests of individuals. This political role means that it cannot restrict its dynamics to the fulfilment of private interests, ignoring public affairs, and even in some cases noisily and successfully claiming responsibility for that unconcern (Friedman, 1962). On the other hand, management does not structurally determine the semantic contents of existence: it is not through management that the meaning of action is determined; it is, rather, the 'result' of a certain vectorization of action that pre-exists management, and conditions its affirmation and development. In other words, management is always wrapped in a set of paradigms that began before it – but does not determine these paradigms, unless it is reciprocally in a mirror effect. It thus occupies a central role in political life in the noble sense of the term, if only by the power it conceals, and is always the fruit of vectorized logic, without playing a driving role in the vectorization of that logic. While it is born of others in terms of purpose, it engenders others as a condition for the daily concerns of political life. What management does, and causes to be done, relates to thought of which it is always the heir, although its power ranks it among the sovereigns of thought. A sovereign of thought with no thought is sovereign over nothing, a true nihilist, and a thought aired by a traitor to that thought has nothing sovereign, and is powerlessness and silence. For life in its totality to regain meaning, for management in its everyday motivation to remember what it owes to the thought which always precedes it and serve politics in the strong, noble sense of the term, the link between management and power must be disconnected and management must be restored to its principal duty.

Disconnecting this link requires the development, as far as possible, of a genealogy of morals specific to management – in other words, a deciphering of the presuppositions that have become strangers to management as a way of being for man, in the generic sense of the term. Building on this first step of disconnection, making a theoretical contribution to restoring management to its principal duty will involve returning management to its place of honour among the means of expressing and achieving humanity in the strongest sense, including the ultimate possibility of nihilism which will if possible be neutralized beforehand.

In the first part of this chapter, we examine the sources of the movement through which management comes to life and defines itself; this leads us to examine the emergence of contemporary anthropology which has yet to be understood in the light of Greek anthropology, and its political, epistemological, and moral consequences. We then deduce the consequences of this genealogy, with a nod towards what could represent a provisional morality that can assist humans in a tranquil appropriation of management that for a while forgot the irreducible political meaning that makes life human (Aristotle, 1998).

THE HIDDEN ANTHROPOLOGICAL FOUNDATIONS OF MANAGEMENT

That management exists by differentiating itself from other human activities has become self-evident. That it imposes itself as one of the most important human activities for individual and collective life is no longer in any doubt, and is expressed through the contemporary power of the paradigms manufactured, presupposed, and conveyed in turn by management theories founded on the modern notion of rationality. Behind the term management, on both a practical and theoretical level, lies the cultural inheritance received by Europe and now the whole world from the US. The English-language term management first gained its current importance during the industrialization of the nineteenth and twentieth centuries in the US (Freeman and Soete, 1997; Freeman and Louçã, 2001; Chandler, 1990). Behind management's contemporary ideological (that is, 'cultural') power lies the growing force of US power. This power in turn results from the affirmation, after the pioneers Hobbes and Locke, of the modern values of European moral and political philosophy derived from the Renaissance (Diamond, 1987). Management's current power as an activity and the source of values is rooted in the political revolution of the European Renaissance. Disconnecting the link between management and power in order to restore management to its principal duty first requires explanation of the movement that introduced the moral and political values underlying management, to demonstrate how these values are not as obvious as they may seem.

INTELLECTUAL ORIGINS OF MANAGEMENT AS AN AUTONOMOUS PRAXIS

Transparency and Control

The emergence of European moral and political thought owes a fundamental debt to authors such as Machiavelli and Descartes. One after the other, and in different ways, they contributed to the movement instituting man (in the generic sense of the term), against contemporary authorities, as the centre and the goal – in fact the ultimate value – of life, and therefore of all possible action. Descartes and Machiavelli, along with others, are thus at the origins of humanism, if this 'ism' is understood as the claim to finally make man at home in the world he inhabits. In this sense, humanism primarily consists of the decision to make man 'master and possessor of nature' (Descartes, 1956), so as to detach him permanently from the theological-political power of the time, pre-Reformation Judeo-Christianity, by releasing him from his natural chains. In other words, the humanism that eventually engendered management as the dominant contemporary praxis is primarily a dual struggle, against the Judeo-Christian political and religious authorities on one hand, and 'nature' on the other.

All struggles involve interaction, and all interaction involves coexistence on the same level. In other words, struggling against something in one way or another comes down to being on the same level and participating in the same ontic region as the opponent in the struggle. Struggling is simultaneously attempting to negate the other and asserting its existence, as long as the struggle has not ended that existence either temporarily or permanently. Setting itself up against the religious authorities of the time, and against eternal nature, humanism contributes in some way to reconfer existence on the contents that make up Judeo-Christianity and the said nature. From another angle, it was definitely, and for the first time, in the West that an intellectual and political movement against both religion and nature was asserted, and therefore that humanism arose; religion and nature were to be considered from an entirely new viewpoint from the time of what was to become the European Renaissance.

While the Judeo-Christian tradition and 'nature' were confirmed in their existence by humanism, which instituted them as its enemies, this took place in a completely new way that led to the advent of 'management' as a *praxis* in the Marxist sense of the term – that is, both as science or theory, and as a practice, central to our time.

The central aim of humanism is to give man his place in the world he inhabits. At the time, the world belonged to God, and its operation, which could at first sight appear spontaneous, was sooner or later governed by the will of He who created heaven and earth (Saint Thomas, *Somme théologique*, II. I., q.79, a.2). Humanism was thus fundamentally instituted against divine authority. Man would at last be free, and happy, finding himself no longer placed in a world that does not belong to him, that he does not understand, and which in return fails to understand him – or, as it is written in the sacred texts, understands him by enveloping him and determining him without his knowledge, maybe even against his will. Man finds himself in a bleak prison where he controls none of the machinery, or is only a plaything – a plaything *par excellence*, but nevertheless a plaything (Acts 21: 5–6; Isaiah 66: 22). The main way for man to free himself of this world while remaining alive in it is to understand it, envelop it in its turn, and force a passage through it, make it his own. This is the fundamental meaning of Descartes' famous expression quoted earlier. Humanism involves the voluntary decision to take an active part in the affairs of the world. It should not be forgotten that a few lines after asserting that man could, in certain circumstances, become like 'a master and possessor of nature' in his *Discourse on Method*, Descartes calls medicine the queen of sciences, to be invented and developed in the model of the new science he is instituting in the place of scholastics which was taught in schools at the time (Descartes, 1956). Around a century earlier, Machiavelli in *The Prince* mentions in passing at the end of chapter XXV that 'fortune is a woman' and that to lead a successful life she should be 'beaten and ill-used' rather than treated 'coldly' and with excessive caution. Fortune smiles on the adventurous like the woman she is, preferring them over men who are too tender (Machiavelli, 1981).

Machiavelli and Descartes are saying the same thing: the 'beating and ill-using' of fortune described by one is what the other sees as being 'master and possessor of nature'. For both these great authors, each in his own way a hero of modern philosophy, the reference to women on one side and medicine on the other relates to the same underlying reality, that of the human body, and of a 'controlled and possessed' human body, a 'beaten and ill-used' female human body. In considering fortune feminine, what Machiavelli has in mind is not of course the feminine that is subjected to human male prejudice and scorn; what he has in mind is the feminine as a symbol, the ultimate harbour of the mystery itself of the world where man – in the generic sense of the term – finds himself: what Machiavelli has in mind is the feminine as the place of man's very advent against the impersonal, senseless backdrop of the world, the feminine as the place of gestation. The feminine as a place of gestation is, until a new biotechnological order arrives, exclusively feminine. It is the place where all places, all bodies, and all ultimate possibilities of human thought are formed. When Descartes talks of medicine, and Machiavelli of the feminine, both are referring to total control over the world by man, as it is control over its most elusive mystery, control over the very source of human thought and will. In aiming for a world from which 'god' would disappear, instituting for that purpose a world over which man becomes master, humanism sweeps aside whatever is not man in the world, and tendentially, whatever in this world escapes man. In other words, the world of humanists is a world where man is master, and which is totally transparent to man. More radically, it is a world where man is master *because* the world is totally transparent to him, and vice versa. The world of humanists is totally transparent to man because he has made himself its master.

To clear the ground on which management has instituted itself as the sovereign *praxis* of our time, it would be necessary to consider the provenance of the ultimate possibility of the advent of such a world, through a consideration of the two terms of humanist negation: the Judeo-Christian tradition, and nature. Such a genealogy is presented in Bibard (2005a). Let us here recall the following.

Judeo-Christianity consists in a lowering of understanding or theoretical knowledge, considered limited, below the infinity' of will or practice – later on, in this strict paradigmatic vein, managerial action.[1] The Judeo-Christian tradition represents the most favourable intellectual breeding ground for asserting the infinity of the power of man's will over things. Man created in the image of the god considered all-powerful, man who sooner or later will himself bring the birds of the sky, the fish of the sea, the beasts that crawl along the ground and the others under his dominion (Genesis 1: 26).

Humanism, which opposes the power of Judeo-Christianity on both the levels of thought and action, also wants to institute man as 'master and possessor of nature'. In separating from Judeo-Christianity, humanism isolates, and erects as an essential foundation of the anthropology of the future, the all-powerfulness of wanting over understanding or knowing. 'From now on, what man wants will be', thanks to total knowledge of the world in which he finds himself. Here again, 'nature' is acknowledged in its ultimacy, but as a starting point for what is its sovereign, the will that puts nature at its service. The humanist laicisation of Judeo-Christianity institutes man's will as absolutely sovereign, as a means and an end, to the detriment of nature now contemplated with lucidity in its own laws, in order to better beat and ill-use it, and transform it now that such transformation is considered both possible and desirable. To improve the human lot.

Consequences: The West as Praxis

All philosophies that both reflect and determine the development of humanism illustrate the fact that nature gradually loses its original status or specific spontaneity as the source of man's existence, and becomes a medium for the active will of man with its power to transform. From the Renaissance onwards, a new 'virility' of man is instituted, gradually abandoning the conception of 'nature' as something that should be understood in order for man to conform with and live in as well as possible, founded on what this virility is not: it is not considered 'natural' but increasingly a mere means of man's trials, at the service of human desire. What surrounds man, including at his own level as a body, increasingly becomes external to him in view of the internal which he recognizes as his being; this 'internal self' becomes pure will. As Descartes had already remarked, on one hand is the 'understood' and on the other thought, whose truth is man's will. The 'truth' Descartes is concerned with is not truth as the 'appropriateness' of things to the way men conceive or represent them. 'Truth is, rather, the product of transformation by man of things according to his desire'.[2] Understanding involves 'handling' or 'transforming', in other words understanding is making the object to be understood a means of satisfying man's will. Behind all modern science is the anthropology that Hegel labelled 'negativity': understanding shall no longer be receiving and bowing to the few laws detected; understanding becomes fundamentally wanting and doing. Hence, when man knows, he simply invests into things what he wishes them to be – even if he cherishes the illusion that he is objectively open to the purpose they appear to have initially. Several aspects are characteristic of the new epistemology born after the Renaissance.

a)   *Things are never as they appear at first sight.*

Without embarking on a detailed discussion of a fundamental analysis such as Descartes' discussion of refraction (Descartes, 1956), this point calls for the following comments. The spontaneity of perception is fundamentally called into question: perceiving does not confer understanding, and therefore the truth of things. The laws presiding over the dynamics of causal relationships form a structured dynamics that also confer structure, and their terms are to be found beyond the immediate appearance of all phenomena. Truth is never 'on the actual surface of the given'.

b)   *The 'core' of things is made up of series of measurable relationships, which eventually authorize action on them. The science of all the sciences that make it possible to describe the reasons for possible relationships between things is mathematics.*

'Behind' phenomena lie structures that act alternately as causes and effects of apparent dynamics: the tool available to man for explaining the reasons for things is the ultimate rational tool, the calculation of the infinite number of combinations governing the structural relationships underlying appearances. This is the tool of mathematics, which ultimately turns out to lead to formal logic as such, ushering in both the birth and spread of metamathematics and metalogics in the nineteenth and twentieth centuries (Kline, 1980).

c)   *What is important in 'nature' is not what it is 'in itself', but what it means for man when placed 'in his reach'.*

'Nature' ceases to be a reference, a support, a source of guidance, a basis, because it is a language. It becomes a medium for man's will. What is important now on the level of the phenomena nature presents is that on that basis man receives, thinks and transforms how he calculates, interprets, manipulates and decides. Naturally, from this point the notion of nature comes to be diluted into the notion of the will of the subject who wants and acts. Therefore, the underlying structures allowing development of calculations, which in turn will enable man to intervene in causal relationships, are the ultimate structural expression of the subjectivity which wants and acts as such (Klein, 1986; 1992).

d)   *The very basis of knowledge is man's desire: the object of the ultimate science itself is the very desire for knowledge. It is called 'reason'.*

Science which questions what it does as science sooner or later discovers that knowledge depends on its will and operations – the ultimate object is neither the object the subject attributes itself, nor the subject itself, which is constantly travelling towards its autonomous sovereignty, but the relationship between the two. This relationship is first understood as the relationship of 'reason' to 'another' totally devoid of its own meaning (Kant, 1999).

e)   *The science that reason develops by itself is the science of what reason ultimately is, that is, will. The science of reason is a science of freedom seeking and wanting itself through the 'clashes' of encounters with whatever resists it. What 'resists' reason-freedom is what it objects as counterpoints or 'others' in view of its subjective desire for itself. Reason holds as the science of itself the knowledge of its attempts at affirmation among the objects it attributes itself, or history.*

When reason understands that it is the redeeming effort of tearing nature away from its thick, silent spontaneity, it interprets the dynamics of this separation as the teleology of its liberation. This liberation is its history, or 'History'. Montesquieu, in *De l'Esprit des Lois,* was the first to assert the pre-eminence of history over the natural identity of human things.

f)   *Mathematics, with formal logic as a background, and history are the two extremities of the total spectrum of modern sciences, built on the humanist anthropology that derives from Judeo-Christianity as described earlier.*

Asserting the power of the human in a world that belongs to him leads man to a concept of nature that has no meaning. This concept is concomitant with the disappearance of the God of nature (Koyré, 1957). Henceforth, 'nature' no longer means anything specific and autonomous, and man receives and understands himself as the desire for his freedom, or as Kant said, free will which seeks itself (Kant, 1965; 1996), served by an understanding of things centred on mathematics on one hand and history on the other as drivers, bases and tools of all possible respectively objective and subjective knowledge. They are ultimately space as the place of man's action, and time as expression of man's will which emerges and is imposed to constitute the new reference for living, the will to live, and living well.

Control over all things by man, the underlying foundation that determines what becomes possible and desirable, is the destiny all humanity dreams of: against gods and nature, there is a desire everywhere for man to be free and live in happiness and sovereignty. Only the 'West' in the event of deciding through humanism that it is not only desirable but possible that man should become master of the world and even of the universe affirms the ultimate possibility and desirability of leading everything. Seen in this way, the West can be summed up as the 'spontaneous attitude of control over all things', and the 'goes-without-saying' exercising of will as its own goal. 'Globalization' begins as the Western attitude, compared to the prudent positions of other worlds and other civilizations, spreads throughout the world over time. The point shared by other civilizations is that their cultures assert the need to rein in human desires; more radically still, that even when man's total dominion over the world, conferred by a tendentially exhaustive knowledge of the given, is in fact possible, it is not desirable because it is dangerous for both life and the meaning of life. The tension between control and non-control, voluntarism and listening, prudence and receptiveness, the West and what is not the West, is thus played out within each man and each woman. This tension eminently concerns management, an attitude or method of conducting economic life that is currently undergoing globalization.

Being born of the will to serve man as will here below (see above), 'management' as a useful and efficient organization method eventually involves rationalization of production methods for goods and services. More radically, with the aid of worldwide competition, it is reflected in private economic life not only by a tendency to maximize profit, but fundamentally by the tendency to total control of production operations: everything must be transparent, controlled, with maximum efficiency (Bibard, 2005b; 2005a). On the other hand, particularly due to competition played out on a level where sometimes radically different cultures interpenetrate each other before the West as an attitude of control, organizations need the capacity to be 'receptive to the unknown' which is in complete contradiction with the desire to control all operations. At the level of organizations, this results in the dynamics of the relationship between the West as a *praxis* assuming and seeking to achieve that everything is subjected to man as will and the 'rest' of the world and possible ways of living.

Management *theories* neither describe nor explain this tension totally, far from it, since they fail to see it, being by their origins at the service of wanting for wanting's sake, or control for control's sake. Only slowly and hesitantly are efforts of the sort beginning to emerge.

Let us now briefly examine the moral and political paradigm underlying this 'state of the art' of management.

MORAL AND POLITICAL CONSEQUENCES: THE 'MANAGERIAL' THEORY OF MAN

The most decisive and comprehensive political expression of the advent of humanism is found in the writings of Hobbes. The fundamental presupposition of political thought from the Renaissance onwards is that not only morally, but also politically, the individual is the ultimate entity. In modern political philosophy, the notion of community loses its status as the ultimate entity. As a collective life, political life is no longer, as it had been since the Greeks, considered spontaneous or natural. Collective life results from a 'contract' between individuals. The anthropology underlying modern political thought is that humans are free individuals, equal between themselves with innate independence and a sovereignty of desires common to all men, and calculators of their interests, in other words rational beings.

a)   Free individuals

They are the ultimate moral and political entity: contrary to what political thought had hitherto asserted (Aristotle, 1998), the collective takes no precedence over them. Individual freedom comes down to a set of rights and duties: fundamentally, the duty and right to live. If there is a collective, it is necessarily the result of an agreement to that end between individuals if they think it is more valuable than their own interests, or more strictly, a requirement for better satisfaction of their own interests.

b)   Equal among themselves

The equality of individuals among themselves is an equality of principle before the right and duty to live. Each individual has the right and duty to implement all the means necessary for living. There are two decisive points:

   i) 'Nature' counts for nothing in the theoretical thematization of the foundations of the political: it does not matter that individuals may be women, men, young or old, black, white or any other colour. Each person's rights and duties are the same (this is one of the reasons behind the growing power of children's rights in respect of their parents, for example).

ii) Sooner or later, due to hunting the same prey because they share a desire for the same object (even if this is only because others also desire it), a contradiction arises between different people's interests, a conflict, a war pitting all against all (Hobbes, 1982). Man's 'natural' state is a permanent state of war that sharpens individual awareness of war, peace and the ways of gaining peace by living as well as possible in peace.

c) Rational beings

'Rationality', or humans' fundamental ability to calculate, is initiated in the calculation that living at war on all sides is eventually more costly than a collective form of organization. The ultimate type of collective organisation for a life that is, as far as possible, peaceful is having everyone's interests defended by a single individual such that it becomes his duty, right and monopolistic expertise: Hobbes' Leviathan.

The state's inaugural individual calculation is a calculation that must be presumed universal within and for the community formed in this way: if only a few will delegate protection of their interests to the state, they will be eliminated sooner or later by those who continue to rely on the use of their own force for living.

It must be clearly borne in mind that the modern theory of political sovereignty is a theory that assumes the state is always the result of individual wills, rather than the opposite. In other words, the political expression of humanism lies in a theory that unambiguously grants primacy to the individual over the collective, that is the social and the political. Modern politics is a politics of individuality for each person's individuality. The state in this context merely plays a role as supporter and guarantor of the satisfaction of private interests, whose founding expression in economic and legal terms is private ownership (Locke, 1690).

Despite the decisive importance of the political debate between centrally planned and free market economies that lasted until the war, the principal modern founding trend, in moral and political terms, because in anthropological terms, is towards globalization of free market economic and political individualism, concomitant with the globalization movement in the anthropology of control encountered earlier. Globalization does not mean a result, but a trend and a tension: that States exist, that pressure groups are constantly emerging to disturb the supposedly totally homogeneous logic of the markets, simply indicates that what Hobbes describes as man's natural or pre-political state at the basis of all 'true' empirical politics is in fact the normative description of what should be, or of the 'duty' of all politics consequently by definition logically destined to disappear as such.[3]

In other words, at the basis of the politics of humanism if such exists, lies the 'ultimate devaluation of all politics to the benefit of the (only) political guarantee of satisfaction of interests that are ultimately individual and only individual'. The free market economics, utilitarianism and individualism at the origins of managerial understanding of man, all derive from the same theoretical paradigm resulting from the humanist transformation of the old political philosophy into modern political science.

TOWARDS A CORPORATE POLITICAL RESPONSIBILITY

The shift from the old political philosophy to the modern political science hides the fact that behind corporate social responsibility lies the more complete and demanding notion of corporate political responsibility. Reasons for this are presented below.

Disorientation and Selfishness of Management

Of course, the advent of a particular structure, ideology, prejudice, accepted truth, or paradigm is governed by many isolated, local events. Nevertheless, the fundamental source of both contemporary 'free market' economics and politics, and the logic of control governing the operation of organizations, is ultimately the totally original, exceptional reversal consisting of the advent of humanism as an ideology and a founding aim at the time of the Renaissance in Europe. This underlying cultural movement that defines the 'West' by specifically differentiating it from other civilizations is found at the source of management at the heart of worldwide economic life as a method of conducting organizations. The two consequences of this state of affairs are action for action's sake as the ultimate logic guiding the management of organizations, and a generally implicit sovereign indifference towards the political, or the collective good as such.

Indifference towards the Political

An enterprise is supposed to satisfy its owner's interest. The owner's interest is basically to make a profit from the operations of the organization, and therefore that the organization should be profitable. In view of what we have seen of the anthropological basis of modern morals and politics, it has naturally been forgotten that the first well-known managerial theory had the dual aim of satisfying the worker, or the employee in general, as well as the enterprise's owner: Taylorism was initially intended as a theory of social justice as well as economic efficiency (Taylor, 1947). Only the second intention was paid attention by managers, whether business owners or not, and by economic theory itself, taking the logic of modern anthropology to its extreme limits (Friedman, 1962). From this standpoint, although managers have occasionally taken an interest in the lot of their workers and/or employees, they see it from a strictly utilitarian view of the economic efficiency of the organization, in order to maximize the profit expected as a result. The fears engendered by the human relations movement born in response to Taylorism, with their aim for 'fulfilment' in their jobs for workers and employees (Mayo, 1933; Etzioni, 1961), should be understood from this same standpoint. If developing a science of man capable of explaining behaviours makes improved control and governance appear possible, it is not from a collective standpoint as developed in the human relations movement, but in order to ensure collectives are as efficient as possible. Thus managerial knowledge is shot through with a theoretical activism that is cryptic to varying degrees, but fundamentally active. The history of the theory of motivations illustrates and reflects this difficulty perfectly (Sievers, 1990).

A short diversion is necessary here on the relationships between theory and practice. While theory fundamentally governed practice until the arrival of humanism which inaugurated the reversal of values in favour of practice, or will, over 'speculation' or the contemplative or theoretical life in general, when the implementation of will, and therefore will itself, gained a greater value than any theory, theory as such only carried value if it was 'useful' in some way for practice. This is what happened both in and for management. While theories exist, they are in the end only developed to serve managerial practice or practices. In management, if it is taken seriously for its own sake and not considered from the point of view of management theories, 'it is ultimately practice that counts – not "research" as such'. This shows that management is still awaiting management knowledge, and that this knowledge thus has nothing to gain by developing autonomously. Or that to gain, it must detach itself from its objective and field of exercise. This is the case because in management, theory has the particularity of developing much faster than the object it concerns, which suffers from inertias specific to organizational life as such. The inertias of organizational life mean that intellectual development arising from new issues is constantly held back by the grim, banal coarseness of the repetition of things, and the attached issues. Management theories, as in any other field of human sciences, play the role of the 'fly in the ointment'; revealer or driver of change, but change cannot be brought about by force alone. Managerial change always takes place in an environment of repeated operations that form and guarantee the performance of organizations (Bibard, 2005b; Bibard and Jenkins, 1999; Bibard, 2005a).

Innovation is far from easy in organizations, for tendentially that would mean being unaffected by any organizational inertia, which is by definition impossible for both organizations and their networks (Callon, 1992). To put it differently, the speed with which managers or management in general are capable of taking on board management theories efficiently – that is, in a relevant way for management – is more than limited. It is thus by no means in the interest of management theories to accelerate the pace of production and existence, to the point and at the risk of becoming totally detached from the object of their studies, the very object they are supposed to serve. If management theories are totally detached from their object, they (re)turn into theories 'for theories' sake' responding to an unconscious but deeply efficacious wish, losing the link they had with what they are supposed to thematise, and consequently their theoretical and practical relevance (Bibard, 2005b).[4] As they are after all only the children of fundamental, legitimate 'scientific' theories such as mathematics on one side, and psychology and sociology on the other; as they are otherwise the fruit of management itself when of a directly operational nature, if management theories or management knowledge lose their link with their object, they no longer have any legitimacy, any recognition or existence. It is from this standpoint that the epigraph to this article must be understood: the movements of the elements must be known 'as distinctly as we know the various crafts of our artisans' (that is, of industry, particularly the agri-food industry which works with 'nature' in nature itself, and services). The jobs of our workmen are the basic reference of knowledge in management, not some sort of 'nature' to be contemplated or considered in a 'speculative' manner. It is human beings' *action* – even non-political and exclusively labour-related – that is the model, object and final basis for theories of management, rather than any kind of theoretical reference. The problems addressed by management theories will eventually be those of management, not those arising from management theories as theories. Sooner or later they will be hooked onto the founding axes of the modern anthropology of man, considered as an individual indifferent to politics except as they relate to his own private interests, in an environment of equality and perfectly rational calculation.

Action for Action's Sake

Indifference to things political eventually also conditions the second aspect of managerial nihilism, which is action for action's sake, or acting to contribute to the accumulation of wealth, without ever taking the time off necessary to enjoy it. Independently of Weber's analysis of the relationship between the spirit of capitalism and the Protestant ethic, among other observations pointing out that a Protestant capitalist will very probably not allow himself to enjoy the fruits of his work, instead reinvesting them and therefore feeding the tendential growth in the profit rate (Weber, 2001) – independently of this analysis, it can and must be observed that capitalism, and free market economic life in general, typically displays a constantly growing tension between a population working ever harder to earn ever more money, and a tendentially marginalized population, unemployed and excluded from contemporary economic and social life, whether local, national or global. In other words, some are doing more and more to become richer and richer, among other aims, while others, generally against their will, are doing less and less, and becoming increasingly poor as a result, on the three levels of material comfort, purpose of life and recognition. The most unhappy are not always those we would expect: suffering at work is continuing to rise and intensify, becoming measurable medically (Hirigoyen, 1998; Dejours, 1998), while on the other hand calls are being made for a different way of life from that endured in the situation as it appears here. In other words, the problem of the *meaning* of work is becoming increasingly alarming, reflecting a fundamental lack of meaning in everyday managerial action at the heart of contemporary worldwide economic life. There is willingness to work, but for what purpose apart from survival?

RE-EMERGENCE OF THE QUESTION OF MEANING, LEGITIMACY OF THE POLITICAL

Ethics, Sustainable Development, Corporate Social Responsibility

The 'West's' discovery of the efficiency of 'Japanese-style' management was a true revolution, and significantly contributed to the recognition of the importance of the results of the human relations movement in the management of organizations. The informal relationships between the members of an organization, the various types of relationships with authority, motivation by task enhancement and the focus on working in teams, or by project, were dominant themes of management throughout the 1970s and 1980s. The virtues of Japanese management were not restricted to these teachings. Gradually, independently of the then decisive thematization of the fragmentation of power, and the relationships between powers within organisations through what was known as strategic analysis (Crozier and Friedberg, 1980), the notion of 'culture' linking managerial knowledge to ethnology and anthropology, taking as its object the spontaneous emergence of organization 'culture', a new object of management sciences, sometimes presented as the solution to all the problems of management (Aktouf, 1990; Dupuis, 1990; Thévenet, 2006).

Despite its importance for management, this omnipresent desire to find a potentially ready-made solution to management difficulties in all thematizations did not become the main feature of the discovery of the notion of 'culture'. The most decisive discovery was that of the 'collective as such', based on the most empirical, legitimate reality that exists, that of the businesses themselves. The theory of the collective was nothing more than an arbitrary sociological holism, seeking to impose the 'traditional' viewpoint of a Durkheim on discipline and on management. This holism derived from the most rigorous possible observation of how enterprises operate, diametrically opposed to 'Western' logic – in all senses of the term, the generally accepted sense related to Europe and European culture, and the sense we identified earlier. In other words, once 'Japanese-style' management had been discovered, the 'West' began its contemporary opening up to new managerial concepts, in the perspective of a renewed problematization of the question of its moral and political foundations.

For over twenty years, various events and the emergence of objects new for management and for managerial theories have contributed to 'destabilisation of the epistemological basis identified', described earlier as the intellectual, moral and political given on which management stands as master of worldwide economic life, and of life in short. These events are as discussed earlier, but also the series of three themes that in turn provide ideological pretexts and real questions – but so vast and complex that no serious attempts are made to answer them: ethics, sustainable development, and corporate social responsibility.

The theme of *ethics* asserts itself through the painful contradiction deemed to be underlying and obvious: that economics or business life has nothing to do with ethics. On one side is ethics, and on the other the amoral and occasionally ostensibly immoral hell of economic life. The question that is immediately raised is where ethics is to be found, when clearly economic life is tending to invade all life: what remainders are concerned by ethics?

More precisely, the common sense intuition on this question is that defence of individuals' interests, or any categorical interests, is incompatible with certain rules of collective behaviour that can contribute to the reality of a respectable, happy, in short a good social and even political life for all. The presupposition that there is an incompatibility between ethics and economics or business comes down to the idea that business never takes any notice of the collective nature of men and women's existence, that is, of the political in the noblest sense of the term. As seen earlier, this is not entirely untrue, and may even be constitutively true, at least for a while.

Exactly the same can be observed of the theme of *sustainable development*. This theme in particular has been imposed on managerial life and management sciences via the controversy raised by the thinning of the ozone layer, which was progressively attributed to the emission of CFCs into the atmosphere (Godard, 2004). First in the US then worldwide, this debate made a decisive contribution to the introduction of the precautionary principle, under which the burden of proof, in the event of a scientific debate over environmental threats that could turn out to have irreducibly significantly damaging consequences for future generations, lies with the party that claims the danger has not been shown to exist, rather than the contrary. This second thematization of sustainable development as a necessary objective, or even priority, of enterprises and organizations (public and private), enjoins managers to be capable, in the midst of the storm of interests and ever fiercer global competition, of taking a long view, seeing 'strategic' rather than merely tactical interests, and exercising a certain form of generosity towards future generations.

Just as on its own level, the notion of ethics calls into question the individual nature of the interests of economic actors, the theme of sustainable development calls into question managers' long-term capacity to consider in a balanced, 'fair' way the long term and the short term, the fundamental priorities for the future and the most urgent concerns.

The emergence and imposition on management of the first two themes gradually brought about the advent and imposition of a third theme, *corporate social responsibility* (CSR) which in its content combines and complements the first two, even though it does not directly result from express positioning in relation to them.[5] Historically, CSR, sometimes treated as a thematic duly defined and bounded by the law, comes from consideration of the rights and duties of enterprises, beyond the rights and duties of shareholders and management. Customers, suppliers, political, social, scientific partners, users and consumers, and so on, were progressively integrated into reflection on the interactions between enterprises. In other words, the initial reflection on ethics progressively brought the enterprise or management back into a wholly natural world with just as much existence as the world of profit, and as the world of corporate private life and a tendentially exclusively Western logic explained earlier. In other words, the thematization of CSR is both an illustration and a reflection of renewed awareness of the existence of the political or the political nature of existence, by those who had forgotten it.

CSR illustrates and reflects the rediscovery that economics is not the be-all and end-all, and that the structure of collectives is sometimes much more complicated, uncertain, threatening, heterogeneous and multifaceted than we would like to believe in the logic of an economy that is perfectly controlled for the service of rational shareholders. This can appear very naïve: action makes people forget, and think as they act, to the detriment of acting as they think or believe or want to think (Bibard, 2005c; 2005b).

There is no End to the Political

The imposition of ethics, sustainable development, CSR, and all sorts of other ancillary or future themes both displays and brings about the renewed emergence of the political, in the strongest sense, at the heart of the economic as described earlier. This can be expressed differently, in saying that management rediscovers, or discovers for the first time (given its origins and the beginnings of its development as the dominant practice in economic life), its political nature. Its political nature, that is, the fact that contemporary economic life can in no circumstances – even ultimately or fundamentally – ignore the political in its fundamental question of what justice is, the political which brought it into existence but which it has denied since birth. True, Hobbes' thematization of natural law inaugurates a new, non-political way of seeing the political or men's shared life, 'but this non-political way is sooner or later overtaken by what it sets out to negate'.

Eventually, the political nature of the assertion that economics is a non-political modality of life and men's actions contradict its intention (affirming the reality of a non-political life in the classical sense of the term), verifying its fundamental nature (being a decision of a political nature, or one which concerns the shared life of men according to essential structures and dynamics). Ultimately, there is no 'simply' economic life independent of political life, and willingly or unwillingly, management bears not only a social but a political responsibility towards humans. This point will now be considered in terms of content and consequences, as it concerns management knowledge.

The political is never-ending: this is what we have seen and explained with regard to content. Observing that the political never stops is equivalent to declaring the re-emergence, or a certain form of re-emergence, of one of the most important aspects of Greek thought in its own eyes. The political question defines the core of what is analysed by Plato based on Socrates' experience and the event it represents, the relationship between nature and convention, or the relationship between thought that was subsequently called 'classical' and modern political thought of the social contract (Strauss, 1964). Plato, who re-thinks what Socrates tries, has no more belief than Aristotle in a convention detached from the nature of things. When men believe and think that political life or collective life results from arbitrary or convention-based choices, as opposed to a nature identified and acknowledged on the level of its spontaneous vitality, they are mistaken. 'Being mistaken is part of the nature of things' for nature conceals in itself the possibility of error, as exemplified in monstrosities in living things (Aristotle, 1912). Nature is not restricted to the mineral and life in animal or vegetable form. Men have never left nature, even when they are the primary place of excess, or eminently contain in themselves the possibility of error. Men are just as much part of nature as animals, vegetables and minerals. They are simply 'sick animals', says Aristotle (Aristotle, *On the generation of animals*), that is, animals that are sometimes not quite suited to the nature of things – their own nature or their own disposition (Aristotle, *On the generation of animals*). Philosophy is the method and the tension through which men can strive towards their true nature, which is conformity to the nature of things in general. And 'political' philosophy is the method or the tension through which they can strive towards the fulfilment of the political in conformity with its nature. Conformity of the political to its nature is that things should be in their place, so that the collective can live in peace. Clearly the issue is knowing what 'its place' is for each thing, and who is entitled to state or impose that place if necessary, for the good of each individual and the collective good. This is all the more complicated because it is natural for man to be the potentially lethal disease of nature: man is by nature an outsider, or is 'the outsider par excellence of nature' (Kojève, 1980). This is to say that he contains in himself the possibility of both bad and good. There is a constant assessment to be made be made between good and bad, justice and injustice, truth and error.

Confusion is a constant feature of human life – particularly in its political or collective aspect, which requires relationships between humans to be adjusted and readjusted. Humans are constantly called on to separate the wheat from the chaff, and this requires a sense of justice that no formal law as such can by definition force into existence, for all laws are sooner or later inappropriate, weak or unjust (Aristotle, 1998). True law, the natural law of which Aristotle carefully avoids saying anything other, in his *Nicomachean Ethics*, than that he intends to talk about it because it is vital (Aristotle, 1985), is a law that is constantly reinvented according to the circumstances that characterise the action to be judged. No law or formula is possible for action. Knowledge of the political is of a 'practical' just as much as a theoretical nature. Theory makes it possible to set out correctly the questions, practices or experience of proposing prudential measures to guide judgement, decisions, and action. Teaching of political philosophy involves listening to what is being done in natural political life – even if it has 'gone astray', for the nature of the political contains just as much its potential to go astray as its adjustment to its end or ultimate form. Political philosophy requires observation, totally devoid of moral and political prejudices, of the political as it gives itself spontaneously, or naturally. It would be a constitutive error to think or believe it possible to understand the political, or politicians, better than they understand themselves. The ultimate given for understanding the political is the spontaneity with which it gives of itself, that is, exists and is exercised in everyday life and at times of exceptional events. Nothing needs to be added to the political to understand it theoretically, and to learn to distinguish true and false, just and unjust, good and bad. On the contrary, what is required to foster the best possible knowledge of the political is an intellectually or theoretically totally open and receptive attitude – an attitude comparable to what for Husserl is the eidetical parenthesis – being at the disposal of what is, or 'the thing itself' (Hegel, 1977).

What is then discovered is the spontaneous nature of the collective, rooted in sexual life: for communities to exist, communities must be made up of living human beings, and humans that reproduce. The fundamental constitutive entity of the political is the couple, or heterosexual conjugal life, which guarantees the necessary supply of citizens capable of making the city live, running it on a day-to-day basis, and dying for it. The two extremes of the political are making love and (for) making war when necessary. And it is always necessary, because it is in man's nature to be in an excess that eventually leads one to aspire to what another owns or enjoys. It is thus essential that at least for defence, every community should have soldiers.

This is a world away from modern political thought, which affirms the individual pre-existence of men, and the fundamentally contract-based nature of collectives of any sort. It is a world away from modern political thought, which accepts that theory precedes practice, chronologically, and also axiologically and logically, for thought detects the truth under the surface of things, individuals and social contracts under the collective, blind mechanisms of desires under the collective. For the elders, desires, excesses and their opposites are exercised and animated 'quite naturally' at the level of state or city life, or community life.

For the Greeks, it is quite natural that management should return after a certain time of forgetting, which formed an epistemologically and historically constitutive element, to the political. A little economism removes man from the political, a large amount of economism brings him back to it sooner or later. In correlation with this dynamics, the dynamics of forgetting is exercised and applied on the level of knowledge: a little humanism distances man from political philosophy – by placing him in a keen tension between mathematics and history – while a large amount of humanism will bring him back, willingly or otherwise. Some would have called this a 'trick of reason', using man's 'unsociable sociability' to lead him to self-awareness, and to action that is fairer, truer, better, than the action he took for a while (Hegel, Kant). The term renaissance can be preferred. The renaissance of classical political rationalism (Strauss, 1989). The renaissance of common sense as the basis of a possible scientificity of demanding political thought. Scientificity does not necessarily involve the epistemological act of doubting so as to overturn the contents of common sense (Bachelard, 1985). Just as in the 'hard' sciences, a little removes man from nature, and a lot brings him back (Bibard, 2005b), a little history and political science thematizing history removes man from the political in the traditional sense of the term: a lot brings him back. On the level of corporate life itself, or contemporary economic life, lies the return to questioning the ends, consideration of what makes good and less good lives, the hierarchization of values, the non-equivalence of good and bad. The struggle against the nihilism that is eventually born of cynicism and relativism has no need to be artificially instigated, for instance in this chapter. It is spontaneous or natural.

However, it is equally obvious from political thought of the political as natural that everything possible must be done to prevent the excesses of this struggle: backward-looking movements or the emergence of moralisms that are just as dangerous as nihilism itself. In the end it must be considered, based on the fact that the truth of management is in the counterpoint of its origins, not in an economics unfettered by rules, which for a while thematized profit as the ultimate goal of all action, but in the political that eventually raises the question of ends, and asks not only how profit should be made but equally why it should be made, in what context, and with what sort of newly understood responsibility.

This means that the discussion should not cover only CSR, but corporate political responsibility in the noblest sense of the term – and more broadly of course, the economic life embedded in political life, whether or not it is desired or dominant.

CONCLUSION: EPISTEMOLOGICAL AND AXIOLOGICAL CONSEQUENCES

The moral foundations of management knowledge have lost their way. That way was the path taken by the theology of liberation of man, evacuating his god in order to better circumvent uncooperative nature, in order to find happiness. Humanism's intention was fundamentally liberating, but its progress has been more and more threatening. Its effects were to give free rein to a desire for power bearing in itself all the ambiguity of Nietzchean will: pure good faith; and a flank infinitely open to the twist of painful desires. Wanting to free man as want amidst the things that become like mathematical data to him, in the way that the wise man arbitrarily sets himself an objective, is equivalent to freeing wanting from any other base than himself, by eventually abandoning that wanting to the nothingness of nihilism, where everything is nothing – particularly, the public aspect of living well.

This abandon is marked by a lack of ontological distance between theory and practice. This lack of distance, fundamentally damaging for management knowledge as such, is a constitutive part of management as the science of running organizations. The theory of management is born against a backdrop of the predominantly economicist paradigm of collective life in its assertion as a necessary consequence of the political thought of humanism. If its evolution is carefully observed today, this economism is simply transitory, because it is just as constitutively overtaken by politics as the fundamental structuring of collective human life – of human life in short (Aristotle, 1998). The practical subsumption of the political under the economic is a temporary subsumption, even if it is constitutive of the elevation of management as the queen of sciences of modern practical life. It is transitory in the same way as political science that thematizes the political as a formal procedure designed to serve the conventions agreed on between men to live as they can. Their *view* of the political changes like its object – it is the intention of this path to show and contribute to this change. At the end of the path, two fundamental changes are now visible, carrying along with them a crowd of possible moral changes.

On the *epistemological* level first, political science is leaving the field as political philosophy re-emerges. A political philosophy affected by the same features as those of straightforward philosophy when it seeks to return to the 'thing itself', beyond the interference caused by the modern formalism of post-Cartesian epistemology. The aim is to regain the natural attitude that Husserl refers to in *Krisis* (Husserl, 1970). The aim, as Strauss dramatically wished (Strauss, 1983), is to understand the political as it understands itself, so as to relearn how to prevent tyrannies (Strauss, 1991), even apparently benevolent ones (Tocqueville, 1961). Beyond the contemporary mistrust that constitutes practical political life, based on the supremacy granted to the individual to the extent that nothing of what is public is supposed capable of carrying any value of any kind, to re-hear the eminently humanist possibility of being both good and strong – re-understanding Thucydides (Strauss, 1964).

This renaissance of the classical attitude to the political is eminently fostered by the spontaneous demand of the peoples on one side, tired of being abused, impoverished and misled, and by the spontaneous desire of the powerful on the other side, regularly listening out for ways of saying what they do and presenting its meaning in explanations that might at last preclude mistrust, when it is a parasite rather than a prudent protection. This attitude is finally in action, even only potentially, at the very heart of management sciences, since they began to integrate the efforts of sociology derived from phenomenology. The increasing intermingling of disciplines and the resulting progressive weighting of various scientific paradigms by each other contributes to the 'dissolution of the epistemological homogeneity that resulted from affirmation of the post-humanist epistemology' as detected earlier. The growing number of methodological efforts made to listen to the field in management sciences and all collateral areas; the dissolution of frontiers between disciplines, the resulting fertile interferences, and finally the disappearance of frontiers bringing management sciences back to the political totality of things, all contribute to management's growing self-awareness as political action, in the strongest sense.

Next, on the *axiological* level, the contemporary dynamics of corporate social responsibility, sustainable development, and ethics as themes to be endogenized into managerial issues, or considered as central themes of management, contribute, despite the inevitably occasionally ideological aspect of the affirmation, to the moral renaissance of political conscience, and therefore to surpassing the nihilism that threatened managerial action and the research that describes and explains that action.

Finally, it was suggested earlier that internalization of the new issues of corporate social responsibility, sustainable development and ethics was contemporary with internalization of the fundamental uncertainty inherent to action – managerial and otherwise – as a paradoxical given of management. Globalization, as described earlier, leads in one way or another to confrontation of the Western logic of control with the *non*-Western logics of listening (including Jewish, Greek, Christian and Muslim logics), and the emergence of the unexpected, the qualitative variance, and chaos as irreducible givens of management at the level of a worldwide complexity. This acknowledges the impossibility of controlling everything that early humanism had sought to evacuate. It acknowledges, at further cost, the irreducible obscurity of things, invading alternatively the field of the reasonable and – worse – the rational. It fundamentally acknowledges that control by man over the world has boundaries, or can only ever be *local* (Bibard, 2005c). Management's error, in fact, given its history, was that for a long time it presumed both on the practical and theoretical levels, and practical because theoretical on the basis of the modern praxis, that total control by man over his actions and effects was both possible and desirable. It is in fact both undesirable and impossible; the former precisely because of the latter. This is reflected in the threats overhanging the durability of life on earth, considering the vulnerability of certain nuclear safety systems (waste processing), or manipulation of living things (GM organisms for instance, or the issues raised by the possibility of human cloning). In becoming political once again, in the strongest sense, management reinternalizes or for the first time internalizes the *chaotic, impersonal uncertainty of things*. This is reflected, for example, in the work of persons such as Karl Weick on what he calls 'the cosmic episode' of an organizational dynamics (Weick, 1993), or Latour on sciences (Latour, 2004).

An explicit reference is relevant here to the anthropological basis on which ultimately awareness of uncertainty in terms of the political is worked out, that is the sexual difference – and then the gender difference – of humans

(Bibard, 2005). This is the appropriate basis for radical assessment of the orientation required for the paradoxical renaissance of a phenomenology of management that is simultaneously unborn and ontologically inevitable.

NOTES

1. Whether they concern structures, organizational strategy, culture, power, or rationalization of tasks or human relations, managerial theories are the fruit of the prior development of human sciences and mathematic economics, rooted in modern epistemology that makes sciences an aspect of wanting – see elsewhere in this article.

2. This is illustrated in enigmatic form by the Machiavellian statement that 'men, *in universali*, judge with their eyes rather than their hands, for everyone can see but few can feel' (Machiavelli, 1981): from Bacon's first *Virile production of the century* it is established that understanding takes place through the hands, not through the Greeks' classical contemplation with its emphasis on looking as the primary sense of knowledge.

3. We have seen elsewhere how the dynamics of political education according to the modern political science inaugurated by Hobbes relates to a fundamentally economic reasoning (Bibard, 2005a).

4. This problem applies for all 'modern' sciences, that is, sciences born of the epistemological revolution that formed the Renaissance. One highly eloquent example is the very symbol of genius in the twentieth century, Einstein, who not only wanted to, but did, develop 'theory for theory's sake' at the most demanding level, and who, although he was a *pacifist* theorist, was belatedly overtaken by politics and against his own will enlisted in the eventual production of the first atomic bomb. It is in its *content* that the modern way of knowing nature tends towards active transformation by manipulation in the strongest sense: it is impossible to imagine a follower of *theoretical* (in the Greek sense) contemplation having the same end effect: on this point, see above on the Machiavellian distinction between the use of the senses of sight and touch in knowledge.

5. The corporate social responsibility theme carries with it the theme of the fairness of business, which is not in itself a fourth theme separate from the other three on the level at which we encounter them here. 'Fair trade' is in fact a constituent part of corporate social responsibility.

BIBLIOGRAPHY

Aktouf, O., (1990), 'Le symbolisme et la "culture" d'entreprise – des abus conceptuels aux leçons du terrain', in J.-F. Chanlat, (ed.), *L'Individu dans l'Organisation*, Les presses de l'Université Laval / ESKA, Laval.

Argyris, C. and Schön, D., (1996), *Organizational Learning: A Theory of Action Perspective,* Addison-Wesley Longman, Boston.

Aristotle, (1998), *Politics*, Oxford University Press, New York.

Aristotle, (1991), *The Metaphysics*, Prometheus Books, New York.

Aristotle, (1985), *Nicomachean Ethics*, (translation Terence Irwin), Hackett, Indianapolis.

Aristotle, (1912), *On the Generation of Animals*, The Oxford Translation of Aristotle.

Bachelard, G., (1985), *The New Scientific Mind*, Beacon Press, Boston.

Bacon, F., (1603), *Philosophy of Francis Bacon, An Essay on Its Development from 1603 to 1609, with New Translations of Fundamental Texts*, B. Farrington, London.

Ballot, A., (2005), 'Pour une conduite responsable des affaires', in *L'Ethique Individuelle: un Nouveau Défi pour l'Entreprise*, L'Harmattan, Paris.

Bibard, L., (2003), *Entreprise, Ethique et Politique*, 5° Université de printemps de l'audit social, Audit social et responsabilité sociale de l'entreprise, Corté.

Bibard, L., (2005a), 'The ethics of capitalism', in Daianu D. and Vranceanu R., (Eds.), *Ethical Boundaries of Capitalism*, Ashgate, Aldershot.

Bibard, L., (2005b), *Gestion, Sciences et Politique*, Editions du Centre de Recherche, ESSEC, Cergy.

Bibard, L., (2005c), 'L'éthique et la question du temps', in *L'Ethique Individuelle, un Défi pour l'Entreprise*, L'Harmattan, Paris.

Bibard, L. and Jenkins, A., (1999), *Leadership, Uncertainty and Management Education*, Actes du 9th colloquium on Business and Economic Ethics, IESE, Barcelona.

Boltanski, L. and Thévenot, L., (1991), *De la Justification, Les Economies de la Grandeur*, NRF, Essais, Gallimard, Paris.

Callon, M., (1992), 'Variety and irreversibility in networks of technique conception and adoption', in Foray d'a and C. Freeman (eds.), *Technology and the Wealth of Nation*, Frances Printer, London.

Chandler, Alfred D., Jr, (1990), *Scale and Scope. The Dynamics of Industrial Capitalism*, The Belknap Press of Harvard University Press, Cambridge, Mass.

Clarke, R., (2004), *Against All Enemies*, Free Press/Simon & Shuster, New York.

Cropsey, J. and Strauss, L., (eds) (1987), *History of Political Philosophy*, The University of Chicago Press, Chicago.

Crozier, M. and Friedberg, E., (1980), *Actors and Systems: The Politics of Collective Action*, University of Chicago Press, Chicago.

Cyert, R. and March J., (1963), *A Behavioural Theory of the Firm*, Prentice Hall, Old Tappan.

Dejours, C., (1998), *Souffrance en France : la Banalisation de l'Injustice Sociale*, Seuil, Paris.

Descartes, R., (1956), *Discourse on Method*, Prentice Hall, Old Tappan.

Descartes, R., (1680), *Six Metaphysical Meditations*, Penguin Books, New York.

Diamond, M., (1987), 'The federalist', in J. Cropsey and L. Strauss (eds), *History of Political Philosophy,* The University of Chicago Press, Chicago.

Dupuis, J.-P., (1990), 'Anthropologie, culture et organisation – vers un modèle constructiviste', in J.-F. Chanlat, (ed.), *L'Individu dans l'Organisation*, Les presses de l'Université Laval / ESKA, Laval.

Etzioni, A., (1961), *A Comparative Analysis of Complex Organizations: on Power, Involvement, and their Correlates*, Free Press, New York.

Eyssalet, J.-M., (1990), *Le Secret de la Maison des Ancêtres*, Trédaniel, Paris.

Freeman, Chris and Louça, Francisco (2001), *As Times Goes By: From the Industrial Revolution to the Information Revolution,* Oxford University Press, Oxford.

Freeman, Chris and Soete, Luc (1997), *The Economics of Industrial Innovation,* MIT Press, Cambridge, Mass.

Friedman, M., (1962), *Capitalism and Freedom*, University of Chicago Press, Chicago.

Girard, R., (2006), *Des Choses Cachées depuis la Fondation du Monde*, Garnier-Flammarion, Paris.

Godard, O., (2004), *Savoirs, Risques Globaux et Développement Durable*, Cahiers, CNRS Ecole Polytechnique, 2004-009.

Hegel, W., (1998), *Hegel's Science of Logic,* Prometheus Books, New York.

Hegel, W., (1991), *Elements of the Philosophy of Right*, Cambridge University Press, Cambridge, Massachusetts.

Hegel, W., (1977), *Phenomenology of Spirit*, The Oxford University Press.

Hegel, W., (1953), *Reason in History*, Prentice Hall, Library of Liberal Arts. Old Tappan.

Hirigoyen, M.-F., (1998), *Le Harcèlement Moral: la Violence Perverse au Quotidien*, La Découverte & Syros, Paris.

Hobbes, T., (1982), *De Cive: Or The Citizen*, Greenwood Press Reprint.

Holy Bible, (1990), Riverside World Pub Co, New York.

Husserl, E., (1970), *The Crisis of European Sciences and Transcendental Phenomenology*, Northwestern University Press, Evanston.

Iribarne (d'), P., (1993), *La Logique de l'Honneur, Gestion des Entreprises et Traditions Nationales*, Point Seuil, Paris.

Kant, E., (1999), *Critique of Pure Reason*, Cambridge University Press, Cambridge, Massachusets.

Kant, E., (1965), *Roundwork of the Metaphysics of Morals*, Perennial, New York.

Kant, E., (1996), *Critique of Practical Reason*, Prometheus Books, New York.

Kant, E., (1963), *On History*, Prentice Hall, Library of Liberal Arts.

Klein, J., (1986), *Lectures and Essays*, The MIT Press Classics Series, Cambridge, Massachusetts.

Klein, J., (1992), *Greek Mathematical Thought and the Origin of Algebra*, The MIT Press Classics Series, Cambridge, Massachusetts.

Kline, M., (1980), *Mathematics, the Loss of Certainty*, Oxford University Press, Oxford.

Kojève, A., (1980), *Introduction to the Reading of Hegel*, Cornell University Press, Ithaca.

Kojève, A., (2000), *Outline of a Phenomenology of Right*, Rowman & Littlefield Publishers, Lanham, MD.

Koyré, A., (1957), *From the Closed World to the Infinite Universe*, The Johns Hopkins University Press, Baltimore.

Latour, B., (1988), *Science in Action, How to Follow Scientists and Engineers Through Society*, Harvard University Press, Cambridge, Massachusetts.

Latour, B., (2004), *Politiques de la Nature*, La Découverte, Paris.

Locke, J., (1690), *Of Civil Government*, Ntc Contemporary Publishing Company, New York.

Machiavelli, N., (1981), *The Prince*, Penguin Books, New York.

March, J. and Simon, H., (1958), *Organizations*, Wiley, New York.

Marx, K., (1995), *Capital*, Oxford University Press.

Mayo, E., (1933), *The Human Problems of an Industrial Civilization*, MacMillan, New York.

Montesquieu, Ch., (1989), *The Spirit of the Laws*, Cambridge University Press, Cambridge, Massachusetts.

Nelson, R. and Winter, S., (1982), *An Evolutionary Theory of Economic Change*, Harvard University Press, Cambridge, Massachusetts.

Petrick, J. and Quinn, J., (1997), *Management Ethics: Integrity at Work*, Sage Publications, London.

Plato, (1968), *Republic* (trans. Allan Bloom), Basic Books, New York.

Plato, (2000), *Timaeus*, Hackett Publishing Company, Cambridge (USA).

Sievers, B., (1990), 'La motivation : un ersatz de significations', in J.-F. Chanlat (ed.), *L'Individu dans l'Organisation*, Les presses de l'Université Laval / Editions ESKA, Laval.

Strauss, L., (1991), *On Tyranny*, The University of Chicago Press, Chicago.

Strauss, L., (1989), *The Rebirth of Classical Political Rationalism*, The University of Chicago Press, Chicago.

Strauss, L., (1983), *Studies in Platonic Political Philosophy*, University of Chicago Press, Chicago.

Strauss, L., (1964), *The City and Man*, The University Press of Virginia, Charlottesville, VA.

Strauss, L., (1953), *Natural Right and History*, The University of Chicago Press, Chicago.

Strauss, L., (1935), *Philosophy and Law*, The Jewish Publication Society of America, Philadelphia.

Taylor, (1947), *Scientific Management*, Harper & Row, New York.

Thévenet, M., (2006), *La Culture d'Entreprise*, PUF, Paris.

Tocqueville, A. de, (1961), *Democracy in America*, Oxford University Press, London.

Thucydides, (2005), *The History of the Peloponnesian War*, Penguin Classics, New York.

Weber, M., (2001), *The Protestant Ethic and the Spirit of Capitalism*, Routledge, Oxford.

Weber, M., (2004), *The Vocation Lectures: Science as a Vocation, Politics as a Vocation*, Hackett Publishing Company, Cambridge, Mass.

Weick, K., (1993), 'The collapse of sense-making in organizations, the Mann Gulch disaster', *Administration Science Quarterly*, **38**, 628–652.

2. Reverse Engineering of Moral Discussion: From Symptoms to Moral Foundations

Evandro Bocatto and Eloisa Perez de Toledo

In 1958 I wrote the following: There are no hard distinctions between what is real and what is unreal, nor between what is true and what is false. A thing is not necessarily either true or false; it can be both true and false. I believe that these assertions still make sense and do still apply to the exploration of reality through art. So as a writer I stand by them but as a citizen I cannot. As a citizen I must ask: What is true? What is false? (Harold Pinter, 2005)

INTRODUCTION

Literature reveals groups of reasonably convergent assumptions about moral foundations that affect individuals, organizations and societies. Sometimes, these groups present complementary assumptions and arguments and, at other times, they exclude each other. As examples we discuss several groups of authors: the first considers moral foundations such as revealed truth or religious doctrines, for example, Plato, Galileo, Hobbes, Kierkegaard, Gabriel Marcel, Teilhard de Chardin; the second assumes morality to be a characteristic of the psychological apparatus, for example, Freud, Horney and Jung; the third views morality as the conditioning of an organism or any resulting insight, for example, Watson, Skinner and Kohler; the fourth assumes that ethics are socially constructed and relative to time and situation, for example, Sartre and Foucault; the fifth avoids moral discussions, for example, Popper; and the last group tries to link some of the above assumptions, thus combining doctrine, dialectics, rationality, logic, reality and so on, for example, Plato and Hobbes again and, Maslow, Fromm, Frankl, Lorenz. This list could go on but it is long enough to evidence the existence of different groups with distinct assumptions.

After this classification, the next step is to analyse the impact of each ontological premise on the epistemological view of social and human sciences, theory building and management practice. Those who take part in these types of analyses present different levels of criteria and awareness. Whatever the conclusions might be, they are still in a pre-paradigmatic phase which leads to a miscellaneous moral theorizing and practising. Indeed, how can a particular individual sustain that his/her assumption is better than the others?

We have already found this issue in Hobbes ([1640], 2004). In the letter addressed to his protector, the Earl of Devonshire, the author accuses the philosophers of morality who did nothing to enhance knowledge of the truth and who used circular rhetorical argumentation in their own interests instead of competent principles. Hobbes, then, sustained his moral argumentation on the principle of self-preservation and rationality, which according to him were two ontological bases of humans. Moreover the author relied on the sacred texts of the Holy Bible, the incontestable ethos of his epoch, to demonstrate and confirm his conclusions. Even before Hobbes, Plato ([around 300 BC], 2004) struck against the rhetorician's manipulation of the truth and considered gods' wishes a well-founded argumentation on which to construct his dialectics. Nevertheless neither Hobbes nor Plato was able to convince the majority.

In that sense, as there is still a variety of moral approaches and perceptions, it is difficult, with the present amount of information about some subjects, to prove, for instance, that the stakeholders' approach in management is superior to that of the shareholders; or that in economics humanistic and communitarian capitalism prevails over neo-liberalism.

Kuhn ([1962], 1996: 10) refers to paradigm as '...a term that relates closely to "normal science". By choosing it, I mean to suggest that some accepted examples of actual scientific practice – examples which include law, theory, application, and instrumentation together – provide models from which spring particular coherent traditions of scientific research.' However, the author was not sure if the same dynamics of natural sciences would occur in social issues. He stated ([1962], 1996: 15): '...and it remains an open question what parts of social science have yet acquired such paradigms at all'. And, as Perelman (1982) notes, the main difference between argumentation and a demonstration is that in the case of argumentation the status of axioms are not self-evident. Thus, argumentation is concerned with gaining adherence to sets of theses presented to an audience. Morality belongs to the realm of argumentation and, as a result, is hardly provable.

On this point, we sustain some integration of epistemological views and an instrument capable of making such integration. The objective is to avoid the struggle between Socratic non-rhetorical claims versus 'bad' rhetorical argumentation. The non-rhetorical claim anchored on the trust in evidence, such as rational evidence for Cartesians or tangible evidences for empiricists, is at best rare within the theme of moral discussion. On the other hand, it is common sense that the rhetorical discourse without moral criterion can manipulate minds depending on the context in which it is applied (Chomsky, 1997). As Perelman (1982: 9) puts it, 'all who believe in the existence of reasonable choice, preceded by deliberation or discussion where different solutions confront each other cannot avoid a theory of argumentation'.

If we consider both Perelman's claim and Pinter's challenge quoted in the beginning of this paper, '...but as a citizen I must ask: What is true? What is false?', we verify the need of an integrative instrument that helps building a moral based theory of argumentation and responds to the moral aspect of such a challenge. Such an instrument or model needs minimum criteria in order to be built. Although acknowledging that it is still a matter of argumentation.

PREPARING THE FIELD IN ORDER TO BUILD THE MODEL

Two of the most quoted articles in management are Coase's *Theory of the Firm* (1937) and Milton Friedman's attack on the social responsibility of the firm (1970). Four features of moral discussion can be identified in them, they are: *logical* – that is, based on a series of facts, reasons, and ideas that are connected in a correct and intelligent way; *amoral* – that is, have no moral standards at all; *relativist*; and *pragmatic*. These features, in our opinion, are the ones which often pervert management practice and research if moral considerations are taken into account. In general, they are the ones that originate confrontations such as employees' strikes, corporation or union inflexibility, and labour or commercial processes in courts of law.

Our criteria, then, will be amoral and logical because our aim is to avoid ontological beliefs: that is to say, our intention is to stay out, as much as possible, of the groups mentioned in the beginning of this paper. Our criteria will also be pragmatic, though only partially, but not relativist, although, relativism will be still an option for the final conclusion if it is considered appropriate. The reason for this is given below.

Pragmatic decisions in management are commonly confounded with opportunistic decisions, and expressions such as maximization, efficiency and so on become rhetorical terms for this opportunism. Expressions such as 'let us be pragmatic' receive various meanings including some which lead to naïve decisions based on short-term considerations. If we go back to the basis of the term pragmatism and take a look at the best known philosopher of American pragmatism, John Dewey (1910), we find that the term is related to a form of empiricism, based on the conception that experience is oriented towards the future and guides our activities by providing rules of action. Besides, Dewey's pragmatic approach requires reflection (see also Schön,

1983) which involves not only a sequence but a consequence of ideas, in which each idea determines its proper outcome. Thus, the model defended will avoid short term opportunistic ways of thinking and reinforce pragmatism based on reflexive thought about future consequences of moral beliefs and action.

Nevertheless Charles Peirce gives us our first reason to dismiss the relativist character of our model. He used the term pragmatism for his theories and was attempting to build a theory of signs (Bonet, 2003: 42). According to him, a sign involves a triadic relationship: the sign with the object it signifies and with the people for whom the sign refers. So, maximization, for instance, can refer to the interest of the shareholder and not that of all society in some settings, but in others it can refer to maximizing the welfare of all, shareholders included. Again, this example goes back to what we try to avoid in this chapter (that is to say, assuming a belief to be true) and for this reason we avoid relativism.

The second reason why we avoid relativism is a matter of empathy or, at least, an 'intelligent selfishness'. As adult people, we know that while we comfortably write this essay some people have been taking moral decisions which unfairly and harmfully affect other people. In this chapter, we will make specific reference to some recent published data that are often labelled as 'conspiracy theories' or something similar, and that at present can be used as evidence of morally 'sick' decisions. So, we reject relativism because we advocate that relativist decisions were the motives behind citizens such as the Sandinistas being killed in Nicaragua by the leadership of a local government sustained by an important Western country (Pinter, 2005); workers being exploited as 'modern slaves' in the Gap and Nike plants in Indonesia, while the World Bank was calling the dictator Suharto: 'the model pupil' (Pilger 2003: 17); policymakers seeing their decision-taking sovereignty being threatened by the International Monetary Fund's agreement of intentions in Ethiopia (Stiglitz, 2003). Hence, if we were in these people's place we would reject any relativist moral judgement, and many are known to have been made under spurious interests, either by the media, organizations or governments, because in the end our lives or the lives of our children would be jeopardized. This latter statement is not a matter of naïve sentimentalism, but a decision to believe and respect United Nations' Universal Declaration of Human Rights: Article 2, which agrees that 'Everyone is entitled to all the rights and freedoms set forth in this Declaration, without distinction of any kind...' If we have such rights, we empathically believe in the rights of everybody else. For both of the above reasons we dismiss relativism as a criterion in our model, thus the question of what is true and what is false made by Pinter will come out.

THE MODEL

The model was named 'reverse engineering of moral discussion'. It refers to a contemporary metaphor of software technology, called 'reverse engineering', which is the capacity of an intrusive software to revert the flow of other designed processes and identify how they were engineered. The idea, then, is to create a procedure that, from symptomatic data (that is, abnormal morality in action), sufficiently deconstructs the sequence of acts to their moral constitutions. Hopefully, this method will shed some light not only on the theoretical discussion of moral foundations but also on the practical need for day-to-day decisions that involve moral issues.

Moreover Dewey's assumption that thinking is the operation in which present facts suggest other facts (or truths) in such a way as to induce beliefs in the latter on the grounds or the guarantee of the former is reverted in such a way that the consequential facts are no longer warranted by previous beliefs, but such beliefs are critically examined on their basis instead of being taken for granted.

The inverted process (1) starts with the symptoms which are sometimes evident, but at other times are not clear enough, in this case the symptom can be inferred by the intuitive feeling of 'something seems to be wrong'; then, (2) tries to attain moral sensibility (that is, it tries to answer the question: is it a matter of morality?); (3) changes the failed moral belief and replaces it by a new 'good' belief and/or behaviour; and (4) goes back to the symptom to see whether it has changed and, if so, how. A negative result, which is either the persistence of the first symptom or the emergence of a different but still negative one, (5) restarts the process. If it all ends happily and the symptom disappears, a (6) 'stand by' phase is proposed to confirm that the change is sustainable in the long term.

If the abnormal morality in action is not perceived as a symptom, the inverted process would not start. For that reason, this perception is the key element which makes possible that the whole process develops well. However are individuals intuitive enough to perceive the symptom as a symptom? It seems so. The biological *a priori* capacity to intuit is assumed in several theoretical approaches. Rogers and Freiberg (1994) refer to this intuitive capacity when they define the concept of 'operative values'. Operative values are oriented by inborn capacities common to all human beings who have complete freedom to choose their own value directions, regardless of cultural influences and cognitive or conceptual thinking. Maslow (1962) illustrates the intuitive capacity by arguing that if the humans' inner nature tells them that aggression against others is wrong, then no amount of persuasion by anyone who argues that it is justified under certain circumstances would dissuade the individual from his/her inner conviction. Churchill and Wertz (2001) believe that it can be done in a controlled manner suggesting a methodological approach which starts with the 'direct existential contact'. They suggest that the evidence for this kind of psychological insight can be obtained from all kinds of expressions such as verbal testimony, written protocols, observed behaviour, gestures and drawings, artworks, cultural artefacts and so on.

We, thus, would have to assume health conditions on the perceiver and on the organizational setting he/she belongs to. If this basic condition is not met, the process will hardly start. The Third Reich could be a good illustration of a lack of health conditions, that is, the totalitarian regime along with a sick leadership did not perceive the abnormal morality in action and, thus, did not start the moral discussion.

THE MODEL IN ACTION

Following the rationale described above, some examples of phenomena will be given which we assume to be 'negative' social, organizational and individual symptoms: social depression (Frankl, 1984), stress (Lockwood, 2003) and burnout syndrome (Maslach et al., 2001). We will avoid the natural tendency to enter into a never-ending causal search for moral foundations, and our best 'when to stop' criterion is the change in the symptomatic consequence. In that sense, the model analyses the beliefs directed related to the symptom under scrutiny and if necessary, it analyses the beliefs that support the first beliefs and so on, until the symptom changes.

Social Depression

The first example of the model in action is its use on symptomatic social depression. The model suggests that the discussion about whether society lives in a depressive state or not should be abandoned, instead the model relies on the individual's intuition as an indicator that 'something is strange'. Following the sequence proposed by the model, the academic, the policymaker and the ordinary citizen can assume that this symptom is in fact related to moral issues. Then, we change the failed belief by all kinds of socialization procedures, directing the reformulation towards new beliefs, values and, thus, culture. Let us assume that we increase the belief that money brings happiness by maximizing consumerism. The socialization process creates expressions like 'winners' who are the ones who have a lot of money and consume most, and 'losers' who have not. Morality is constructed on 'having' instead of 'being' as Fromm (1980) analyses. Then we observe if the richer individual or the richer society are the less depressed ones. If the answer is yes, the conclusion is that struggling for money and consuming is the 'right' moral choice. But, if it is not, another belief and/or behaviour should be welcomed.

By rejecting the belief about 'money' and such resulting morality as 'the end justifies the means', the problem of social depression can be interpreted differently, as Horney did (1937: 284) with her description of hypercompetitive societies which were producers of psychopathology: 'Our modern culture is based on the principle of individual competition... The advantage of the one is frequently the disadvantage of the other... [This] competitiveness and the ... hostility that accompanies it, pervades all human relations. ... [and present] a fertile ground for the development of neurosis.' This interpretation was later confirmed by Rogers (1977: 264) who compared the life of the pathologically competitive businessman/woman to a 'rat race'. Rogers insists on the need of freeing professionals from these conditions because, unfortunately, such pathologies produce more pathological behaviours. These professionals, during the process of career development in which they cannot easily move to another job, often face various kinds of job harassment within the autocratic informal culture while they are thinking about the bills they have to pay. This is the kind of moral dilemma in which people live today. And finally, we go back to Frankl's positioning on the problem. He argues (1984: 165): '...as to the causation of the feeling of meaninglessness, one may say, albeit in an oversimplifying vein, that people have enough to live by but nothing to live for; they have the means but no meaning... The truth is that man does not live by welfare alone.' Hence, the societal or individual welfare state would be the initial point, the basis from which the possessor builds his/her meanings of life.

The model, then, refuses present beliefs, in this case about 'having money', by deconstructing the beliefs on which they are built; by practising reverse engineering, a moral discussion is started that attempts to replace the failed sequence of beliefs. This replacement is tested and a better conclusion drawn. As a result, new morality emerges.

As an illustration of the whole process, we could take Frankl's intuition with the symptomatic social phenomenon as a first stage of the model. The second stage is when the author elaborates the problem as a concept. The author (Frankl, 1984: 128) calls this social depression the 'existential vacuum' and analyzes it by saying that: 'No instinct tells him [the individual] what he has to do, and no tradition tells him what he ought to do; sometimes he does not even know what he wishes to do. Instead, he either wishes to do what other people do [conformism] or he does what other people wish him to do [totalitarianism].' After that, Frankl (1984: 129) brings awareness to the morality the phenomenon is built on: 'Moreover, there are various masks and guises under which the existential vacuum appears… [like] the will to power, including the most primitive form of the will to power, the will to money.' The next step replaces the failed moral belief with a new conjecture, for instance, a new belief which states that 'being' is better than having and the search for being 'cooperating' is better than competing.

This first example of the model in practice highlights some of its marginal gains. In the first place, the model allows everyone interested in the subject to confront the *status quo*. Many theories of group dynamics recognize that people get used to bad situations and end up using defence mechanisms to interpret them as 'the only' possible reality to live in. It also respects even the most naïve reasoning and system of beliefs. In the example above, we mixed the belief of 'having' and thus 'being happy', or non-depressive, because this unfortunately seems to be the reasoning of a considerable part of the Western society. In fact, a great deal of advertising uses this belief to convince people to buy things. However when the hypothesis of 'buying more' is submitted to the individual's own reflexive test, it can be easily rejected. The third gain follows the last one in the sense that the inquirer finds that naïve beliefs can lead to 'unfruitful', to use a euphemism, consequences and that complex systems of thought and morality might be worth a personal effort. And finally, the insight gained can provide personal motivation for the difficult struggle which aims to change social, organizational and individual moral assumptions. These marginal gains are in consonance with the gains of transformative education proposed by Mezirow (1991) and the pedagogical approach proposed by Freire (1992).

Stress and Burnout Syndrome

Stress and burnout syndrome, our next examples, are contemporary matters of concern in organizational practice. Lockwood (2003: 4) declares that:

> …increasing levels of stress can rapidly lead to low employee morale, poor productivity, and decreasing job satisfaction. Some of the specific symptoms that relate directly to productivity in the work environment are abuse of sick time, cheating, chronic absenteeism, distrust, embezzlement, organizational sabotage, tardiness, task avoidance, and violence. Other serious repercussions are depression, alcohol and drug abuse, marital and financial problems, compulsive eating disorders, and employee burnout.

Famous business magazines all over the world regularly treat the theme (for example, Benson, 2005). The solution often suggested is that as stress is an 'inevitable reality', the executive who wishes to succeed on moving up the corporate ladder should 'deal' with it, and sometimes they present lists of 'success prescriptions' containing such ideas as 'practising labour gymnastics', 'leaving the job on time' or, amazingly, 'saying no to the boss'. And they 'prove' that these ideas work by presenting one or two executives who followed the suggestions and triumphed. Again, the model can be used to evaluate what is happening with the morality of 'the duty of dealing with the inevitable'. However our experience in dealing with young executives that belong to the so-called X-generation provides evidence about their lack of commitment to their corporations. This moral system is very different to that of their parents who would 'die' for their firm. This evidence evokes our moral sensibility and leads us to a source of information that is different from that of the magazines. We rely on scientists who agree that in moderate amounts stress can be beneficial and that most people are equipped to deal with it. This leads to the new moral of 'the right to accept stress only if it comes in moderate amounts'. We start questioning those magazines by making reference to the work of authors like Ketz de Vries (1979) who explores the phenomenon of 'folie à deux', an aberrant relationship between manager and subordinates that is characterized by shared delusions, leading to the loss of 'normal' rationality and morality in the decision-making process, or to the School of Critical Theory that denounces organizational theories that take for granted biased facts, present them in textbooks and teach them in business schools. These approaches have provided business managers with expressions like 'producers' of ideologies that legitimate and strengthen specific social relations. They have also provided management academics with labels such as 'ideologists' who serve interest groups by implementing the socialization process in business schools, providing managers with ideas and vocabularies that aim to control the culture and ideology of the work setting and thus creating a scientific aura that supports the introduction and use of domination techniques (Alvesson and Deetz, 1998). So we conclude that the moral discussion on stress and burnout syndrome is complex. Workers start to reflect on and confront present beliefs about the 'inevitability' of stress and job burnout anchored in questionable supportive beliefs such as the inevitable global economy and the global competition that comes with it. They then place them in a new hypothesis, which inevitably leads to new morality.

DISCUSSION

Three points still remain to be stressed: the first one is associated with the possibility of achieving a 'better truth'; the second with the mistaken desire of institutions to maintain unsustainable beliefs that lead to actions full of moral inconsistencies or even illegalities; and the last reflects about the capacity of the model of being used as an integrative epistemological tool which provides knowledge within moral discussion and about moral action.

A 'Better Truth'

In relation to the first point, a 'better truth', some considerations must be made. Post-modern hermeneutical perspectives on science refer to the identification of the social construction of all, or at least the most relevant, aspects of human experience and the relativism of truth claims (Josselson and Lieblich, 2001). This statement is anchored in evidence and analogies. One of the most important analogical anchors is the theory of evolution; or rather, the part of this theory which believes in the non-orientation of evolution. However this non-orientation is more an assumption than a certainty.

Actually, there are three problems to be considered when the subject is evolution (Nogare, 1994): the fact of evolution which is widely accepted by the scientific community; the mechanism of evolution which places the synthetic theory (that is, an integration of mutation, selection and adaptation), as the most commonly accepted; and the direction of evolution. Scientists are divided on the third of these problems, the direction of evolution, which is the subject we are going to discuss. This inductive belief (that is, the direction of evolution) affects the basis of a variety of other theories, including those marked by moral discussions. Philosophers and scientists give three different responses to the problem of direction: 1. The evolution has no direction: it is a random effect (for example, J. Monod); 2. The evolution has a direction, purely immanent and terrestrial, explained by the dialectical laws of nature (for example, Engels and A. Oparin); and, 3. The evolution has directions, which are immanent and transcendent, terrestrial and ultra-terrestrial (for example, Hobbes, Chardin and Kierkegaard). Therefore, the 'non-directive' approach leads to the belief in 'adaptation to reality'. Such analogy was rapidly undertaken by postmodern approaches and theories such as neo-liberalism as an argument to justify their beliefs. The second hypothesis, evolution has a direction, is used by Marxists, Keynesians and some humanistic psychologists to justify the need to establish a communitarian order working for social interests. These approaches can be considered to be modern. We are going to skip the third possibility because it deals with revealed truth which, although being worthy of respect, is beyond the scope of this chapter.

If we take the historical evolution, direction can be supported. In ancient Greece, for instance, war prisoners, women and slaves were broadly considered to be sub-races. Nowadays, after a cultural 'directed evolution', this is not the case because international agreements and common sense took care of this precarious type of morality. Thus, when ordinary citizens realize that war prisoners such as the ones in Guantanamo Bay are still being held without any rights or that women are still being bought and sold, they tend to consider it absurd, in Hobbesian terms. As far as slavery is concerned, there is still a kind of moral flexibility, as is the case of Indonesians and Chinese workers who seem to work for food. In these cases, world citizens seem to believe that the path towards rights and welfare is just in its initial phase, and so they hope for the evolution towards the freedom of choice. In any case, the belief in a 'better' truth and morality is a relevant competing system of thought.

The model proposed leads to the conclusion that evolution has direction. Interestingly, although the model resembles a postmodern procedure (that is, the deconstruction of discourse), it is forced to question some postmodern assumptions such as the relativism of beliefs. The examples given suggest that better morality, and thus a better belief, is possible, which means that there is a clear orientation towards something. This does not mean we are Marxists, Keynesians or humanistic psychologists by *a priori* assumption but we might become one or another through *a posteriori* reasoning.

Unsustainable Beliefs

The second point to be discussed is related to the mistaken desire of governments and corporations to maintain unsustainable beliefs. There is evidence showing that governments and corporations still take morally weak and short-term decisions and they will be better interpreted as mistaken if one makes a longitudinal analysis. In Rome, near the Coliseum, there is a map showing the geographical expansion of the Roman Empire, from the city state to the known world of that time. This empire eventually crumbled, so it is reasonable to assume that other empires will also crumble and that the morality on which they were built is a significant explanatory factor.

Dewey (1954: 89, 90) presents an interesting evolutionary sequence about the change from mercantilism to the roots of a global economy. The author states:

> [The] use of machinery in production and commerce was followed by the creation of new powerful social conditions, personal opportunities and wants. [however] The legal regulations so affected every phase of life which was interested in taking advantage of the new economic agencies... [this] established custom of states, expressed intellectually in the theory of mercantilism against which Adam Smith wrote his account of 'The [True] Wealth of Nations,' prevented the expansion of trade between nations... .

Smith's truth was a reaction to old mercantile morality. Nevertheless this new establishment is built on another fragile morality which may explain the present urge for changing the way the global economy was devised. Dewey (1954: 90) explains:

> The economic movement was perhaps the most influential because it operated, not in the name of the individual and his inherent rights, but in the name of Nature. Economic 'laws,' that of labour springing from natural wants and leading to the creation of wealth, of present abstinence in behalf of future enjoyment leading to creation of capital effective in piling up still more wealth, the free play of competitive exchange, designated the law of supply and demand, were 'natural' laws.

Thus, our model considers the governments' and corporations' decisions as symptomatic and invites us to think about the beliefs which support such decisions. In the model, the belief that assumes 'economic laws' as 'natural laws' is confronted, then new moral beliefs are hypothesized, and so on.

In this respect, the little empires of international organizations namely the World Bank and the International Monetary Fund are criticized by the authors quoted in this chapter, because of the tendentious morality on which they were first built. When, for example, John Maynard Keynes, the British representative at Bretton Woods, proposed a tax on creditor nations, designed to prevent poor countries falling into perpetual debt, 'he was told by the Americans that if he persisted, Britain would not get its desperately needed loans' (Pilger, 2003: 120).

Unfortunately, the decline of empires and the moral beliefs in which they sustained are not natural per se. Lorenz ([1973], 1988: 17–18) observes that the homeostatic regulation of organic systems is made possible by feedback mechanisms, in which circuits of positive feedback are followed by negative feedback, which in turn leads back to the steady state. Breaking this mechanism is a great risk: an unblocked circuit of positive feedback can lead to disaster. The pathological perturbations of human social life represent this kind of positive circuit and therefore must be taken seriously and be confronted by concerned citizens. In fact, Smith took a stand against mercantilism and Pilger, Pinter and Stiglitz are attaining moral sensibility as well and criticizing the morality of the label 'global economy' and how this dubious morality is used in the foreign policies of developed countries, the objectives of international organizations and the ethics of corporations.

Integrating Epistemological Approaches

The third, and last, point is a self-reflection about the capacity of the instrument in integrating epistemological approaches once thought mutually exclusive and in providing knowledge for moral discussion and action. If we consider knowledge as 'justified true belief', as Von Krogh et al. (2000) thought about it, the question of justification regarding truth is not about data, or of confirming or ruling out evidence, but of the criteria set up and used to establish the confirmation procedures and then how these criteria are legitimized. Accordingly, the model works on analysing with reflection the criteria set up and used to establish the confirmation procedures of the present moral belief and action felt as symptomatic and also to understand how these criteria were legitimized. Both understandings being confronted deconstructed and changed leads to a revitalizing search for enhancement of the present moral. We insist on the confrontation of the moral interpretation of the symptoms. That is, the symptoms are there: civilians are killed in wars, poor people starve to death, employees suffer stress and so on. All of this is reality. However the interpretation of the motives of why the symptom is happening is broad, and thus flexible enough to be confronted, changed and tested. And that is what the model does.

In summary, it is amazing to observe how international organizations, governments and corporations take decisions as if world citizens or employees would respond with a kind of *ceteris paribus* attitude; we mean by that, they expect passivity, they expect them to act as if nothing had changed. Moreover these decisions do not invite more profound moral discussion as the reverse engineering model presented here does; in fact, the simplest invitation to think about the moral issues involved can decisively shake their bases. The assumption that justification regarding truth is about the criteria set up and used to establish the confirmation procedures is true, however, it is not rigid. Being thus stated, any instrument can bring new and 'better' knowledge to moral discussion and action.

USE, RELEVANCE AND LIMITATIONS OF THE MODEL

Academic settings are appropriate places in which the model can be used. Business management congresses and seminars can benefit from the model, particularly because the extreme technical interest of management knowledge minimizes important discussions on the moral foundations of their acts. Moreover the simplicity of the model means that it can be used to encourage reflection in all sorts of groups belonging to schools, unions, churches and so on. Neither is age a restriction: children, adolescents and adults can benefit from it because it relies on the part of the brain that is logical and rational permitting the observation of what is decided by emotions and traditions (Berne, 1961). The simple task of using the symptom to deconstruct beliefs that were once guarantees of the belief in the symptom, and then choosing and testing a new belief and morality makes it easier to spread moral discussions throughout society.

We agree with the existentialists who argue that truth must not be treated as if it were detached from human experience. In that sense, Kierkegaard advocates: 'The subjective man can never be separate from the object which he observes' (May, 1958: 26). However we have argued that perceptions, experiences and subjectivities are not completely rigid, so beliefs, morals and truth can not only change but can 'get better'. Frankl (1984: 154–155) tells the story of Dr. J. who was the only person he could qualify as a 'satanic figure'. Dr. J., in fact, was known as the 'mass murderer of Steinhof' (the large mental hospital in Vienna) who followed the Nazi euthanasia programme and tried not to let a single psychotic individual escape the gas chamber. After many years, Frankl received the impressive information that Dr. J. was a prisoner in Lubianka, where he eventually died. While he was there, he was described as 'the best comrade one can imagine', he gave consolation to everybody and lived up to the highest conceivable moral standard. In our opinion, Dr. J. found a better truth. Moral choices between a totalitarian or manipulative government versus a democratic one, individual and paranoid competition versus teamwork, and bad-quality products and services in contrast to total quality can be made and tested. In short, we believe that there are an infinite number of ways in which humans can learn and change their perceptions and experience, although we do not discount biological and psychological restrictions. In the end, the truth, or the relational truth in Kierkegaard's terms, between subjectivity and the external object, can be enhanced.

The relativist moral decision is a mistake for many reasons. In the long run relativist decisions can harm every person or institution that they affect, if not in this generation, in future ones. In fact, it cannot be forgotten that any psychopath in charge either of companies or governments can take advantage of the relativistic claim in order to institutionalize their pathological desires. Therefore, as we intend to consider a minimum health as a prerequisite for taking moral discussions, as Maslow et al. (1998) point out, we would prefer a decision-making process that considers the impacts on the human beings as specie in present and future times. Sometimes a relativist decision is inevitable, due to the difficulty in finding the truth. Nevertheless this decision should always be under suspicion and taken as a conjecture waiting for confirmation. The reverse engineering model determines that, if confirmed, the conjecture will receive the status of a stronger conjecture (Lorenz 1973, 1988), but still subject to future confrontation.

The model does not claim to be universal. In fact we see some of its limitations in the bioethics discussions, for example. Besides, there are some controversial issues nowadays in which moral discussions are not welcomed. The model is also limited by these controversies.

REFERENCES

Alvesson, Mats and Deetz, Stanley (1998), 'Teoria crítica e abordagens pós-modernas para estudos organizacionais', in S. R. Clegg, C. Hardy and W. R. Nord, (Eds), *Handbook de Estudos Organizacionais*, Atlas, São Paulo, 227–266.

Benson, Herbert (2005), 'Are you working too hard? A conversation with Herbert Benson', *Harvard Business Review*, **83** (11), 53–61.

Berne, Eric (1961), *Transactional Analysis in Psychotherapy: A Systematic and Individual Psychiatry*, Grove Press, New York.

Bonet, Eduard (2003), *Arts of Reasoning in Knowledge, Action and Learning, Lecture notes and readings*, ESADE/URL, Barcelona.

Chomsky, Noam (1997), *Media Control: The Spectacular Achievements of Propaganda*, Seven Stories Press, New York.

Churchill, Scott D. and Wertz, Frederic J., (2001), 'An introduction to phenomenological research in psychology: historical, conceptual, and methodological foundations', in Kirk J. Schneider, James F. T. Bugental, and , J. Fraser Pierson (eds.), *The Handbook of Humanistic Psychology: Leading Edges in Theory, Research and Practice*, Sage, London, 247–262.

Coase, Ronald H., (1937), 'The nature of the firm', *Economica*, **4** (16), 386–405.

Dewey, John (1910), *How We Think*, Prometheus, New York.

Dewey, John (1954), *The Public and Its Problems*, Swallow Press, Chicago.

Frankl, Victor (1984), *Man's Search for Meaning*, Square Press, Washington.

Freire, Paulo (1992), *Pedagogia da Esperança: Um Reencontro com a Pedagogia do Oprimido*, Editora Paz e Terra, São Paulo.

Friedman, Milton (1970), 'The social responsibility of business is to increase its profits', *The New York Times*, 13 September 1970.

Fromm, Eric (1980), *Ter ou Ser?*, Editora Zahar, Rio de Janeiro.

Hobbes, Thomas (1640), *De Cive*, reprinted in T. Hobbes, (2004), *Do Cidadão*, Editora Martin Claret, São Paulo.

Horney, Karen (1937), *The Neurotic Personality of Our Time*, Norton, New York.

Josselson, Ruthellen and Lieblich, Amia (2001), 'Narrative research and humanism', in Kirk J. Schneider, James F. T. Bugental, and J. Fraser, Pierson (eds.), *The Handbook of Humanistic Psychology: Leading Edges in Theory, Research and Practice*, Sage, London, 275–288.

Ketz de Vries and Manfred F. R., (1979), 'Managers can drive their subordinates mad', *Harvard Business Review*, **57** (4), 125–127.

Kuhn, Thomas S., ([1962], 1996), *The Structure of Scientific Revolutions*, University of Chicago Press, Chicago.

Lockwood, Nancy R., (2003), 'Work/life balance: challenges and solutions'. *HR Magazine*, **48** (6), 2–10.

Lorenz, Konrad (1973), *Die acht Todsünden der zivilisierten Menschheit*, reprinted in W. Eitel, (ed.), (1988), *Os Oito Pecados Mortais do Homen Civilizado*, Editora Brasiliense, São Paulo.

Maslach, Christina, Schaufeli, Wilmar B. and Leiter, Michael P., (2001), 'Job burnout', *Annual Review of Psychology*, **52**, 397–422.

Maslow, Abraham H., (1962), *Toward a Psychology of Being*, Van Nostrand, New York.

Maslow, Abraham H., Stephens, Deborah C. and Heil, Gary (1998), *Maslow on Management*, John Wiley & Sons, Inc, New York.

May, Rollo (1958), 'The origins and significance of the existential movement in psychology', in R. May, E. Angel, and H. F. Ellenberger (eds.), *Existence: A New Dimension in Psychiatry and Psychology*, Basic Books, New York, 3–36.

Mezirow, Jack (1991), *Transformative Dimensions of Adult Learning*, Jossey-Bass, San Francisco.

Nogare, Pedro D., (1994), *Humanismos e Anti-humanismos*, Editora Vozes, Petrópolis.

Perelman, C., (1982), *The Realm of Rhetoric*, University of Notre Dame Press, Notre Dame (IN).

Pilger, John (2003), *The New Rulers of the World*, Verso, London.

Pinter, Harold (2005), *Art, Truth & Politics*, Nobel Lecture, 8 December. (http://nobelprize.org/literature/laureates/2005/pinter-lecture-e.html), accessed on 9 December 2005.

Plato, (300 BC), *Republic*, reprinted in Plato (2004), *A República*, Martin Claret, São Paulo.

Rogers, Carl R., (1977), *Carl Rogers on Personal Power*, Delacorte Press, New York.

Rogers, Carl R. and H. Jerome Freiberg, (1994), *Freedom to Learn*, Prentice Hall, New Jersey.

Schön, Donald A., (1983), *The Reflective Practitioner*, Basic Books, New York.

Stiglitz, Joseph E., (2003), *Globalization and Its Discontents*, W. W. Norton and Company, New York.

Von Krogh, Georg, Ichijo, Kazuo and Nonaka, Ikujiro (2000), *Enabling Knowledge Creation*, Oxford University Press, Oxford.

3. From Hunter-gatherer to Organizational Man: A Morality Tale

Kathryn Gordon and Raymond-Alain Thietart

Man, with all his noble qualities, with sympathy which feels for the most debased, with benevolence which extends not only to other men but to the humblest living creature, with his god-like intellect which has penetrated into the movements and constitution of the solar system – with all these exalted powers – Man still bears in his bodily frame the indelible stamp of his lowly origin. (Darwin [1879], 2004: 689)

INTRODUCTION: THE EVOLUTIONARY BASIS OF MORALITY

This chapter begins with a long-term view of the topic of the moral foundations of management.[*] This view stretches back into the primordial past to the time when human beings lived as hunter-gatherers in small, durable groups of closely-related individuals. During this early phase of human evolution, the cognitive and emotional traits that permitted the formation and spontaneous enforcement of behavioural norms were essential for the survival of humans as a group-dependent species. It could be argued that such a long-term perspective is not needed to understand the moral foundations of the management of business organizations in modern market economies.

The value of this long term perspective is that it permits the development of a micro-analytical theory of morality (a system of ideas of good or right conduct).[1] It sheds light on both the sources of ethical principles (that is, norms by which people judge the appropriateness of their own and others' actions) and on sources of obligation (that is, how ethical principles are made to influence behaviour in group settings, including the modern business

---

[*] The views and opinions expressed in this chapter are not necessarily shared by the OECD or by its member governments.

organization). As such, this perspective provides a basis for modelling moral obligation and group behaviour for modern man. Evolutionary psychology (EP) is the discipline that analyses animal and human psychology by considering them to be evolutionary adaptations. The implications of this body of theory for understanding ethics has been extensively developed (see, for example, Alexander's *The Biology of Moral Systems*, 1987) and the current chapter draws on this body of literature.

In particular, it uses the EP perspective to elaborate, in the final section, the views that: 1) there is no such thing as an ethically neutral business organization; all business activity is fraught with ethical choice; 2) crafters of formal managerial and regulatory control systems would do well to take into account the spontaneous group coordinating capacities that are built by evolution into the human mind; and 3) 'soft' managerial measures designed to cement affiliation and identification with the organisation can be as powerful as the contractual and financial incentives that are the focus of mainstream economic analyses of the firm.

MAN AS A SOCIAL ANIMAL: ETHICS, COOPERATION AND COMPETITION

Evolutionary success depends on success in two (inter-related) spheres: somatic activities and reproduction. Through their somatic activities, animals seek access to the basic material resources that they need to survive (food, shelter, defence). These in turn create the conditions in which reproduction can take place – ability to leave surviving offspring is the ultimate measure of an organism's evolutionary success. Reproduction requires: 1) surviving until the age at which procreation is possible; 2) gaining access to reproductive opportunities; and 3) successfully creating the conditions in which someone (often one or both parents) makes the investment needed for the survival of their offspring (humans are one of several animal species that require extremely high investments in their young).

Man in his ancestral state of nature was largely dependent on his group. In the environment in which our ancestors evolved, group activities included hunting, gathering, finding or building shelters, caring for children and group defence against animal predators and hostile, competing bands of humans. There was 'an overriding need (and commensurate rewards for) mutualism and reciprocity...' (Corning, 2004: 4). Life within these groups of hunter-gatherers was undoubtedly subject to fierce internal competition (for resources and reproductive opportunities), status rivalries and social conflicts. However, a common interest in the durability and success of the group joined all group members in a 'shared enterprise of collective survival' (Boehm,

2000). There was no 'social safety net' other that provided by the group itself. The ancestral environment created high evolutionary stakes for successful cooperation and for finding the right dynamic balance between individual and group interests.

Thus, the prototypical hunter-gatherer was continually confronted with a particular class of moral questions – should he seek to advance group interests or his own self-interests? For the highly social, group-dependent human species – evolving as hunter-gatherers faced with numerous environmental threats – the nature of self-interest was and is complex. Self interest in humans obviously includes concern for one's own material, sexual and psychological well-being. In addition, there is an obvious evolutionary logic for showing concern for genetically-related individuals (kin selection would promote the propagation of genes that promote individuals engaging in behaviours that benefit other individuals who share some of the same genes). Altruism within families is a readily observable feature of all human societies and casual observation shows that altruistic behaviour weakens as kinship ties weaken (for example, parents care for and protect their own children more than those of others).

However for human beings (and other social animals) the individual's well-being was closely related to that of his group – individuals in the ancestral environment could not expect to survive without the production efficiencies afforded by rudimentary division of labour in hunting, gathering and household production; without the mutual protection afforded by the group when confronting animal and human threats; and without the social insurance opportunities provided by intra-group group sharing (this allowed for pooling of the food availability risks associated with hunting and gathering). All of these sources of benefit – division of labour, mutual protection and social insurance through sharing – would have required the formation and enforcement of social norms in order to work in a coordinated manner and to control free-riding (via both self-control and group control).

Many animal species cooperate and some have evolved complex systems for cooperation. Ant colonies have elaborate divisions of labour and bees pool information (Ridley, 1996). The characteristics that distinguish the human approach to cooperation are its elaborateness and, above all, the flexibility of human cooperative (or non-cooperative) behaviours. The pronounced cooperation in human societies and the wide repertoire of possible human responses to external stimuli (a trait that resembles free will), is, in the EP perspective, a product of emotional and cognitive programming by the processes of evolution.

Charles Darwin's *The Descent of Man* makes explicit the tight link between human evolution and moral choice. More particularly, he was one of the first to document how humans have been endowed through evolutionary processes with 'social and moral faculties' that allow them to be both cooperative and competitive in an evolutionary sense. Chapter 5 ('Moral Faculties') of *The Descent of Man* develops an evolutionary model of morality which sets forth themes that have occupied evolutionary psychologists ever since: the relation between moral sentiments and human evolution; how evolution overcame the penalties associated with the self-sacrifice of altruism; natural selection of groups versus natural selection of individuals; the role of 'self-regarding' and social emotions in self-regulation and group regulation.

Darwin states that:

> In order that primeval man, or the ape-like progenitors of man, should become social, they must have acquired the same instinctive feelings which impel other animals to live in a body; and they no doubt exhibited the same general disposition. They would have felt uneasy when separated from their comrades, for whom they would have felt some degree of love, they would have warned each other of danger and have given mutual aid in attack or defence. All this implies some degree of sympathy, fidelity and courage. Such social qualities, the paramount importance of which to lower animals is disputed by no one, were no doubt acquired by the progenitors of man in a similar manner, namely, through natural selection... (Darwin [1879], 2004: 155).

In a nutshell, the argument is that evolutionary processes created emotions and related cognitive processes in man because these reinforced group behaviours that were 'fit' in the ancestral environment (that is, that provided a mix of competition and cooperation within the group that permitted individuals having such behaviours to leave surviving offspring). Love, loyalty, sympathy, sociability and fear of exclusion were the emotional glue that held the ancestral bands together (more or less). Disdain, anger and 'moralistic aggression' allowed people to 'punish' perceived transgressions of norms (for example, that one's cousin's gift of meat is not generous enough) while other sentiments in the transgressor (embarrassment, shame, fear of loss of esteem or status) enhanced the effectiveness of such spontaneous, emotion-based punishment. On the positive side, praise, encouragement, desire for status and esteem would have promoted pro-group norms. This subject is discussed in more detail in the section below on the 'emotional and cognitive bases of cooperation'.

Since many of these capacities allowed human communities to define and to enforce spontaneously (that is, using emotion-based mechanisms) the rights of individuals and duties to family and to the group at large, EP provides an evolutionary perspective on how ethical norms are formed and implemented in groups. To the extent that these capacities are still present in the human mind, they influence the dynamics of group behaviour in modern organizations and they constitute the most basic moral foundation upon which all organizations in all cultures rest. Wenegrat et al. (1996: 404) state that 'while norms and the cultural emphasis placed on compliance may vary, similar processes of compliance with social norms have been observed in all societies'.

The EP literature dealing with this subject is of two types: 1) reports on results of experiments (often based on games played by students) or other empirical studies that attempt to measure the extent of altruism, cooperation and defection (non-cooperative behaviour) and the mechanisms influencing such behaviours; and 2) speculations about which evolutionary processes in the ancestral environment could have led to altruism. The following paragraphs describe the broad thrust of this literature.

Although the conclusions of research measuring the extent and mechanisms for altruism and cooperation are in state of flux, the following results appear to be particularly pertinent. First, experimental results show that altruism and cooperation are extremely common (indeed, they are universal), but the details of these behaviours also seems to be highly dependent on the frame of the experiment. For example, Stout (2001) surveys 'results of experimental games, where propensity toward altruism and cooperation is tested with experimental subjects'. The survey points to a strong tendency toward altruism and cooperation, but also stresses the importance of the framing of the game in influencing outcomes (for example, the game's title, the social context in which the game takes place and the approach of the person administering the game). Another important finding is that altruistic enforcement of rules is an engrained human behaviour. Numerous experiments indicate that humans have a pronounced tendency to punish perceived anti-social, self-serving behaviour, even when such punishment is personally costly to the punisher (see, for example, the survey in Gintis, 2003). Such punishing behaviours may have been adaptive in the ancestral environment as a means of spontaneously enforcing group-supporting norms. They are a form of altruism since the damage caused by spiteful activity to its perpetrator amounts to an investment in the effectiveness of group norms that benefits the group as a whole.

Explanations of how such behaviours might have emerged in humans (that is, speculating on which evolutionary processes might have produced them) are a major topic in EP research and many of the possible explanations remain controversial. There is general agreement that altruism addressed to kin can emerge through processes of kin selection and that the members of the small bands of hunter-gatherers that populated the ancestral environment were probably closely related to one another. However human beings frequently engage in generalized 'other considering behaviour' that cannot be explained by biological relatedness or by a straightforward quid pro quo (that is, it is not a rudimentary barter of good deeds). Indeed, in human beings the extent of altruism (beyond kin) can be dramatic – Johnson (1996), using a record of thousands of acts of extreme heroism kept by the Carnegie Foundation, studies 676 heroic acts that involved rescuers risking (and sometimes losing) their own lives to save the life of another.

A widely-accepted explanation of altruistic behaviour is 'indirect reciprocity' (Alexander, 1987). This model views altruism as being a kind of investment in other-considering behaviour that falls short of direct exchange. In this view, individuals make these investments not because they expect an immediate reward, but because they expect the favour to be reciprocated at some later date. Alexander speculates that incentives for indirect reciprocity could have been quite diffuse – for example the individuals making them might have secured the survival-enhancing benefits of living in a generally well-functioning, tight-knit group (something resembling social capital). Within the group there would have been ample scope for moving ancestral bands of hunter-gatherers toward what might be thought of as a Paretian 'social contract' curve via generalized exchanges in other-considering 'good deeds' – that is, such investments would have been especially enhancing of overall welfare inasmuch as humans have cognitive capacities to judge which 'altruistic' acts have relatively low costs for them and relatively high benefits for others. If such indirect reciprocity conferred survival benefits then the genetic predisposition to this sort of behaviour would have been favoured by the process of natural selection.

'Group selection' is a considerably more controversial (and non-competing) explanation of altruistic behaviour (Rubin and Somanathan, 1998: 449). Group selection occurs when evolutionary pressures operate first on group survival (that is, they select fit groups rather than fit individuals) and, through this mechanism, affect individual survival and the propagation of genes. If group selection was a strong feature of the ancestral environment (for example, because warfare or food shortages tended to wipe out entire bands of hunter-gatherers), then it clearly would have created an evolutionary incentive for individuals to, under certain circumstances, sacrifice their interests for those of the group.[2] In this respect, sexual selection and group selection may have interacted in complex ways – for example, if high status was conferred on individuals making strong contributions to group welfare and if, for example, females preferred to mate with high status males, then the necessary incentives would have been created.

Of course, altruism is not the whole story and human development is not an unremitting tale of concern for others and brotherly love. Man, in addition to being a social animal, has also been evolutionarily programmed to be self-interested – he suffers when he is hungry or thirsty, lust causes him to seek out reproductive opportunities. There is a strong evolutionary logic for him to act to secure material resources and reproductive opportunities at minimum costs to himself and evolution has produced an arsenal of traits that help him to do this.

The human capacity for deception is well developed – humans can deploy an elaborate array of deceitful behaviours. In the ancestral environment, this capacity for deception would have been used to open up free-rider opportunities (for example, for an individual to take more food than group norms say he deserves or to shift dangerous tasks on to others). Control of cheating on group norms for resource allocation (food sharing or task assignments) would have been an important function in ancestral societies. Humans also have a demonstrated capacity for (often violent) coercion. Thus, control of bullying or physical aggression would have been an important function for maintaining the cohesiveness and the durability of the group.

The spontaneous formation and enforcement of social norms (that is, shared rules for assessing behaviour) in primitive societies is crucial to understanding how humans 'solved' (in an evolutionary sense) these challenges (for example, of controlling free-riding and aggression). The formation of norms allowed groups to come up with coordinated answers to a wide variety of questions: How were the fruits of hunting and gathering to be distributed in different circumstances? Who was to undertake what type of productive activity? What duties of protection and care were owed to various members of the community (for example, the sick or injured, the old and the very young)? What rules governed access to reproductive opportunities? How were dangerous tasks to be allocated? Informal social norms are central to anthropological studies of modern hunter-gatherers and, extrapolating from these studies, one palaeontologist concludes that 'Members of the earliest moral communities agreed on behaviours they did not like' (Boehm, 2000: 26). The ability to develop spontaneously shared norms is one of the defining characteristics of the human species – humans are 'a rule-making and rule-using animal' (Dopfer, 2004: 180).

THE EMOTIONAL AND COGNITIVE BASES OF COOPERATION

Of course the ability to form norms is only part of the story – in many respects the most interesting part is how early humans enforced these norms. How did they keep free-riding, cheating and aggression in check? As suggested earlier, the EP answer to this question is that, through evolutionary processes, emotional and cognitive capacities emerged that allowed humanity to solve these crucial group coordination problems. They did this by providing emotion-based punishments and rewards in support of group norms.

From an evolutionary perspective, 'emotions are specific neuro-physiological phenomena, shaped by natural selection, that organise and motivate physiological, cognitive and action patterns that facilitate adaptive responses to the vast array of demands and opportunities in the environment' (Weiss 2002: 35). It is important for EP that certain basic emotions be universal – that is, shared by all cultures (which is not the same thing as saying that culture plays no role in how emotions are expressed or acted on). Darwin's chapter headings in *The Expression of the Emotions in Man and Animals* ([1872], 1999) provide a typology of what he believed are universally-shared emotions: 1) low spirits, anxiety, grief, dejection, despair; 2) joy, high spirits, love, tender feelings, devotion; 3) reflection, meditation, ill-temper, sulkiness, determination; 4) hatred and anger; 5) disdain, contempt, disgust, guilt, pride, helplessness, patience, affirmation and negation; 6) surprise, astonishment, fear, horror; and 7) self-attention, shame, shyness, modesty, blushing.

Some of these emotions would have promoted adaptive behaviours at the level of the individual (for example, fear would have motivated the action of avoiding danger). They would also support, in various ways, humanity's positioning as a social animal. For example, they would have provided the mortar that held human groups together. Chiappe and MacDonald (2005: 42) state that 'the human affectional system is designed to cement long term relationships of intimacy and trust by making them intrinsically rewarding'. Thus, the more social emotions in Darwin's list would have increased the cohesiveness of human groups (for example, love, tender feelings, devotion would have held them together) while also providing counterbalancing motivations for disbanding and forming new groups (anger and hatred).

Human emotions also supported the formation of socially complex (somewhat hierarchical) groups. Pride and the desire for the esteem of others and to have a high status in the group hierarchy would have reinforced investments in group welfare and adherence to group norms. Sexual selection – that is, an evolutionary process that runs parallel to natural selection and that is driven by competition for and choice of sexual partners – would have complemented and reinforced these emotions if mating decisions were also made on the basis of group status and prestige. These emotions would have supported individual actions in support of group welfare and would have provided a positive impetus for respecting group norms.

Other emotions created scope for psychological punishment of transgressions of group norms. On the punisher's side, these would have included emotions such as anger, and self-righteousness (and related behaviours such as moralistic aggression) which would have motivated spiteful behaviours (being willing to give up some of one's own well-being to punish someone else, a habit that is documented in the Gintis study cited in the preceding section). On the side of the punished individual, other emotions that would have enhanced susceptibility to such punishment would have included fear of ridicule or ostracism, embarrassment and shame.

Emotions would also have facilitated communication within the group. Emotions are associated with distinctive physiological states and with characteristic physical displays. These allowed group members to evaluate each others' emotional states and to guess likely responses – thus, emotions were (and are) one of the keys to coordination and regulation of group activities. 'Emotions have a fundamental linkage with social capacities, providing a non-verbal means to communicate through facial expressions, body posture and voice tone' (Lord et al., 2002: 15). Darwin's recognition of the key role of emotions in human and animal evolution explains his interest in the universality of facial expressions and in documenting the links between animal expressions and human expressions of emotion.

Finally, as noted earlier, emotions also made (and make) possible the human species' broad and complex behavioural repertoire by imparting a kind of flexibility and open-endedness to human behaviour – Lord et al. (2002) note that emotions are part of the architecture of the mind which allows the human animal to decouple stimuli and response and to respond flexibly to changing situations.

Human cognitive capacities played an important role in facilitating cooperation and constraining anti-social behaviour. Humans are good at the dissimulation and mimicry needed to fool or cheat others. In response, evolutionary processes created an offsetting cognitive capability – the ability to assess trustworthiness and to predict when one is likely to be a victim of defectors or cheaters. Thus, human evolution has been an ongoing cat and mouse game between opportunists and cooperators – as Rubin and Somanathan (1998: 452) put it 'successful human ancestors deduced ways to behave opportunistically and also to avoid being victimised by opportunistic behaviour'. Because this cognitive capability is of particular relevance to transactions costs economics, the discussion of cheater detection is deferred to the following section.

Another cognitive capacity that is central to humanity's status as a social animal is the ability to identify individuals and to identify degrees of affiliation – this is partly physical (related in particular to identifying faces), but humans also have finely tuned abilities to determine affiliation based on behavioural cues. Group affiliation is therefore closely related to norms because an individual's affiliation to a group is identified in part by his ability to show appropriate adherence to group norms (for example, speaking a language without an accent – that is, applying norms for pronunciation in a faultless manner – is one way of demonstrating one's cultural affiliation).

Rubin and Somanathan (1998) comment on the human species' intriguingly elastic ability to form multiple group affiliations. For example, modern humans might define themselves in terms of their nationality (and/or regional origin), religion, profession, place of employment, allegiance to a particular sports club, which university they graduated from, and so on. This human ability (which has both cognitive and emotional bases) to form relatively cohesive groups, but also the ability to dissolve old groups and to reconstitute or to join new groups may indicate that this flexibility had important survival value in the ancestral environment.

CONCLUSIONS: THE MORAL ANIMAL IN THE MODERN BUSINESS ORGANIZATION

Humankind is now the dominant species on the planet and has enjoyed dramatic improvements in its material and social well-being. Ever deeper and broader specialization in production (now being realised on a global scale) has raised material standards of living for most of humanity. The progressive development of formal systems of law has, in most societies, lowered exposure to physical threats to personal security and to loss of property through theft or confiscation. All in all, human history has been a story of progress.

These benefits have been associated with increased scale in the capacity to cooperate and coordinate in the economic, political and social spheres. With the ingenuity that characterizes it, mankind has developed increasingly complex institutions that allow it to balance the tensions between cooperation and competition and between group and individual interests.[3] Anthropologists and complexity theorists are now trying to understand the evolutionary basis of the transition from informal, norm-based coordination within small, permanent groups to the institutional complexity that characterizes modern societies (see, for example, Jost, 2005 and Corning, 2004). According to Corning (2004: 43), institutional development has involved progressive institutional innovations or '"workarounds" to compensate for the lack of the face-to-face social influences that facilitate cooperation and constrain anti-social behaviour in small groups'.

This progressive development of political, economic and social institutions (what might be thought of as 'civilization') has, among other things, allowed coordination to take place within ever-expanding groups of unrelated individuals. In effect, the scope of human capacity to coordinate has, over many millennia, rippled out in concentric circles from the inner core formed by small, ancestral bands of hunter-gatherers. The development of behavioural norms for economic transactions in markets and within business organizations is an important subset of broader institutional development. This subset contains such diverse elements such as laws, religious strictures, regulatory and administrative procedures and civil channels for communicating with and pressuring the business sector. It covers a vast domain of business behaviours (for example, protections of the rights of various stakeholders, transparency, fair competition, political activity). The behavioural principles and rules embodied in these institutions form an important moral foundation of management, but one that rests on the deeper foundation formed by the capacities and predispositions built into the human mind.

North (1990: 17) states that all 'theorising in the social sciences builds, implicitly or explicitly, upon conceptions of human behaviour'. When thinking about formal systems of managerial and regulatory control, therefore, it is useful to keep in mind the behavioural patterns and cognitive and emotional capabilities bequeathed to us by our ancestors. As Cosmides and Tooby (1994: 329) put it, 'biological evolution is a slow process and the modern world has emerged within an evolutionary eye-blink'. Thus, the humans interacting in modern business organizations bring these mental capabilities to work with them. Organizational man and his hunter-gatherer forefathers have much in common – while the former is usually better dressed and heavily influenced by formal rules, most of the mental tools he uses to manage his interaction with others are identical to those of his forefathers. What is interesting is to attempt to understand how the emotional and cognitive capacities that are part and parcel of this evolutionary legacy interact with formal institutions of managerial and regulatory control.

The remainder of this section develops some thoughts on this matter. Before beginning, it is worth recalling the definition of ethical principles given earlier in this paper – 'norms by which people judge the appropriateness of their own and others' behaviour'. It is also worth establishing a definition of organization as a group of people intentionally organized to accomplish an overall, common goal or set of goals. Several conclusions about the link between our evolutionary legacy, ethics and organizations emerge.

No such Thing as an Ethically-neutral Business

Business organizations are *inter alia* social contexts in which ethical considerations inevitably come into play; there is no such thing as an ethically-neutral business. The argument in support of this proposition has many layers. For example, even the apparently straightforward proposition that the purpose of the firm is to maximize profits (or shareholder value) is not ethically-neutral. Managers working toward such a goal face a multitude of weighty ethical questions (for example, what is the meaning in the manager's particular business context of exercising due care in honouring duties to shareholders?)

Seen through the lens of EP, business organizations (indeed, all organizations) are intrinsically ethically-charged social contexts because, as suggested earlier in this chapter, the people involved in them have been programmed by evolution to make moral judgements about a particular class of fairness problems and to create and enforce related group norms when they engage in durable group activities. The evolutionary programming of the human mind will direct individuals operating in business organizations to focus their cognitive and emotional resources on particular classes of ethical problems, especially those dealing with fairness of resource and task allocation, cheating, not honouring commitments and free-riding. Systems of formal management control within organizations and of formal regulation by governments ignore this moral programming at their peril.

Formal Control Systems and the Legacy of our Hunter-gatherer Past

Formal systems of managerial or regulatory controls can be either undermined or reinforced by the informal group controls that will arise spontaneously in the course of repeated human interactions in a durable group setting (such as that created within business organizations). One of the testable managerial implications of the EP perspective is that, in small businesses whose sizes resemble those of the hunter-gathering bands in the ancestral environment and for transactions complexities that are similar to those found in that environment, few formal management controls are needed to produce coherent group action.

Dunbar (1993) argues that the species-specific maximum group size for humans is about 150 individuals (that is, this is the maximum number of relationships that an individual can keep track of, given human neurological constraints, in a complex and continuously changing social world). This suggests that small organizations of 150 or fewer people should be able to rely extensively on spontaneous, informal mechanisms in order to pursue organizational goals in a more or less orderly way. EP details the architecture of the human mind that explains why and how smaller business groups can be very cohesive and directed, just as our hunter-gatherer ancestors were when facing external threats or opportunities.

A closely-related implication is that the mental capabilities conferred by evolution can be used to form smaller sub-groups (say, 150 individuals or fewer) within larger business organizations. These would emerge in the context of repeated interactions in the context of team production or other formal sub-units of the organization; they could emerge as a result of shared affiliation with some other group (for example, among employees of the same race or the same religion); or they could emerge informally and spontaneously.

Regardless of the context in which these sub-groups form, their members will use their inherent cooperation and coordination abilities to create their own group behavioural norms and ways of informally enforcing these norms. Indeed, it is possible that these subgroups will establish a cohesive sub-group ethic (that is, group identification, group behavioural norms and associated, largely emotion-based enforcement) that exerts a more powerful influence on members' behaviour than the prevailing ethic in the broader organization. The sub-group may be extremely effective in accomplishing sub-group goals and there can be no guarantee that these will be congruent with broader organizational goals.

According to EP, the challenge for crafters of formal organizational controls is to recognize that such mezzo-level sub-groups will inevitably arise within large organizations (merely by virtue of the fact that the organization provides a context for repeated interactions among more or less stable sub-groups). Moreover, organizational advantage can be had from harnessing these groups' inherent coordination and motivational capabilities and using them to pursue organizational goals.

Management control in large organizations can be seen as an aggregation problem – how do individual and sub-group behaviours get aggregated into overall organizational action? The contribution of EP is to point out that these subgroups will inevitably arise and to provide insights into the concerns and motivations that will animate them – it sheds an interesting light on the power, cohesiveness and behavioural dynamics of the sub-group level of large organizations.

The Moral Animal as the Subject of Managerial and Regulatory Controls

Just because the evolutionary niche of mankind in the animal kingdom is that of the 'moral animal' doesn't mean that all men are moral (in the human evolutionary sense that they readily adhere to pro-group norms). Indeed, the fact that mankind has evolved its elaborate neurological apparatus for coordinating the collective aspects of life within groups is, in itself, a testament to the strength of the threats coming from other humans in the ancestral environment (not just human threats from outside the group, but threats of opportunism from members of the group).

In effect, just as evolution produces dynamic, but fairly stable equilibria between predator and prey in natural environments (for example, the numerical relationship between lion and gazelle on the African savannah), it has also produced an equilibrium between the exploitative capabilities of opportunists (who can deploy an impressive arsenal of anti-social mechanisms such as violence, deceit, indifference to group emotional pressures, and so on) and the defensive capabilities of pro-social individuals (who can also be very successful in discerning trickery, deceit, or true levels of effort and resource allocation).

EP, in this sense, puts a new, biological spin on an age-old story about the battle between good and evil. What is interesting in the EP version of this story is the neurological basis for the struggle and the fact that all humans (except perhaps a born sociopath) are endowed with the mental capabilities to be, in an ethical sense, either predator or prey, opportunist or cooperator. This is the EP equivalent of the concept of free will – the complex neurological underpinnings of human behaviour have endowed humans with the possibility to choose between good and evil (meaning, in this context, either complying with pro-group norms or transgressing them).

This characteristically human flexibility in deciding whether to engage in pro-group or opportunistic behaviours undoubtedly increased the fitness of humans as they were evolving – it allowed them to switch behaviours in response to changes in the evolutionary environment. To take a basic and extreme example, it would have allowed individuals (even those with strong attachments to the group) to make the evolutionarily 'fit' choice of abandoning injured or ill comrades in the face of extreme external threats instead of making heroic efforts to save them. This flexibility also means that the mental tools that human use when making behavioural decisions in a group context are extremely complex.

EP sheds light on how this choice is made by individuals. Decision-making processes involve complex calculations regarding both the individual's and the group's needs or desires, feelings of duty and emotional attachment to the group and a weighing of the risks of alternative behaviours (including strategic calculations of one's own competencies in either cheating/free-riding or defending against cheating/free-riding as well as the same competencies of the other members of the group).

The complexity of the human ethical apparatus (at least in relation to individual/group behaviours) and its importance in determining outcomes of group interactions within business organizations means that crafters of management controls need to pay close attention to these matters. Managers interested in controlling organizational outcomes face employees and groups of employees who are capable both of extremely selfless behaviour in pursuit of group objectives and of the most subtle trickery and stealth in the pursuit of private interests at the expense of the organization.

The EP perspective on this issue complements and adds nuance to mainstream economics analyses that deal with similar issues (for example, Williamson, 1979; Jensen and Meckling, 1976). The principal value added of the EP approach is to highlight the importance and the potential power of 'soft' measures (as opposed, for example, to contractual or money incentives) in getting individual employees to pursue group objectives and to honour their commitments to the organization. It argues that, while being mindful of contractual and other formal incentives, employees will also be attentive to and motivated by measures that influence perceptions of fairness and that reinforce attachment and affiliation to the organization. According to the EP perspective, these are not marginal considerations – they are central to how group behaviour within business organizations will play out.

NOTES

1. See Webster's II University Dictionary (1984: 769).
2. Johnson (1996) uses the database of the Carnegie Hero Fund Commission (the Commission that gives Carnegie Medals for heroism) to study acts of outstanding heroism (where rescuers risked their own lives to save the lives of others and, in some cases, lost their lives). He finds that, although their appeared to be a slight kinship dimension to these acts, group selection was the most likely source of these extreme altruistic behaviours.
3. An institution is defined here as a non-physical and durable constraint on individual behaviour – generally the institution will be limited in its scope of action to a particular group of people (for example, citizens of a country, members of an ethnic group or club, practitioners of a profession).

REFERENCES

Alexander, R., (1987), *The Biology of Moral Systems,* Aldyne de Gruyter, New York.

Boehm, C., (2000), 'Interactions of culture and natural selection', unpublished working paper, University of Southern California.

Chiappe, D. and MacDonald, K., (2005), 'The evolution of domain-general mechanisms in intelligence and learning', *Journal of General Psychology,* **132** (1), 5–40.

Corning, P., (2004), 'The evolution of politics', in F. Wuketits and C. Antweiler, (eds) *Handbook of Evolution*, Volume I, Weinheim: Wily-VCH Verlag Gmbh, 6–47.

Cosmides, L. and Tooby, J., (1994), 'Better than rational: evolutionary psychology and the invisible hand', *American Economic Review*, **84**, (2), 327–332.

Darwin, C., ([1879], 2004), *The Descent of Man*, Penguin Books, London.

Darwin, C., ([1872], 1999), *The Expression of the Emotions in Man and Animals*, Fontana Press, London.

Dopfer, K., (2004), 'The economic agent as rule maker and rule user: homo sapiens oeconomicus', *Journal of Evolutionary Economics*, **14**, 177–195.

Dunbar, R. I. M., (1993), 'Coevolution of neocortical size, group size and language in humans', *Behavioral and Brain Sciences*, **16** (4), 681–735.

Gintis, H., (2003), 'Strong reciprocity and human sociality', *Journal of Theoretical Biology*, **206** (2), 169–179.

Jensen, M. and Meckling, W., (1976), 'Theory of the firm: managerial behaviour, agency costs and ownership structure', *Journal of Political Economy*, **3**, 305–306.

Johnson, R., (1996), 'Attributes of Carnegie medalists peforming acts of heroism and of the recipients of these acts', *Ethology and Sociobiology*, **17**, 355–362.

Jost, J., (2005), 'Formal aspects of emergence of institutions', unpublished working paper, Santa Fe Institute.

Lord, R., Klimoski R. and Kanfer, R., (eds.), (2002), *Emotions in the Workplace: Understanding the Structure and Role of Emotions in Organisational Behaviour*, Josey-Bass, San Francisco.

North, D., (1990), *Institutions, Institutional Change and Economic Performance*, Cambridge University Press, New York and Cambridge.

Ridley, M., (1996), *The Origins of Virtue*, Penguin Books, London.

Rubin, P. and Somanathan, E., (1998), 'Humans as factors of production: an evolutionary analysis', *Managerial and Decision Economics*, **19** (7/8), 441–455.

Stout, L., (2001), 'Other-regarding preferences and social norms', Georgetown University Law Center, Working Paper Series in Business, Economics and Regulatory Policy, Working Paper No. 265902.

Weiss, H., (2002), 'Conceptual and empirical foundations for the study of affect at work', in R. Lord, R. Klimoski and R. Kanfer, (eds), *Emotions in the Workplace: Understanding the Structure and Role of Emotions in Organisational Behaviour*, Jossey-Bass, San Franciso.

Wenegrat, B., Abrams, L., Castillo-Yee E. and Romine, I. J., (1996), 'Social norm compliance as a signalling system: studies of fitness-related attributions consequent on everyday norm violations', *Ethology and Sociobiology,* **17** (6), 403–416.
Williamson, Oliver (1979), 'Transactions cost economics: the governance of contractual relations', *Journal of Law and Economics,* **22** (2), 233–261.

PART II

Economics and the Question of Moral
Foundations

4. Economics, Ethics and Anthropology

Antonio Argandoña

INTRODUCTION[1]

In the beginning, economic science, while at the same time searching for its own identity and methodology, coexisted harmoniously with ethics.[2] However, with the advent of the neoclassical paradigm, the cooperation and understanding between the two disciplines came to an end, even though numerous attempts have been made since then to restore the former harmony, particularly in recent years. This task has been rendered particularly difficult, first, by the lack of clarity about what ethics is and, second, by the changes that economic science has undergone in the course of the attempts to expand and refine and, for some, surpass and transform its conventional paradigm.[3]

This chapter seeks to contribute a few ideas to the endeavour to restore the interrelation between economics and ethics. My starting point will be the theory of human action and I shall explain the points of contact that this theory offers between the economic and ethical approaches, with particular emphasis on the limitations of the treatment given to the theory of human action in conventional economics. I will then discuss the theory of human action and its ethical dimension, indicating some of the areas where an attempt can be made to bridge the gap that has formed between the two disciplines, in particular in the choice of ends, learning, motivation, and individual ethics. The chapter will close with the conclusions.

HUMAN ACTION[4]

Human action is intentional: by acting, a human being tries to achieve some end that she has set for herself. This end may have arisen from changes in the environment but is not caused entirely by such changes. In other words, a human being may react to outside events but this reaction has a purpose or intention, which is what gives meaning to the action. This is why it is said that the ends of human action are subjective, insofar as they are proposed by the agent herself.

The goal pursued by any action is to solve a problem, that is, a situation that is less desired, less satisfactory or less pleasant for the agent, and, possibly, lead to the attainment of satisfaction or the disappearance of dissatisfaction (Pérez López, 1991: 25). All actions share in common a series of elements:[5]

1) One or several ends, goals or objectives which induce people to act. As a general rule, everything starts with: a) the identification of a less satisfactory situation, a need, which may be within the subject or outside of her but which, in any case, affects her, b) the possibility of transforming it into a more satisfactory situation, and c) acknowledgement of the desirability of this transformation, which is the action's purpose. Therefore, ends are not given but originate from the agent's evaluative actions (Parsons, 1998). In turn, through the agent's intention, an action's meaning is defined by its ends.[6]

2) The deliberation, in which the subject: a) identifies the means or resources available; b) formulates the possible alternatives for achieving the end;[7] c) analyses the consequences that can be expected from their implementation, that is, she formulates a representation of the situation that is expected to prevail after the action has been performed and compares it with the original situation; d) establishes criteria (economic, but also ethical, social, political, etc.) under which the means will be appraised, and e) carries out the appraisal.

3) The motive that leads to implementation of the action. In all actions, there is a potential motivation, which is the satisfaction of needs, which must be turned into an actual motivation before the specific action is performed.[8]

4) The decision or choice of the means to carry out the action. In complex actions, the means may be lower-order ends, that is, the results of other actions.

5) The performance of the action, an act of will by which the agent puts into motion the means that she has chosen: the 'transforming efficacy of action' (Polo, 1996).

6) The action's consequences or results, in other words, how and to what extent the planned end is achieved or other effects are obtained, including effects that are not expected or not wished.

7) The evaluation of the action's consequences in the light of the results attained and the resulting learning for the agent.

8) The correction of the decision, if the action will be repeated in the future or forms part of a broader plan.

Action is determined by decision-making, so decision-making is the keystone of human action. Therefore, the theory of human action is above all a theory of decision-making. But, as we shall see later, this does not mean that the other elements are irrelevant.

In neoclassical economics, the theory of action follows the previous model, with certain refinements:

1) The action's end is also the satisfaction of a need felt by the agent, in accordance with a function of preferences which the agent takes as given.

2) The deliberation consists of looking for alternatives (means) and appraising them. This process is usually carried out in terms of the subjective values attributed by the agent to the expected or anticipated results (objective values) of her choices, within a plurality of possible states. By inserting all preferences in a single function (utility function or order of preferences), under the assumption that the values are commensurable, it is possible to perform (mental) comparisons between the expected subjective outcomes using a single comparison unit (ordinal), which is the expected utility in each case. This establishes the decision criterion that the agent will use, which is the maximization of her utility, in accordance with the 'economic' or 'efficiency principle': the agent always tries to obtain the best result that can be obtained with the limited means available – or, alternatively, the agent always uses the lowest possible quantity of means to obtain a given result.[9]

3) The motivation for the action is the satisfaction of a need and that alone is sufficient to start the process. No distinction is made between potential and actual motivation.

4) The decision consists of the choice of means for maximizing the expected utility. This is centerpiece of the theory of action.

5) The economist usually does not consider the execution phase: the fact that the agent is considering the possibility of acting implies by itself the will to act – and the capacity to do so, if she has the necessary resources.

6) The action's consequences are also of little interest to the economist, at least in non-repetitive actions or actions which do not form part of complex plans: the agent made her decision based on the appraisal (utility) attributed to the action's expected consequences, in accordance with a given, unvarying function of preferences; therefore, the fact that the action's actual consequences do not match its expected consequences cannot influence her decision, which has already been made. In other words, either the agent does not learn from the consequences of her action or such learning is irrelevant because it has no effect on the decision that has already been made.

7) Therefore, the evaluation of the action's consequences is not relevant either.
8) And neither is the correction of possible future decisions, at least in the case of non-repetitive actions.

THE INADEQUACY OF THE ECONOMIC VIEW OF HUMAN ACTION

Let's say an agent (active agent) who has a problem (for example, she's hungry) starts an action (buying food and eating it) whose purpose is precisely to resolve her problem. In the deliberation phase the agent assesses the resources she has available and the relative prices of the food she can buy, based on her experience, her knowledge of the nutritional properties of different foods, her tastes, and so on. To start with, let's accept that the criterion she uses to make her decision is that of maximizing the utility of the action, as represented by a preference function which, for now, we shall assume is given and constant over time. With these givens, the decision as presented in economics textbooks is very simple: it is a matter of allocating available resources to the consumption of different goods until all available resources are exhausted, so that the expected or forecast marginal utility of the last unit of income spent on the purchase of any one good is equal to the utility derived from the last unit spent on the purchase of any alternative good.

What happens after that is of little interest to an economist. The agent made her decision in such a way that, at least potentially, her need was satisfied (the action was 'effective') and its utility was maximized (the action was 'efficient'): given the agent's preferences and existing constraints, no other combination of consumptions could have given her greater utility (whether or not she actually obtains the expected utility does not affect the decision, which is already taken). The only consequences relevant to the action are the forecasted or expected consequences that the agent included in her deliberation. But is this true?

Let's imagine our agent comes back home after lunch. Her hunger has been satisfied and she enjoyed the meal, having experienced greater satisfaction than she would have with any other use of her limited resources (her income and the time she had available). These are the 'extrinsic' results obtained as a consequence of the reaction of the environment to the agent's initiative.

However, two other types of results are possible. First, the 'intrinsic' results of the action; for example, what the agent learns from the action, which is (at least partly) a consequence of her limited knowledge. Learning is relevant to future decisions for at least two reasons: 1) because it may change the agent's decision rule in that she does not have to make the same choice the next time, even if all else is equal; and 2) because the active agent may seek such expected (though uncertain) 'intrinsic' results as part of the purposes of her action, that is, she may act in order to learn.

Also, when the action involves another person (whom we shall call the reactive agent, as opposed to the active agent who performs the action), there are what we might call external effects,[10] which are the effects on the other person. These are also relevant, as they will modify the reactive agent's willingness to engage in similar actions in the future. That happens, for example, if the reactive agent feels cheated, making future interactions unlikely if not impossible.

Simply taking these three types of effects of an action into account – extrinsic (the response of the environment or the reactive agent to the active agent's action), intrinsic (the effects of the action on the active agent: learning, satisfaction, and so on) and external (the effects of the action on the reactive agent) – forces us to broaden our view of action beyond that of traditional economics. The situation is further complicated if we take into account the fact that actions do not occur in a vacuum, because agents act in society or in organizations, or simply because the active agent (and other agents) learns from her decisions, leading to changes in her personal preferences and decision rules,[11] and changes in the decision rules of other agents, that is, changes to the rules of the game in organizations and society.

Now we are in a better position to understand the nature of the problems the agent faces. The agent is forever seeking satisfaction, because she is continuously faced with problems that offer opportunities to obtain satisfaction by performing certain actions. Every time she performs an action, the agent experiences a satisfaction, as economics acknowledges, and starts a learning process that changes her expected future satisfactions. At this point at least two problems emerge.

The first is the possibility that, in seeking present satisfactions, the agent will reduce her expected future satisfactions by setting in train negative learning processes within herself (this is very clear in the case of addiction: drug consumption today may yield high present satisfactions, but serious future dissatisfactions). The second problem is that the active agent's actions may bring about changes in the environment (the reactive agent's behaviour) that make it unlikely that her future needs will be satisfied (for example, the actions of an organization's members may make it increasingly difficult for the organization to operate).

In the language of conventional economics, these problems suggest that maximizing the active agent's utility at any given moment may not guarantee that the agent will be able to maximize her utility in the future, not because of exogenous changes in relevant variables (resource availability or relative prices, for example), but as an endogenous consequence of the agent's own actions or as a consequence of endogenous 'perverse effects' in her environment (changes in the reactive agent's decision rule). Therefore, taking a dynamic view of human action forces us to broaden the anthropological model beyond the simple assumptions of conventional economics, which, as we have just shown, may be useful in some simple cases of non-repetitive action by non-learning agents in non-human environments, but not in other more realistic circumstances.[12]

In the next few pages we shall show how ethics may help to broaden the anthropological paradigm of decision-making adopted by conventional economics.

THE ETHICAL DIMENSION OF HUMAN ACTION

Economics provides an excellent framework for understanding the role of ethics, because economics is, above all, a theory of human action (efficient human action), and ethics is the normative side of the theory of human action.[13] Ethics is built on an anthropology, a complete conception of man, and economics is also built on the same anthropology (or, at least, on one of its aspects, that which refers to the efficient action of man in the presence of scarce resources).[14]

The economic theory of action considers that decisions are made for the efficient satisfaction of needs, defining efficiency as the obtainment of the best possible results with the resources available, or the use of the least possible resources to obtain a result, within certain restrictions that include the resources and information available and other constraints, which can include law and ethics.[15]

However, this assumes that ethics is a restriction imposed from outside on an economic conduct that is geared towards efficiency. This way of bringing in ethics is common, particularly in applied economics and organization management. But, at the same time, it is not the best way of bridging the gap between economic science and ethics.

The description of the theory of action suggests a number of natural ways of bringing about this integration. Put simply, we can say that human action implies that an agent considers an end which motivates her to carry out a particular action. This action is performed and certain results are obtained, tempered by the environment's reaction (as a general rule, other agents who interact with her) and from which certain consequences arise.[16] This assumes that there are a number of places (that are not independent from each other) where one can attempt to link ethics and human action: in the choice of ends, in the agent's motivations, in the decision (and its implementation), in its consequences and in the agent herself.[17]

Ends[18]

Neoclassical normative economics is based on the concept of welfare or well-being; the action's results are assessed in terms of welfare, not because that is the only morally important concept but because economics offers particularly useful tools for dealing with welfare issues, and because it is considered that it is possible to separate welfare issues from other ethical issues that are also important, such as equality, freedom and justice.[19]

The different ethical outlooks attribute an important role to the agent's welfare – and this is applicable both to the utilitarians, who believe that moral correctness seeks to maximize the agent's welfare, and to the non-utilitarians who, for example, attribute a role to benevolence, altruism or solidarity, including not harming others and taking their interests into account. The outlook of the neoclassical economists on this point has moved from hedonism (which identifies the agent's good with a mental state of pleasure or happiness) to identifying well-being with the satisfaction of her preferences. If the agent has a consistent order of preferences, she is well informed and takes care of her personal interests, then the satisfaction of her preferences implies achieving maximum well-being for the agent, which is considered to be a normative requirement.

However, there are a number of criticisms that can be made to this outlook: preferences can be based on mistaken beliefs; the agents may prefer to sacrifice their own well-being to other ends that are considered to have higher value; preferences may be a consequence of past manipulations, or reflect disruptive psychological influences, and so on. (Elster 1983). There are also reasons for not using this criterion as a basis for public policies because, for example, individual preferences can be manipulated or too much importance can be given to extravagant preferences, and so on. In other words, we need a theory of the formation of preferences as a result of psychological, sociological and ethical influences, first on a positive (descriptive) plane in order to be able to base a normative theory on it.[20] And ethics must have a lot to say on the subject of choosing ends.[21]

Learning

To talk about ethics, it is necessary to talk about the agents' learning, at least within certain schools. Economic science has paid a certain amount of attention to operational learning (for example, that which increases skills in the performance of actions) and cognitive learning (the acquisition of theoretical and technological knowledge) but it has not taken sufficiently into account the impact that this may have on the agents' preferences. And neither has it considered the learning of attitudes and values, which obviously modify these preferences.[22]

As we have already explained, the agent undertakes action with the aim of producing a reaction in the environment (normally, another agent) from which will ensue the satisfaction of a need. This is the most important consequence, from the economics viewpoint, and we have called it the action's extrinsic result. However, another two types of result are obtained: some that affect the agent herself (intrinsic results) and others on the environment, which have no significance when the environment is immaterial (its changes will appear as restrictions or costs in the agent's decision), but which are important when another rational agent is involved (external results).[23]

As we noted before, these results are important for at least three reasons: 1) because they can change the agent's decision rule (her choice does not necessarily have to be the same the next time, even if the other conditions are the same),[24] 2) because the active agent may seek intrinsic results (expected although uncertain) as part of the ends of her action (which are not commensurable with the agent's other preferences), and 3), because she may seek directly her action's effects on the other agent (the external results), which also has an effect on the choice of ends beyond what is permitted by her preference function – and this is particularly important in organizations.

Therefore, as we explained before, the problem of action lies in the possibility that, in the quest for present satisfactions, the agent may start negative learning processes that close the door to any possibility of satisfying her future preferences. Consequently, the theory of action needs to account for the mechanisms by which the agent can internalize this learning. And this is where ethics will have an important role.

Motivations

We have already said that the motivational structure in neoclassical economics is very simple: the agent acts moved by 'extrinsic' motives, to achieve the satisfaction produced by the extrinsic effects of his action.[25] However, in actual fact, there are another two types of motive that must also be considered. One of them is the 'intrinsic' motive: the agent seeks to achieve the learning that will enable her not only to obtain present satisfaction, but also future satisfaction – that is, she is willing to accept the costs of performing an action that does not optimize her present preferences in order to optimize future preferences.[26] And there are the 'transcendent' motives, when the agent tries to attain certain results in the other agent with whom she interacts, or with the other agents in an organization.[27]

The interest in discussing the existence of the different types of motive lies in the fact that conflicts may arise within and between each type. We all know, for example, that certain foods that we like cause us indigestion, or that smoking may cause diseases. Conventional economics acknowledges the existence of these motivational conflicts but, since it is confined to a single type of motivation (extrinsic motivation), it simplifies the solution of these conflicts by proposing trade-offs between them, which are always possible due to the existence of a single scale for comparing the satisfaction gained from the action's results.[28]

If there are intermotivational conflicts, the agent must have a mechanism that enables her to settle them, implementing intrinsic and transcendent motivations. This implies that the agent must be capable of appraising a priori both the extrinsic results (the expected satisfaction from her preferences) and the intrinsic (her personal learning) and transcendent results (her action's effects on the other agent), that is, the results of something that she has not yet experienced.[29] And when the agent makes the decision to act moved by intrinsic or transcendent motivation, whether it confirms or is contrary to her extrinsic motivation, her ability to continue learning, that is, her ability to assess the intrinsic and transcendent effects of her actions, grows.[30]

How does the agent acquire this ability to appraise his actions? She not only has the experience gained from previous decisions but also what we could call 'abstract knowledge':[31] for example, the information she has received over time from different sources about the suitability of the means for achieving the ends, social and religious norms, scientific and technological knowledge, and so on,[32] and also ethical rules and principles. Ethics plays an important role here, because moral norms constitute important knowledge about what should or should not be done, depending on the results that these actions may have on the agent herself or on other agents and, therefore, on the changes that will take place in the agent's decision rule and in the other agents' reactions, on which the results of present and future actions depend, particularly in organizations.

However, the use of abstract knowledge in general and ethical knowledge in particular, poses an additional problem: the agent needs a mechanism that is capable of transforming this knowledge into actual motivation. For example, why do different agents, or the same agent in different circumstances, react differently to the knowledge they possess, for example, about the harmful effects of smoking or about the ethical rules that they consider adequate for guiding their behaviour? This leads us to the development of abilities.[33]

INDIVIDUAL ETHICS: VIRTUES

The fact that the agent is capable of learning means that she is capable of developing intellectual and operational habits that facilitate future learning and behaviour in accordance with this learning. Intellectual habits or virtues develop the ability to correctly use the information obtained from learning or abstract knowledge to adequately judge the alternatives that the agent can choose between. Moral habits or virtues develop the agent's ability to act, empowering her to effectively want what seems desirable or suitable to her, even if it does not appeal to her from the viewpoint of what she spontaneously feels.[34]

Consequently, virtues are not altruistic preferences that are added to those that the agent already has. Virtues determine what she is capable of performing even if it does not bring her any immediate satisfaction; they grow as a consequence of learning processes, and change with experience. They are the agent's self-control instruments and model the range of alternatives available: even though in theory the agent is capable of performing any action provided her resources are sufficient to bear its opportunity cost in physical or monetary terms, in practice there will be actions that are not feasible due to a lack of internal potentiality that prevents her going beyond her spontaneous motivation.[35]

Virtues are acquired by repetition of acts, driven by a higher motivation: a person who lets herself be swayed by anticipated satisfaction (extrinsic motivation) will not acquire virtues (moral habits), while a person who acts out of intrinsic (to develop her abilities) or transcendent motivation (for other people's good) will acquire them, to a greater or lesser extent, irrespective of whether this will make her act in favour or to the detriment of her extrinsic motivation. We can conclude from this that the formation of virtues in the agent broadens the range of possible learning, generating what we could call a non-diminishing return on learning, unlike the learning that takes place under spontaneous motivation. This leads us to the consideration that an agent's virtues can be likened to a stock of moral capital, accumulated over a period of time.[36]

CONCLUSIONS

All social sciences, including economics, are based on an explicit or implicit anthropology. Essentially, economics is a science of human action, at least from the viewpoint of instrumental rationality, while ethics is a normative science of human action, from the viewpoint of speculative rationality (Melé,

2000). Therefore, economics and ethics should share their paradigm of man, even if they then differ in the methodology and scope of their propositions. However, as we have seen, the conceptions of human action on which they are based are not the same, which justifies the effort to establish a link between them.

If ethics and economics must share their conception of human action, economics must have a lot to contribute to the review of the anthropological basis of ethics – not because economics is an appropriate base for ethics but because it is the science that studies and discusses most the theory of human action (albeit often on a limited plane, as we have pointed out earlier).

The various ethical theories usually focus on one of the three anchor points of the theory of action: the agent, the action itself and its consequences (Solomon, 1998). This gives rise to theories based on intention or motivation and on virtues, duties or rules (deontology) and on consequences (consequentialism). However, our reflections lead us to conclude that an ethical theory must include all of the elements of action, that is, an ethics that encompasses goods, norms and virtues,[37] not by adding recommendations but by developing a comprehensive explanation of what human action is and what its normative consequences are. This is by no means an easy task, given the plurality of viewpoints on ethics, but would no doubt be made easier by a deeper study of human action.

In fact, since human action seeks what is good for man, ethics should study those things that are good that are the goals of his action. Economics assumes that the agent has sufficient knowledge of her preferences and is better qualified than anyone else to act in accordance with her own interests. However, our previous reflections on learning and changes in decision rules suggest that this is not always achieved. This raises the role of ethics as a long-term 'equilibrium condition' for the agent and for all human systems (Argandoña, 1989). This does not necessarily imply a role for the state, but rather for institutions and ethical standards.[38] These have a primarily negative role: do not make – they tell us – immoral decisions because you will deteriorate as a person, you will harm the systems or society to which you belong, and you will limit your opportunities for future action. This is the first role of the ethics of norms: to place limits on human action, insofar as it can lead to negative learning – voluntary limits, of course: moral standards may be abided by or not but this does not detract from their normative content. However, ethical standards are above all positive: do, do good, try to do all you can, and do it well – a message that is consistent with the economic viewpoint of human action. To do this, the agent must develop human capabilities for ethically correct action, that is, virtues – and their rational component: because virtues enable agents to improve their capacity for analysis, judgement and appraisal.

However, our conclusions do not point only towards ethics but also towards economics. As we have already said, economics is based on a theory of human action. However, it is an incomplete theory, based only on means, because it has little to say about the ends, beyond accepting, without questioning them, the agent's preferences (Koslowski, 1990). The theory we currently have is useful but incomplete. Its revision is both possible and necessary, and ethics may contribute interesting suggestions about how to revise that theory of action, so that it endogenously includes the long-term 'equilibrium condition' for the agent and human systems that we have identified with ethics.

NOTES

1. This chapter is part of a research project undertaken by IESE's 'la Caixa' Chair of Corporate Social Responsibility and Corporate Governance. It is an enlarged version of an article entitled 'Economía, teoría de la acción y ética', published in *Información Comercial Española*, **823**, June 2005, 31–38 and reproduced here with permission.
2. This is clearly seen when the two main works of Adam Smith, *The Theory of Moral Sentiments* (Smith [1759], 1976) and *The Wealth of Nations* (Smith, [1776], 1937), are viewed in juxtaposition.
3. In the following pages, I will focus my attention on neoclassical economics, which continues to be the predominant branch, while at the same time acknowledging the contribution of other schools (particularly the Austrian school) and the many extensions that have been attempted of the neoclassical paradigm.
4. What follows is based on Argandoña (2003, 2005). The vital role played by the theory of action has been extensively developed by the Austrian school; undoubtedly the classic reference is Mises (1949).
5. This list has been drawn from Yepes (1996) ch. 5, and Polo (1996).
6. Mele (1997: 19), summarizes the role of intention in five points: 1) start and sustain action, 2) guide the agent's intentional conduct, 3) coordinate this conduct over time, 4) coordinate relationships with other agents' actions, and 5) start (and end) practical reasoning in the decision-making process. At least one more point would have to be added to this: 6) order and prioritize the action's ends or purposes, when there are more than one (Parsons, 1998).
7. Although neoclassical theory considers that they are given, in fact they are discovered by the agent. See Huerta de Soto (1999).
8. See Pérez López (1991: 80–81).
9. Certain hypotheses are added, such as that of continuity (to avoid lexicographic preferences), that of the preferences' internal consistency (to assure the decision's

rationality), and that of the preferences' quasi-concavity and the infinite divisibility of goods (to guarantee the existence of a single optimal result when the range of feasible solutions is convex). It is possible to deal with situations of uncertainty if it is assumed that the agent is able to identify mutually exclusive and exhaustively possible states of the environment, each one of which is associated with a probability. See Casson (1988).

10. The terminology used here to designate the three types of effects is taken from Pérez López (1991).

11. This applies in particular to actions that are part of 'plans' (Parsons, 1998), but also, as we shall see, to all actions to the extent that the agent learns from them.

12. The fact that we human beings learn shows that we are not stable systems, unlike machines which do not learn. The example of drug addiction shows that we are not ultrastable systems, either, which only ever learn positively, that is, they are trial-and-error systems that automatically self-correct whenever they deviate from the optimal path. Rather, we are free systems in which learning can be positive or negative. Hence the importance of 'discovering' the rules of behaviour of free systems, which is the task of ethics. The description of these systems given here is taken from Pérez López (1991: 43–45).

13. Our view is that the description, explanation and prediction of actions with an ethical content do not pertain to ethics, which is a normative science.

14. According to the traditional definition given by Robbins (1932), as a science that is concerned with the allocation of scarce (given) resources among alternative (also given) ends. This definition is very limited but provides a suitable starting point for our discussion.

15. For example, Friedman (1970: 138), states that the responsibility of the person who is charged with the firm's management is 'to conduct the business in accordance with their desires [of the owners], which generally will be to make as much money as possible while conforming to the basic rules of the society, both those embodied in law and those embodied in ethical custom'. On the role of ethics in this type of decision, see Argandoña (2006a).

16. This version of the theory of action is drawn from Pérez López (1993), Polo (1996) and Solomon (1998).

17. Other approaches can be found in Broome (1999), Hausman (1996), Koslowski (2001) and Krelle (2003).

18. Hausman (2003) develops the theses that are discussed in this chapter.

19. This is justified by the second theorem of welfare economics: given any initial distribution of income, there is a competitive equilibrium that is Pareto-optimal. In other words, it is possible to discuss issues related with efficiency (currently understood as the satisfaction of preferences, not as the minimization of the

resources used to attain a certain level of output: see Legrand, 1991), without going into issues of fairness in distribution.

20. Relating economics with psychology, behavioural economics, sociology, neuronomics and other interdisciplinary contributions seeks to solve this problem; see for example, Rabin (1998), Loewenstein et al. (2003), Camerer et al. (2004, 2005). However, they are not sufficient because they are based on theories that are not general enough, are deterministic and have a purely empirical rationale.

21. See the contributions by Sen (1987, 1992) for a discussion outside of the line of identifying welfare with the satisfaction of preferences, and Nussbaum and Sen (1993) and Sen (1999) for a definition of welfare in terms of capacities. For other interesting contributions, see Hausman (2003).

22. For example, altruism is presented as one of the agent's preferences but no analysis is made of its origin (beyond generic references to culture, education, etc.) or its development (positive or negative) in the agent, as a result of her own altruistic or selfish behavior. See Stark (1995).

23. I have taken this terminology and the explanation of learning from Pérez López (1991, 1993). The fact that actions do not have just an external effect (production, *poiesis*), which we have called the extrinsic result, but also an internal effect (action, *praxis*) on the agent, is widely known in philosophical literature.

24. The theory of tastes formation is relevant here (see for example Stigler and Becker, 1977; Becker, 1996), although its scope is limited, as I have explained in Argandoña (2005). On the role of education in the formation of preferences, see Morse (1995).

25. The terminology is again taken from Pérez López (1991, 1993). Insofar as economics is focused on choice, motivation is irrelevant; however, as Parsons (1998) points out, any theory of choice must include a reflection on motives.

26. This is considered by neoclassical economics, which assumes that the agent optimizes a function of preferences over time. However, it cannot introduce preferences that vary in accordance with previous decisions and, above all, preferences whose direction of change is unpredictable (because the learning can be positive or negative).

27. There has been extensive discussion in economics about selfishness and altruism. Considering the different motivations may help bring order to this debate. There may be blind selfishness, which only considers the actions' effects on the agent, and also a blind altruism, which omits any consideration of the agent's needs. And there is also an 'intelligent altruism' which should not only be compatible with 'intelligent selfishness' but in fact demands it. See Pérez López (1993: 176).

28. A considerable body of theoretical and empirical literature has been building up for some time on the existence of 'intrinsic motivations'. For example, it is found that when an agent obtains direct satisfaction from her work, or from an altruistic

activity ('intrinsic motivation'), a decision to pay for performance of that activity or a change in the amount paid or the terms under which it is paid ('extrinsic motivation') may interfere with the degree or amount of such satisfaction. For example, there are well-documented cases of blood donors who reduce their generosity when they are paid for donating (Titmuss, 1970), or residents who protest against locating a waste disposal site in their area when they are offered some kind of financial compensation (Frey, 1999), the experiences of cooperation and the requirements of certain fairness rules in prisoner, dictator or ultimatum games, even if they are only played once (Kahneman et al., 1986) and so on. Likewise, the use of the agent's abilities as a source of satisfaction (Rawls, 1972: 426, note) or the self-esteem obtained from achieving difficult goals (Hirschman, 1984: 91) are examples of 'intrinsic motivations'.

29. Note that this is not equivalent to including other agents' well-being in the first agent's preferences function, because what is pursued is the result in the second agent, not the satisfaction or utility generated in the first agent.

30. See Pérez López (1991: 102–105).

31. Pérez López (1991: 64) calls it 'rational knowledge'. We prefer not to use this adjective because part of this knowledge may be emotional or even irrational and because it may divert our attention towards the discussion of rationality, which is beyond our field of interest.

32. Not all of this knowledge is scientific, validated and reliable: it may be 'critical' knowledge (scientific or verified) but it can also be 'paradigmatic' knowledge (intuitive, received by tradition or by trust in others: see March, 1991); it may be 'substantive' (about what is known and what must be done) or 'procedural' (about how to observe and find what must be done: see Anderson, 1983) and it may be 'implicit' (knowledge that the agent knows although she is unable to explain it) or 'explicit. On these varieties of knowledge, see Grandori (2001).

33. Neoclassical economics does not consider this problem because, as we have already pointed out, its motivating mechanism is very elementary: anything that can satisfy a need is capable of driving the action.

34. See Pérez López (1993: 163). The classic reference in the ethics of virtues is Aristotle (1980) and, in its application to the firm, Solomon (1992).

35. See Argandoña (2006b, 2007), Rosanas (2006).

36. The existence of a moral capital, its formation and significance is discussed in Sison (2003).

37. This is Polo's thesis (1996).

38. On the role of ethics in institutions, see Argandoña (2004).

REFERENCES

Anderson, J.R., (1983), *The Architecture of Cognition*, Harvard University Press, Cambridge.

Argandoña, A., (1989), 'Relaciones entre economia y ética', *IESE Research Paper*, 166, April.

Preferencias y aprendizajes', in *De Computis et Scripturis. Estudios en Homenaje a Mario Pifarré Riera*, Real Academia de Ciencias Económicas y Financieras, Barcelona, 51–77.

Argandoña, A., (2004), 'Economic ethics and institutional change', *Journal of Business Ethics*, **53** (1-2), 191–201.

Argandoña, A., (2005), 'La teoría de la acción y la teoría económica', in R. Rubio de Urquía, E.M. Ureña and F.F. Muñoz Pérez, (eds), *Estudios de Teoría Económica y Antropología*, Unión Editorial, Madrid, 615–646.

Argandoña, A., (2006a), 'Economía de mercado y responsabilidad social de la empresa', *Papeles de Economía Española*, **108**, 2–9.

Argandoña, A., (2006b), 'Ethics in economics and in organizations: can they be fully integrated', *Occasional Paper*, IESE, No. 06/17, July.

Argandoña, A., (2007), 'Integrating ethics into action theory and organizational theory', *Journal of Business Ethics*, forthcoming.

Aristotle, (1980), *The Nicomachean Ethics*, Oxford University Press, Oxford.

Becker, G.S., (1996), *Accounting for Tastes*, Harvard University Press, Cambridge.

Broome, J., (1999), *Ethics out of Economics*, Cambridge University Press, Cambridge.

Camerer, C., Loewenstein, G. and Prelec, D., (2004), 'Neuronomics: why economics needs brains', *Scandinavian Journal of Economics*, **106** (3), 555–579.

Camerer, C., Loewenstein, G. and Prelec, D., (2005), 'Neuronomics: How neuroscience can inform economics', *Journal of Economic Literature*, **43** (1), 9–64.

Casson, M.C., (1988), 'Economic man', in McCloskey D., (eds.), *Foundations of Economic Thought*, Blackwell, Oxford.

Elster, J., (1983), *Sour Grapes: Studies in the Subversion of Rationality*, Cambridge University Press, Cambridge.

Frey, B.S., (1999), *Economics as a Science of Human Behaviour. Towards a New Social Science Paradigm*, 2nd edition, Kluwer, Dordrecht.

Friedman, M., (1970), 'The social responsibility of business is to increase its profits', *The New York Times Magazine*, September 13, reproduced in W.E. Hoffman, and R.E. Frederick, (eds), (1995), *Business Ethics.*

Readings and Cases in Corporate Morality, 3rd edition, McGraw-Hill, New York.

Grandori, A., (2001), *Organization and Economic Behavior*, Routledge, London.

Hausman, D.M., (1996), *Economic Analysis and Moral Philosophy*, Cambridge University Press, Cambridge.

Hausman, D.M., (2003), 'Philosophy of economics', in Zalta, E.N., (eds), *Stanford Encyclopedia of Philosophy*, http://plato.stanford.edu/ entries/ economics (visited in July 2006).

Hirschman, A., (1984), 'Against parsimony: three ways of complicating some categories of economic discourse', *American Economic Review*, **74** (2), 88–96.

Huerta de Soto, J., (1999), 'The ethics of capitalism', *Journal of Markets and Morality*, **2** (2), 150–163.

Kahneman, D., Knetsch, J.L. and Thaler, R., (1986), 'Fairness as a constraint on profit seeking: entitlements in the market', *American Economic Review*, **76**, 728–741.

Koslowski, P., (1990), 'The categorical and ontological presuppositions of Austrian and Neoclassical economics', in A. Bosch, P. Koslowski and R. Veit (eds), *General Equilibrium or Market Process: Neoclassical and Austrian Theories of Economics*, J.C.B. Mohr, Tübingen.

Koslowski, P., (2001), *Principles of Ethical Economy*, Kluwer, Dordrecht.

Krelle, W., (2003), *Economics and Ethics*, Springer, Berlin.

Legrand, J., (1991), *Equity and Choice*, Routledge, London.

Loewenstein, G., Rabin, M. and Camerer, C.F., (eds), (2003), *Advances in Behavioral Economics*, Princeton University Press, Princeton.

March, J.G., (1991), 'Exploration and exploitation in organizational learning', *Organization Science*, **2** (1), 71–87.

Mele, A.R., (1997), 'Introduction', in Mele, A.R., (eds), *The Philosophy of Action*, Oxford University Press, Oxford.

Melé, D., (2000), 'Racionalidad ética en las decisiones empresariales', *Revista Empresa y Humanismo*, **2**, 213–234.

Mises, L., (1949), *Human Action*, Yale University Press, New Haven.

Morse, J.R., (1995), 'The development of the child', George Mason University Working Paper.

Nussbaum, M. and Sen, A.K., (eds), (1993), *The Quality of Life*, Clarendon Press, Oxford.

Parsons, S.D., (1998), 'Mises and Lachmann on human action', in Koppl R. and Mongiovi G., (eds), *Subjectivism and Economic Analysis. Essays in Memory of Ludwig M. Lachman*, Routledge and Kegan Paul, London.

Pérez López, J.A., (1991), *Teoría de la Acción Humana en las Organizaciones*. Rialp, Madrid.

Pérez López, J.A., (1993), *Fundamentos de la Dirección de Empresas*, Rialp, Madrid.

Polo, L., (1996), *Ética. Hacia una Versión Moderna de los Temas Clásicos*, Unión Editorial, Madrid.

Rabin, M., (1998), 'Economics and psychology', *Journal of Economic Literature*, **36** (1), 11–96.

Rawls, J.A., (1972), *A Theory of Justice*, Oxford University Press, Oxford.

Robbins, L., ([1932], 1935), *An Essay on the Nature and Significance of Economic Science*, 2nd edition, Macmillan, London.

Rosanas, J.M., (2006), 'Beyond economic criteria: a humanistic approach to organizational survival', Working Paper, IESE, No. 654, October.

Sen, A.K., (1987), *On Ethics and Economics*, Blackwell, Oxford.

Sen, A.K., (1992), *Inequality Reexamined*, Harvard University Press, Cambridge.

Sen, A.K., (1999), *Development as Freedom*, Oxford University Press, Oxford.

Sison, A.J.G., (2003), *The Moral Capital of Leaders. Why Virtues Matter*, Edward Elgar, Cheltenham, UK and Northampton, MA, USA.

Smith, A., ([1759], 1976), *The Theory of Moral Sentiments*, Clarendon Press, Oxford.

Smith, A., ([1776], 1937), *An Inquiry into the Nature and Causes of the Wealth of Nations*, Cannan edition, Modern Library, New York.

Solomon, R.C., (1992), *Ethics and Excellence: Cooperation and Integrity in Business*, Oxford University Press, New York.

Solomon, W.D., (1998), 'Normative ethical theories', in D.K. Wilber, (eds.), *Economics, Ethics, and Public Policy*, Rowman and Littlefield, Lanham.

Stigler, G.J. and Becker, G.S., (1977), 'De gustibus non est disputandum', *American Economic Review*, **67**, 11–96.

Stark, O., (1995), *Altruism and Beyond: An Economic Analysis of Transfers and Exchanges within Families and Groups*, Cambridge University Press, Cambridge.

Titmuss, R.M., (1970), *The Gift Relationship*, Allen and Unwin, London.

Yepes, R., (1996), Fundamentos de Antropología. Un Ideal de la Excelencia Humana, Eunsa, Pamplona.

5. The 'Ethics of Competition' or the Moral Foundations of Contemporary Capitalism

Marie-Laure Djelic

INTRODUCTION

A distinctive feature of the contemporary period of globalization is a powerful trend towards marketization in many regions of the world. The term 'marketization' refers both to market ideologies and market-oriented reforms. A market ideology reflects the belief that markets are of superior efficiency for the allocation of goods and resources. Market-oriented reforms are those policies fostering the emergence and development of markets and weakening, in parallel, alternative institutional arrangements.

Since the early 1980s, market ideology and market-oriented policies have spread fast and wide around the globe. The global diffusion of marketization has had, furthermore, an impact well beyond the traditional boundaries of the economy. Marketization implies a redefinition of economic rules of the game but also a transformed perspective on states, regulation and their role. Marketization is questioning all forms of protective boundaries and barriers and having an impact, as a consequence, on social but also on health, cultural or legal policies.

This chapter is not about marketization and its diffusion, though. This has been dealt with elsewhere (Djelic, 2006). Rather, what we want to understand here is the ideological and moral 'ground' on which this powerful marketization trend rests. We want to explore the moral foundations of contemporary marketization with a particular focus on the 'ethics of competition'. The exercise will be one in intellectual genealogy. The current movement towards global marketization has a lot to do, historically, with the development of a particular form of capitalism in the United States and its evolution from the late nineteenth century till today (Djelic, 1998; Djelic and Sahlin-Andersson, 2006). Sustaining and reinforcing those structural developments, we find in the early period a powerful ideological frame. American conservatism towards the end of the nienteenth century was a surprising mix of classical economic liberalism, Puritan doctrine and Social Darwinism. Through a summary pathway, we trace the intellectual lineage of contemporary marketization by considering the ethics of competition as they emerge in turn from Adam Smith and early economic liberalism, the Puritan doctrine and Social Darwinism. We end with a focus on the more recent neoliberal synthesis, considering in particular the Chicago School. We see neoliberalism as both reflecting and embodying some of the ideological influences presented below and at the same time strongly shaping and structuring the normative frame that embeds contemporary marketization.

We explore, on this historical and genealogical path, the definitions of competition and ethical principles associated with those definitions. We hope to underscore in the process the political and ethical message implicitly associated with contemporary marketization and many management practices that go with it. Beyond the neutrality of 'scientific' and 'best practice' discourse, an intellectual genealogy of this kind makes it plain that our structural choices, economic policy-making and associated educational institutions and templates carry with them profound moral implications with a probable impact on the socialization of millions of human beings.

LIBERALISM AND COMPETITION

We start from the premise that the work and thought of Adam Smith have significantly contributed, historically, to economic liberalism. Adam Smith was himself building and expanding upon some of the key ideas of the great founders of political liberalism – John Locke in particular.

Political Liberalism and the Impact on Adam Smith

For John Locke, a state of nature pre-dates the social contract. In contrast to Hobbes, however, Locke's picture of the state of nature is not one of essentially chaotic and destructive anarchy. The state of nature is not a social space – in the sense that it is neither structured by contractual rules nor by a sense of community. For Locke, however, this state of nature is stabilized by natural law – the right to private property based on the work of the individual. In the state of nature, each individual faces nature and interactions between individuals have to do with that interface, with work, the product of work and property. Pre-political man, 'natural' man is before anything else a *homo oeconomicus* – in the simple sense here of economic man (Manent, 1986; Locke, 1997). The social and political contract comes later and its role is merely to create a collective responsibility for the respect of natural law – in other words for the protection of private property and economic freedom.

Adam Smith was strongly inspired by those ideas and was the main bridge, historically, between British political liberalism and classical or neoclassical theory (Manent, 1986). More specifically, Smith appropriated three key propositions of political liberalism. First, building upon the idea of 'natural man' as economic man, he took over the claim of an independence and precedence (both historical and moral) of the economic sphere (Smith, 1999, 2000). What Locke referred to as the 'state of nature', Smith called the 'system of natural liberty'. The systematic disembeddedness and self-contained character of economic activity so characteristic of orthodox economic thinking in the nineteenth and twentieth centuries directly followed upon that. So did the notion that human liberty fundamentally rests upon economic freedom (itself implying competition). Second, Adam Smith took over the idea that this pre-eminent and autonomous sphere is structured by 'natural laws'. Third, Adam Smith also found inspiration in Locke's subtle reading of the social contract. The social contract and the associated polity emerge when the natural order is threatened – but ironically they are themselves potentially dangerous to that order. For Smith as for Locke, the role of the polity is important but it should remain minimal.

Natural Laws of Economic Exchange

The natural propensity of human beings to barter and trade the products of their own work suggests and demands the market. In Smith's thought, the market is in fact a natural, emergent and essential reality of human and social life, stemming from this very propensity. The exchange of goods within that natural space reflects three main principles – the division of labour, the invisible hand and competition.

The propensity to exchange has for direct consequence that each individual does not have to rely simply on herself to provide for the whole range of her needs. She can find the answer to parts of those needs on the market and obtain them in exchange for the things she produces herself. The division of labour leads to the greater productivity of each individual and hence to the maximization of welfare, both for the community and for the individual. The extent and complexity of the division of labour depend upon the scale and density of the market, and the latter are in direct correlation with demographic and infrastructural conditions (Smith, 1999: I, iii). Adam Smith argued that the progressive extension and expansion of markets meant, ultimately, not only greater individual and collective well-being but also moral, social and political progress away from feudalism and tyranny and towards yeomanry and democracy (Smith, 1999: I, i, 109; III).

Another 'natural law', according to Adam Smith, was that markets were orderly. Order did not stem from an all-powerful regulator but from a multiplicity of transactions and their combination (Smith, 1999: I, ii, 119). The collective good is achieved not by planning it but by leaving free rein to the natural propensity of market players to maximize their individual welfare and personal gains. Through combination in the market, the greed and selfishness of individual acts turned into a morally satisfying and welfare maximizing collective order. In *The Wealth of Nations*, individuals were pictured as essentially a-moral; the market, though, was inherently albeit mysteriously producing a progressive and moral order (Nelson, 2001). The miracle of the 'invisible hand' requires, however, specific conditions.

The invisible hand will not come into play, in particular, lest free rein is left to the competitive mechanism. Competition emerges, in the work of Adam Smith (although he rarely uses the word) as a third structuring principle of the market. In a market where competition works, the scarcity of a particular good will naturally lead to the emergence of new providers. This, in turn, will drive quantity up and prices down, thus re-establishing a balance between demand and offer. In turn, when offer is too plentiful, prices will tend to go down, discouraging some of the providers. This balancing mechanism, however, will only work if competition is not hampered. Smith pointed to two types of obstacles. Market players themselves could introduce disruption and 'people of the same trade seldom meet together, even for merriment and diversion, but the conversation ends in a conspiracy against the public or in some contrivance to raise prices' (Smith, 1999: I, x, 232). This part of Smith's argument has often been neglected but it shows deep consciousness that competitive markets were not automatically self-sustaining. Smith also strongly denounced tampering and intervention by political authorities (Smith, 2000: IV, ii).

> No regulation of commerce can increase the quantity of industry in any society beyond what its capital can maintain. It can only divert a part of it into a direction into which it might not otherwise have gone: and it is by no means certain that this artificial direction is likely to be more advantageous to the society than that into which it would have gone of its own accord. (Smith, 1999: IV, ii, 3)

That particular denunciation is an important part of the genetic link between Smith's liberalism and contemporary neoliberalism (Skinner, 1999: 79).

The Ethics of Liberal Competition

Beyond the intuitions and hypotheses of economic liberalism, we can see emerging a deeply consequential reading of human nature and of the character of social life – and this already in the work and thought of early liberals including Adam Smith. Let us try and summarize here this reading, underscoring its main ethical implications.

Man is by nature an economic man. The economic sphere, the sphere of work and property is pre-eminent and all other spheres of human life (social, political and so on) come after in the double sense of emerging later historically and of having to be subservient to the natural laws of the economic sphere.

In the natural state, man is essentially alone facing nature. His (we have no sense of what is happening to 'her') work is his alone and determines his property, which is fundamentally individual. Hence, the notion of individualism is profoundly inscribed in the liberal project. At the core of this project is what could be called a liberal 'Eden' – the situation of equilibrium with so many free and autonomous individuals *qua* producers and property owners, projected as being the state of nature. In this liberal 'Eden', interactions are chosen, they are free and centre on the bartering and exchange of goods produced. The essence of human interaction in this state of nature is, in other words, the 'spot contract'. This liberal 'Eden' is, as in most monotheist religions, at the beginning but also may be at the end of history. In any case, it is a target, a goal that we should be striving for. In the state of nature, the individual is free and independent. Any form of collectivism (whether social – family or tribe; political, moral or religious, cultural or professional) potentially represents a threat to that fragile equilibrium.

The liberal market, in its 'Eden' form, is structured through the division of labour, competition and the invisible hand. Here things become slightly more complex – and there are two potential readings of early economic liberalism and in particular of Adam Smith (Force, 2003: 256ff). If we read only *The Wealth of Nations*, we easily get a sense that the main, if not the only, motor of market dynamics and human behaviour are individual self-interest, selfishness and greediness. The image used by Adam Smith to suggest that has become famous:

> It is not from the benevolence of the butcher, the brewer or the baker that we expect our dinner, but from their regard to their own interest. We address ourselves not to their humanity but to their self-love and never talk to them of our own necessities but of their advantage. (Smith, 1999: 119)

A miracle, though, happens through the mysterious alchemy of the market and its 'invisible hand'. The aggregation of multiple a- and un-ethical individual actions turns into a morally and ethically satisfying collective good. In *The Wealth of Nations*, the market is a moral structure – beyond the dimension of efficiency. This idea is still present today in all variants of neoclassical economic theory, as 'natural law' – hence unquestioned and not to be scientifically demonstrated (Nelson, 2001). Arguably, this is one of the most striking – and consequential – legacies of *The Wealth of Nations*. If the market is indeed a moral and ethical structure, then there is no need to bring in ethical considerations at the level of individual behaviours. Furthermore, the reasoning could well be that if we attempted to do that, we would only distort and disturb the natural regulative mechanisms of the market (Friedman, 1962).

There is, however, a second possible reading of Adam Smith if we focus this time on *The Theory of Moral Sentiments*. In his first book, Smith clearly suggests that the market and its invisible hand reveal a rational (that is, divine) plan and order. Individuals are linked to each other in and through that plan (Nelson, 1991). These individuals are endowed – presumably by the 'Author of Nature' – with certain faculties (such as reason or imagination) and particular propensities (Smith, 1982). There are two such propensities – self-love that expresses itself in the maximization of self-interest but also 'fellow feeling' as the first sentence of the *Theory of Moral Sentiments* shows:

> How selfish soever man may be supposed, there are evidently some principles in his nature, which interest him in the fortune of others, and render their happiness necessary to him, though he derives nothing from it except the pleasure of seeing it. (Smith, 1982: I.i.1.1)

Fellow feeling implies sympathy and empathy. The individual has a natural disposition to form judgements (applied both to herself and others) concerning what is fit and proper to be done or to be avoided. But since this natural disposition may conflict with self-love, it is probably not enough, Smith tells us, as a source of control. It should be strengthened and reinforced by the setting up of socially defined 'general rules concerning what is fit and proper' (Smith, 1982: III.4.8). This code of morality – this ethical project – may be the missing link in *The Wealth of Nations*; the one that could explain that the aggregation of self-interested actions turns ultimately into a morally satisfying collective good. A code of morality that would be deeply inscribed in the individuals themselves – although it may sometimes conflict with and contradict self-love – could create the basis for collective self-restraint and relative harmony. Undeniably, this dimension of Smith's work has been all but disregarded in classical and neoclassical economics.

READING COMPETITION THROUGH THE PROTESTANT ETHIC

The doctrine of divine election and its expression in worldly successes and in the realization of one's calling does in fact fit rather well with the liberal idea of a self-regulated market. We build here, naturally, upon Max Weber's interpretation of the Calvinist religion in its interaction with emergent modern and rational capitalism (Weber, 1930).

When Virtue Implies Virtuosity

Jean Calvin was a Franco-Swiss preacher. Together with Martin Luther, he was a key actor of the Protestant Reformation movement in Europe during the sixteenth century. An important element of Calvinist teachings was the doctrine of predestination. The original version of that doctrine was extremely rigid. The Calvinist God was a stern and all-powerful master planner who had divided humanity from immemorial times between a few that were elect and would be saved and the rest who would be damned. The motives of that almighty God were beyond human understanding. The division between those bound for damnation and those who would be saved was fully predetermined. Good deeds, human merits or repentance could have no impact whatsoever. In this rigid version, the doctrine of predestination was a source of deep existential anguish and pessimistic disillusion. It produced an 'unprecedented inner loneliness of the single individual' (Weber, 1930: 60). Undeniably, it was too harsh and inhuman.

While Calvin himself, as a chosen agent of God, was certain of his own salvation, the double practical question of whether one was saved or not and what were the signs of salvation, was certainly a burning one for regular believers. Hence practical takes on the doctrine of predestination had to emerge. More particularly, two types of pastoral advice appeared. First, it was an absolute duty to consider oneself one of the chosen – *certitudo salutis*. Second, it was possible to look for signs of salvation in a positive contribution to the glorification of God's Kingdom on earth and in 'intense worldly activity' (Weber, 1930: 67). This could be done through an absolute focus on one's 'calling'. The idea of the calling – or *Beruf* – was that each single one of us was put on this planet by the 'Great Master Planner' into a particular position and with a particular duty. Signs of our election could be found in the successful accomplishment of our *Beruf* as it contributed to the prosperity of God's earthly Kingdom and therefore to the Glory of God. In contrast, the refusal to do one's calling turned into a sign of damnation. In contrast to Catholicism, where the highest form of religious sentiment was otherworldly and mystical contemplation, in Calvinism the fulfilment of one's duty in worldly affairs was the highest form that the moral and religious activity of individuals could take (Weber, 1930: 67–70). The distant Calvinist God could not be reached otherwise than indirectly through the interface with his earthly Kingdom. As a consequence, the Calvinist creed was profoundly inner-worldly.

Existential anguish was a permanent state – and the search for signs of election was and should be permanent. The 'God of Calvinism demanded of his believers not single good works but a life of good works combined in a unified system' (Weber, 1930: 71). Virtue – as ultimately symbolized in the *certituto salutis* – implied virtuosity as measured by earthly successes and the production of wealth. The wealth that was being created, though, was not for enjoyment and it should not be used towards self-aggrandizement. In fact, straying away from an ascetic work ethic – through enjoyment, pleasures, unnecessary spending, pride, spite or the use of wealth to exert power – could be interpreted as signs of damnation. Wealth should be created and immediately and forever reinvested to fructify further God's Kingdom on earth. And the greater the possessions, 'the heavier, if the ascetic attitude toward life stands the test, the feeling of responsibility for them, for holding them undiminished for the glory of God and increasing them by restless effort' (Weber, 1930: 115).

The Calvinist Ethics of Competition

The notion of competition does not appear in any direct way in the Calvinist doctrine, whether in its harsher or softer variants. When we connect, however, this doctrine with the development of rational capitalism, we see how the competitive mechanism plays an implicit role.

In its harsher form, the Calvinist doctrine is profoundly and consequentially conservative. The doctrine of predestination, in its strong reading, implies full determinism. Each single one of us is either saved or damned (and implicitly good or bad) by divine decree. Trying to be anything else than what we are, trying to change would simply not make any sense. In this profoundly stable and rigid world, competition does not make sense. The softer variant of Calvinism, however, suggests a very different situation. The Calvinist, in this variant 'creates his own salvation or as would be more correct, the conviction of it' (Weber, 1930: 69). The way he does so is by working to multiply signs of earthly success – excelling in one's calling, helping fructify God's Kingdom on earth, generating wealth. Moral virtue as symbolized by salvation gets translated into worldly virtuosity and in particular into economic virtuosity. Man is not by nature *oeconomicus* but his economic activity becomes indirectly the measure of all things, in particular of his salvation and of his virtue.

The Calvinist doctrine of predestination means profound solitude of the believer in front of his destiny. The fight for the 'conviction of salvation' is a deeply solitary one; not all can be saved and stakes are high. In fact, I can be saved only if others are damned. Hence, competition in gaining the signs of salvation, competition in worldly and economic affairs has very profound even vital consequences. I need to succeed, I need to accumulate riches and others need to lose as two sides of the same coin – the conviction of my own salvation. The Calvinist doctrine suggests essential individualism – the solitary fight of each individual to convince himself of his own salvation. The consequence has been 'the strikingly frequent repetition, especially in the English Puritan literature, of warnings against any trust in the aid of friendship of men' (Weber, 1930: 62). Only God should be your confidant.

A direct consequence of this essential individualism is its associated utilitarianism. All actions and interactions need to serve the broader goal of increasing God's glory on earth and in parallel my own *certitudo salutis*. Any action that cannot be justified in this way is unnecessary distraction at best, sinful enjoyment at worst. Another way to look at this is to underscore the need to reinterpret and recast all our actions, interactions and relationships as contributing to the generation of wealth – hence reassuring us on the matter of our salvation.

Furthermore, nothing should be allowed to distort the aggregation of multiple solitary fights that necessarily impact each other. The Calvinist doctrine, in its softer form, builds upon the notion of an immutable, pre-determined order that will be revealed if those fights are left free play and remain unhampered and undistorted. Parallel to the invisible hand in classical economic liberalism, here a divine scheme in the background generates a profoundly moral order. Salvation is for a minority and salvation is measured by earthly success – hence by the capacity to produce wealth. The majority is damned and the situation in this world reflects the reality of the other world as determined by God. Salvation and wealth are more or less explicitly associated with virtue – being 'good'. Naturally, in contrast, being damned becomes being bad, sinful, 'wicked and ungodly' (Westminster, 1717: Chapter V – *Of Providence*). Still, the good need the bad, the saved need the damned – one category could not exist without the other. Competition is therefore not a fight to the death but a quest for an equilibrium reflecting a predetermined order. As such, the softer variant of the Calvinist doctrine was also quite conservative. More precisely, it generated good conscience about the status quo and a justification for profound social inequalities. The unequal distribution of the goods of this world 'was a special dispensation of Divine Providence, which in these differences, as in particular grace, pursued secret ends unknown to men' (Weber, 1930: 120). It also prevented and de-legitimized any kind of social intervention to correct those inequalities – in particular on the part of the state – and suggested instead the need for *laissez faire*.

At the end of *The Protestant Ethic and the Spirit of Capitalism*, Max Weber suggested however that modern capitalism was, at the dawn of the twentieth century, already in the process of 'losing its soul', in other words its religious and moral backbone. Weber proposed, furthermore, that the Calvinist revolution itself had had the unanticipated consequence of weakening through time the religious dimension of our world. By cutting away any form of direct connection between God and the believer, by judging of salvation through the metrics of economic productivity, Calvinism was significantly contributing through time to what Weber called the rationalization and 'disenchantment of our world' (Weber, 1930: 71).

At the same time, the practical ethics of Calvinism generated their own internal contradictions. In time, the latter were coming to weaken the invisible spiritual structure of developing capitalism. Calvinism, in its doctrinal form, was initially tightly connected to an ethical and religious project that required and implied its own material and worldly translation. Such materialization of a spiritual project, though, inherently generated tensions. Wealth and the materialism associated with its production were seen by Max Weber to have a deeply secularizing influence (Weber, 1930: 124). As a consequence, they were bound, he argued, to weaken the spiritual structure that originally sustained them. This was already in process during the last decades of the nineteenth century, particularly, he argued, in the United States. Capitalism was on its way to 'losing its soul', becoming 'disenchanted' and fully rationalized and in the end capitalism was turning into an 'iron cage'.

> The Puritan wanted to work in a calling; we are forced to do so. For when asceticism was carried out of monastic cells into everyday life, and began to dominate worldly morality, it did its part in building the tremendous cosmos of the modern economic order. This order is now bound to the technical and economic conditions of machine production which today determine the lives of all individuals who are born into this mechanism, not only those directly concerned with economic acquisition, with irresistible force... In the field of its highest development, in the United States, the pursuit of wealth, stripped of its religious and ethical meaning, tends to become associated with purely mundane passions. (Weber, 1930: 123)

DARWIN AND SPENCER: SURVIVAL OF THE FITTEST AND COMPETITION

In his *Origins of Species* (1859), Darwin outlined one general law that 'led to the advancement of all organic beings – namely multiply, vary, let the strongest live and the weakest die'. 'Selection' happened through the 'struggle for life' and advantage was measured by survival and reproductive success. Charles Darwin put competition – the 'struggle for life' – at the centre of natural life and of the evolution of species.

Rapidly, the evolutionary argument proposed by Charles Darwin was adapted and transferred to the social sciences. Although Darwin's original focus had been the biological evolution of species, he did not himself shy away from reading social life through a parallel evolutionary frame. As such, he was one of the first 'Social Darwinians' (Hawkins, 1997; Jones, 1978). The key mechanism here again was competition; competition between institutions, practices, organizations, ideas. The 'fittest' survived and the 'weakest' disappeared. This led to an easy association between evolutionary social change and social, human, or even moral progress. In fact, Darwin came to deduce the superiority of civilized Anglo-Saxon countries over other countries from his general law of evolution (Hawkins, 1997).

Bridging Social Darwinism and Liberalism: The Role of Spencer

Herbert Spencer was another key figure of Social Darwinism. Spencer contributed significantly both to the theoretical explicitation of Social Darwinism and to its diffusion to a broad public across national boundaries. An important dimension of Spencer's contribution was that he was able to create a bridge between Social Darwinism and economics, particularly liberal economics. Spencer was also instrumental in the cross-national transfer of ideas that brought Social Darwinism to the United States.

Herbert Spencer was born in Britain in a family that valued individualism and self-help. He started his professional life as a railway engineer, later becoming a journalist and writer. From 1848 to 1853, Spencer was editor of *The Economist*, the key British financial weekly then already a mouthpiece of liberal economic thinking.

Spencer's theory of cosmic evolution pictured a world in constant flux where the fight for scarce resources meant significant competitive pressures – within species, across species, within nations, across nations. This theory of cosmic evolution was associated in Spencer's thought with a 'theory of inevitable progress'. In his first book, *Social Statics*, published in 1851, Spencer claimed that

Progress, therefore, is not an accident but a necessity... The modifications mankind has undergone and is still undergoing result from a law underlying the whole organic creation. And provided the human race continues and the constitution of things remain the same, those modifications must end in completeness and progress. (Spencer, 1851: Chapter II, par. 4)

The tough pressure of competition meant – everywhere – the disappearance of the weak and the 'survival of the fittest'. Spencer, in fact, coined this expression that later came to be used as an iconic label of Social Darwinism. The harsh discipline of competition had ensured 'a constant progress towards a higher degree of skill, intelligence and self-regulation, a better coordination of actions, a more complete life' (Spencer, 1898, vol. II: 526-8). Competition should also lead to the elimination of the 'unfit'.

Such a Panglossian view of evolution and a deterministic sense of inescapable progress meant that Spencer believed in uninhibited individualism and championed strict *laissez-faire*. Any kind of interference could only be detrimental to the longer term and natural evolutionary process. There was no need whatsoever, in the Spencerian world, for politics, collective bargaining, welfare or charity initiatives. The latter in fact could be highly counterproductive. They were bound to disrupt the natural process that should (including in a moral sense for Spencer) lead to the 'survival of the fittest' and to the shouldering aside of the weak.

In the few years before and after 1870, the Spencerian variant of Social Darwinism got transferred from the old to the new continent. The Spencerian argument did resonate particularly well with the conditions that characterized the United States after the Civil War. Hence, it spread fast and was eagerly appropriated. This was a time of upheaval, turbulence, transformations and unpredictable developments where the old rules were inadequate and the new ones still to be invented (Kolko, 1963). In that context, Spencer's ideas became the intellectual foundation for the Social Darwinism that came to characterize the 'Robber Barons'. The 'Robber Barons' were that generation of businessmen that thrived initially on the chaotic conditions associated with the American Civil War and then established firmly their power and legitimacy during the period of corporate reinvention of American capitalism, at the end of the nineteenth century (Josephson, 1934; Sklar, 1988).

Spencer's ideas also spread within American intellectual circles, with significant impact in particular in American universities. Altogether, the Social Darwinian world-view, particularly in its Spencerian form, became an important ingredient of American social science with a profound and long - term impact (Hawkins, 1997). It was read, interpreted, used and appropriated – and transformed in the process. There were different paths to such transformation. We will just point to an interesting effort at reconciling and bringing together Spencerian evolutionism and the Calvinist doctrine. William Graham Sumner played here an interesting role. Sumner reinterpreted the 'survival of the fittest' as the consequence of a divine scheme and turned, in the process, *laissez-faire* into a natural/divine law.

> The law of the survival of the fittest was not made by man and cannot be abrogated by man. We can only, by interfering with it, produce the survival of the unfittest. (Sumner, 1963: 17)

Sumner also re-affirmed the Calvinist ethic as, interestingly, an instrument of the progressive evolutionary process championed by Spencer

> Labour and self-denial, to work yet abstain from enjoying, to earn a product yet work on as if one possessed nothing, have been the condition of advance for the human race from the beginning and they continue to be such still. (Sumner, 1963: 40)

When Herbert Spencer went to the United States in 1882, he was received with the highest honours. Andrew Carnegie or John D. Rockefeller revered him (Chernow, 1998). Spencerian evolutionism could, in and of itself, justify – including in a moral sense – the brutal tactics that were then characteristic of American capitalism. Violent and rapacious behaviour, in the context of 'free', in the sense of wild competition, were identified as necessary means leading to progress through struggle. The 'elimination' of the weak and the institutionalization of a hierarchical and unequal division of labour were also given legitimacy in this way. According to Spencer

> Not only does this struggle for existence involve the necessity that personal ends must be pursued with little regard to the evils entailed on unsuccessful competitors but it also involves the necessity that there shall not be too keen a sympathy with that diffuse suffering inevitable accompanying this industrial battle. (Spencer, 1890: 611).

Unsurprisingly, the Robber Barons rapidly seized upon an ideology that turned in this way struggle, violence and brutal use of power into necessary steps towards progress.

The Ethics of Spencerian Competition

In his work, Herbert Spencer suggests in fact an evolution of the main mechanisms of evolution. At an early stage of development of humanity, he tells us, warfare and diseases were the main operative mechanisms in the process of selection (Spencer, 1878: 193). Progressively, though, and as the human species evolved, warfare diminished in significance. As hygiene and medical science made progress, diseases and physical weaknesses had less of an impact. Warfare and diseases did not disappear as mechanisms, naturally, but they were complemented and in part replaced by what Spencer calls 'industrial war': 'After this stage has been reached, the purifying process ... remains to be carried on by industrial war and by a competition of societies' (Spencer, 1878: 199).

Hence, for Spencer, man is not by nature a *homo oeconomicus* but a warrior, a fighter. This warrior and fighting spirit originally reflected and expressed a natural law – the law of progressive evolution – through the struggle for life. In time, this spirit was translated into a different kind of mechanism – that of unhampered economic competition. So the profound nature of man remained the same – a warrior fighting for his own survival. But the way this nature expressed itself evolved through time – from warfare to the market. At a later stage of development, man did become a *homo oeconomicus* in the sense that the key dimension of his nature (his fighting spirit) played out mostly through market competition.

Reading Herbert Spencer, we realize that the picture of the market that emerges is one of a ruthless battlefield. Competition should be not only 'free' but in fact 'wild'. The idea that it is a jungle out there and that everything, as a consequence, is and should be possible is very much what comes to mind – strong in the morning, dead in the evening! Competition is all out war. Competition is not merely a struggle against nature. Nor is it enough to think of it as a search for equilibrium where all are needed and find their place. Competition here is a war of all against all – there should be clear winners and clear losers. More often than not, losing means dying in the real sense of the term (for a firm, for a society, even for an individual directly or by lack of posterity).

The violence and the suffering necessarily associated with such an understanding of competition are justified in teleological terms as bringing along human and social progress, a better and more developed society. Where individual units might suffer or disappear, the collective will benefit through reaching a 'higher stage'. In Spencer's reading of it, the freely playing competitive mechanism is progressive and therefore morally good. The argument should even be pushed one step further. Not only is the competitive mechanism morally justified and morally good but so are also all its consequences. Individual suffering becomes morally legitimate since it is a means, a step towards collective progress.

Mitigating that suffering, furthermore, through charity, state intervention or any form of social engineering distorts the natural process and mechanism of selection. Hence, all form of intervention is an obstacle to collective human progress – and as such at the same time both highly counter-productive and morally illegitimate. Absolute *laissez-faire*, whatever its consequences, should be the rule when it comes to market competition. The game is fully and essentially an individualist one and it should remain so – one individual against others; one firm against others; one nation against others.

Interestingly, by pushing a step too far the quest for 'pure' market competition, Spencer opens up a dangerous breach. Wild competition, without bounds, is in fact logically bound to lead, progressively, to a reduction of competition! If everything is possible in the context of economic warfare, then the strong will kill and eat the weak, the strong will get stronger, the number of actors will altogether be reduced and the conditions for competition radically altered. In parallel, the constant struggle of all against all, the possibility to be at the top one day and dead the other create a profoundly distressing situation. History repeatedly shows that individuals or individual units will try as much as they can to mitigate and set bounds to such disturbing pressure. Adam Smith had pointed to the natural propensity of 'people of the same trade' to convene and agree on ways to dampen competitive pressures (Smith, 1999: I, x, 232). While Spencer's ideas were crossing the Atlantic, the temptation was strong in the US but also in Europe for industrialists to counter competition through different forms of collaboration. The last decades of the twentieth century saw a multiplication of cartels, trusts or other forms of association in the United States – the objective of which was to make competition less wild if not to get rid of it altogether. Too much competition, in short, generates an urge to control and reduce it. This urge stems not only from external actors (like the state) but is also to be found amongst the actors in competition themselves. In the end, and if there is no regulatory intervention, the logical evolution is from wild competition to a progressive taming of competitive pressures, in particular through increasing unit size and the decreasing number of actors involved. Wild competition suggests in time an oligopolization (of industries but also potentially of societies, nations or other forms of collectives).

TOWARD A NEOLIBERAL SYNTHESIS

Those three bodies of ideas – economic liberalism, Calvinist doctrine and Spencerian evolutionism – met, combined and influenced each other on

American soil. The encounter was intense and powerful. There were, as Max Weber would have said, powerful 'elective affinities' between those three bodies of thought. We turn now to what appears, in retrospect, a step towards synthesis. Neoliberalism has multiple roots and reflects intermingled influences. We focus here on the Chicago School as one of the key roots and pillars of the neoliberal doctrine as we know it today. The Chicago School was born and developed in the economics department of the University of Chicago. It built upon but also overcame and went beyond classical economic liberalism, the Calvinist heritage and Spencerian insights. It also emerged and developed in a peculiar period, in times when American capitalism was undergoing major transformations. This period saw the emergence of oligopolistic equilibria in many industries, the multiplication of large firms and the spread of collective ownership of the corporate type (Sklar, 1988; Djelic, 1998).

Building the Liberal Temple: The Early Years at Chicago

Created in 1892, the University of Chicago was originally financed by John D. Rockefeller. The 'Titan' of the American oil industry was threading a path followed by many other 'Robber Barons' (Josephson, 1932; Chernow, 1998). After accumulating wealth on an unprecedented scale, including through questionable methods, the 'Great Captains' of American industry were buying social and moral legitimacy by fuelling back some of that wealth into philanthropic activities. In its early years, the University of Chicago was nicknamed the 'Standard Oil University'. The first head of the economics department was J. Lawrence Laughlin, one of the most conservative economists in the country. Laughlin was a combination of neoclassical theorist and aggressive big business apologist – the type that seemed to 'confirm the suspicion of those who regarded the University of Chicago as a tool of business interests' (Coats, 1963).

The liberalism championed by Laughlin differed in important ways from Smithian-type liberalism. His apology of the market was reconciled with the corporate revolution that transformed American capitalism (Sklar, 1988). Laughlin defended the status quo on the grounds that eternal laws of economics were just and progressive. At the turn of the twentieth century, the status quo meant oligopolies in most industries (Bornemann, 1940). This reconciliation between markets and 'bigness' has remained to this day a trademark of the so-called Chicago School of economics (Miller, 1962; Nelson, 2001). The Chicago School has been characterized by its 'willingness, even eagerness, to accept whatever results the free market grinds out' (Bronfenbrenner, 1962: 73) and by its incessant struggle against any form of state intervention.

The Chicago School crystallized during the 1930s around the key figure of Franck Knight (Nelson, 2001). The group that emerged then would make the Chicago School famous – Jacob Viner, Henry Simons, Aaron Director, Allen Wallis, Milton Friedman, Rose Director Friedman and George Stigler (Reder, 1982). Franck Knight championed free markets on moral grounds, as the best arrangements to ensure the preservation of individual freedom. Increased efficiency and utility maximization were positive collaterals, not ends in themselves. (Nelson, 2001)

Chicago – The Post-World War II Generations

The Chicago School of Economics reached maturity in the 1950s. The new generation had appropriated the philosophical insights of their teachers, in particular Frank Knight. There were two features, however, that set that generation apart. First, it jumped on the bandwagon of the 'marginal' or mathematical revolution in economics (Schumpeter, 1983: III, ch. v). It contributed, in fact, to the acceleration of the move to quantitative methods and complex econometrics within the economics profession (Reder, 1982). Second, with Milton Friedman as its main spokesman, this generation re-affirmed the public and polemical role of the economist, originally explored by Laughlin but neglected by the generation of the 1930s.

By the early 1960s, the Chicago School in economics had acquired its unique features. First, one finds an unconditional commitment to and advocacy of the market mechanism. The Chicago economist 'differs in this advocacy from many economists on his dogmatism and in assuming that the actual market functions like the ideal one' (Miller, 1962: 66). Second, one finds a principled rejection of regulation and state intervention that implies acceptation of the evolutionary dynamics of market competition and of their consequences. This has meant, in particular, that the Chicago School has accepted 'bigness'. The fear of concentrated wealth, present in the work of Adam Smith, has had little weight here, much less in any case than the fear of government. Gary Becker summed it up well: 'It may be preferable not to regulate economic monopolies and to suffer their bad effects, rather than to regulate them and suffer the effects of political imperfection' (Becker, 1958: 109).

Third, one finds a Panglossian vision of the world. The market mechanism is seen as progressive – leading to greater efficiency, collective prosperity but also individual freedom (Friedman and Friedman, 1979, xv, 28: 129). Fourth, provided the state does not meddle, the market mechanism should be self-sustaining. For the Chicago Boys, faith in the market is such that monopoly is at most an ephemeral situation that should not threaten the vision of competitive markets (Reder, 1982). Fifth, the associated conception of human nature is that of neoclassical economics – human beings are out to maximize utility. The Chicago School has systematically explored that path by expanding the boundaries of economics, explaining theft, discrimination, marriage, fertility, child-rearing (Becker, 1971, 1991), legal issues (Posner, 1972) or the functioning of the church and religious institutions (Ekelund et al., 1996) through the prism of utility maximization.

Sixth, and finally, an important feature of the contemporary Chicago School has been its capacity to reconcile science and politics (Weber, 1959). The post-war generation contributed to the scientific and mathematical turn of economics. At the same time, though, this generation also became highly involved in policy-making and ultimately in political discussions. The move to politics and policy-making was, at least at the start, partly accidental (Djelic, 2006). Soon, though, the most vocal amongst Chicago economists – in particular Milton Friedman – finding out that there was a 'market' for their ideas, engaged in normative proselytizing. A few of the Chicago economists turned themselves into missionaries of market mechanisms within but also beyond the economic realm. All their proposals for reform

> ... involved either increased use of the price system (e.g. on national markets but also across national boundaries), substitution of private for public production (e.g. in health, education), replacement of legal compulsion by voluntary – financially induced – private cooperation or a mixture of all three. (Reder, 1982: 25)

CONCLUDING REMARKS

In retrospect, the spread, in the United States, of Social Darwinism in its Spencerian form proved to be an important factor contributing to and hastening the secularization of capitalism in that country. The idea of an emergent natural order was a common feature of economic liberalism in its Smithian variant, of Calvinism and of Social Darwinism in the Spencerian version. In all three bodies of thought, that natural order was considered to be beyond human intervention. In fact, in all three cases, that order could only be revealed if natural laws were left free play. Natural laws had a divine dimension both in Calvinism and in a complete reading of Adam Smith. In the version of economic liberalism that forgot the *Theory of Moral Sentiments*, though, as well as in Spencerian Social Darwinism, natural laws were essentially mechanistic. They had no 'deeper meaning', no ethical foundation – they just were there to be reckoned with.

Like Calvinism, economic liberalism and Spencerian Social Darwinism were highly conservative ideologies but they were so in a different sense. Calvinism justified the status quo and the position that all occupied in the divine scheme of things was reflected in the social hierarchies of this world. There was, however, room for all in this world – the weak and the strong, those who would be damned and those who would be saved. Economic liberalism in its mechanistic variant and Spencerian Social Darwinism justified instead the logics of evolutionary dynamics – and the survival of only the fittest and most competitive, which implied as correlate the disappearance, death or disintegration of the weak and the least competitive. Those logics were not (and should not be) mitigated by any form of self-restraint or 'fellow feeling' – as had been the case both in a full reading of Smithian liberalism or in Calvinist capitalism. Instead, the fight of all against all should be given absolutely free play even if it expressed itself in the most violent and brutal manner. In that context, a moral frame was reinterpreted as mere obstacle – just like laws, regulation and state intervention – to the free play of natural, mechanistic, forces. A moral frame and 'fellow feeling' did not belong with economic logics and were in fact bound to disturb those logics.

In the twentieth century, the emergence of neoliberalism represented an emerging synthesis. All three bodies of thought – economic liberalism, Calvinist doctrine and Spencerian evolutionism – were present and combined in this synthesis. At the same time, the neoliberal synthesis pushed forward a process already well under way – the disenchantment of economics and economic activity. Rationalization, individualism, utilitarianism, *laissez-faire* and a belief in progress remained as key building blocks. Neoliberalism also appropriated the reconciliation between competition and size that was mentioned above. The profound meaning, though, the legitimacy and the moral backbone that had been understood to sustain economic activity, at least in classical economy and in the Calvinist world-view, had all but disappeared. Strangely enough, notions like 'invisible hand' or 'spontaneous market equilibrium' carried with them the shadows and echoes of a lost moral frame. This lost moral frame had originally given meaning to a peculiar form of economic and acquisitive behaviour. It also had placed bounds and limits upon it, through notions like 'fellow feeling' as a counterpoint to 'self-interest'. Without the frame, only pragmatic ethics remained – acute individualism combined with utilitarianism; materialism as the only end; an attachment to *laissez-faire* and competition even when those were leading in fact through their own internal contradictions to a weakening of competition; rationalization and the eviction of pockets of irrationality; finally a profound conviction that the evolutionary trend meant 'progress' whatever the associated externalities.

REFERENCES

Becker, G., (1958), 'Competition and democracy', *Journal of Law and Economics*, **1**, 105–109.

Becker, G., (1971), *The Economics of Discrimination*, Chicago University Press, Chicago.

Becker, G., (1991), *A Treatise on the Family*, Harvard University Press, Cambridge, MA.

Bornemann, A., (1940), *J. Laurence Laughlin*, American Council on Public Affairs, Washington.

Bronfenbrenner, M., (1962), 'Observations on the Chicago schools', *Journal of Political Economy*, **70**, 72–75.

Chernow, R., (1998), *Titan,* Random House, New York.

Coats, A. W., (1963), 'The origins of the "Chicago school(s)"?', *Journal of Political Economy*, **71**, 487–493.

Darwin, C., ([1859], 1999), *The Origins of Species*, Bantam Classics, New York.

Djelic, M. L., (1998), *Exporting the American Model*, Oxford University Press, Oxford.

Djelic, M. L., (2006), 'Marketization: from intellectual agenda to global policy making', in M. L. Djelic and K. Sahlin-Andersson (eds), *Transnational Governance, Institutional Dynamics of Regulation*, Cambridge University Press, Cambridge, 53–73.

Djelic, M. L. and Sahlin-Andersson, K., (eds), (2006), *Transnational Governance*, Cambridge University Press, Cambridge.

Ekelund, R., Herbert, R., Tollison, R., Anderson, G and Davidson, A., (1996), *Sacred Trust*, Oxford University Press, NY.

Force, P., (2003), *Self-interest before Adam Smith*, Cambridge University Press, Cambridge.

Friedman, M., (1962), *Capitalism and Freedom,* Chicago University Press, Chicago.

Friedman, M., (1968), 'The role of monetary policy', *American Economic Review*, **58** (1), 1–17.

Friedman, M. and Friedman, R., (1979), *Free to Choose*, Avon Books, New York.

Hawkins, M., (1997), *Social Darwinism in American and European Thought, 1860-1945,* Cambridge University Press, Cambridge and NY.

Jones, G., (1978), 'The social history of Darwin's *The Descent of Man*', *Economy and Society*, **7**, 1–28.

Josephson, M., (1934), *The Robber Barons*, Harcourt, Brace and World, New York.

Kolko, G., (1963), *The Triumph of Conservatism*, Free Press, New York.

Locke, J., (1997), *Locke: Political Essays*, Cambridge University Press, Cambridge, UK.

Manent, P., (1986), *Les Libéraux,* Hachette Littérature, Paris.

Miller, H., (1962), 'On the "Chicago school" of economics', *Journal of Political Economy*, **70** (1), 64–69.

Nelson, R., (1991), *Reaching for Heaven on Earth*, Rowman and Littlefield, Lanham.

Nelson, R., (2001), *Economics as Religion*, Pennsylvania State University Press, University Park, PA.

Posner, R., (1972), *Economic Analysis of Law*, Little Brown, Boston.

Reder, M., (1982), 'Chicago economics: permanence and change', *Journal of Economic Literature*, **20**, 1–38.

Schumpeter, J., (1983), *Histoire de l'Analyse Economique*, NRF-Gallimard, Paris.

Skinner, A., (1999), 'Analytical introduction', in Smith, A., the *Wealth of Nations*, Penguin Books, London and NY, 15–43.

Sklar, M., (1988), *Corporate Reconstruction of American Capitalism, 1890-1916*, Cambridge University Press, Cambridge and NY.

Smith, A., ([1759], 1982), *The Theory of Moral Sentiments*, Liberty Press, Indianapolis.

Smith, A., ([1776], 1999), *The Wealth of Nations – Books I-III*, ed. A. Skinner, Penguin Books, London, New York.

Smith, A., ([1776], 2000), *The Wealth of Nations – Books IV-V*, ed. A. Skinner, Penguin Books, London, New York.

Spencer, H., ([1873], 1878), *The Study of Sociology,* seventh edition. Kegan Paul, London.

Spencer, H., ([1876-96], 1969), *The Principles of Sociology*, Macmillan, abridged, London.

Spencer, H., ([1855], 1890), *The Principles of Psychology*, third edition, William and Norgate, London.

Spencer, H., ([1864-7], 1898), *The Principles of Biology,* 2 vols, Appleton and Co, New York.

Spencer, H., ([1851], 1970), *Social Statics*, Augustus M. Kelley Pubs, New York.

Spencer, H., (1994), *Political Writings*, ed. J. Offer, Cambridge University Press, Cambridge, UK.

Sumner, W. G., ([1881], 1963), 'Sociology', in S. Persons, (eds), *Social Darwinism: Selected Essays of W. G. Sumner*, Prentice Hall, Englewood Cliffs.

Taylor, M., (ed.), (1996), *Herbert Spencer and the Limits of the State,* Thoemmes Press, Bristol, UK.

Weber, M., ([1904-5], 1930), *The Protestant Ethic and the Spirit of Capitalism,* translated by T. Parsons, Routledge, London and New York.
Weber, M., (1959), *Le Savant et le Politique*, Plon, Paris.
Westminster, ([1647], 1717), Westminster Confession, Fifth Official Edition, London.

6. The Ethics of Rationality: Elucidations in the Theoretical Foundations of Economics by Relation to Ethics

Mircea Boari

INTRODUCTION

Views about the relationship between ethics and economic action have been divided for the larger part of modern times, probably since Adam Smith's dual treatment of the subject. However, for early modern philosophers such as John Locke, Spinoza, Montesquieu, as well as for some twentieth century proponents of free trade, such as Ayn Rand, the freedom of economic action was a precondition for the development of moral character.

That there exists an implicit ethics of economic action is also the background thesis of the present chapter. This ethical core is constitutive to economic rationality and to the model of the rational maximizing individual. Without this ethical built-in component, production, exchange and the whole range of indirect benefits of economic action could not exist. This implicit ethics is minimalist: which means to say that it will not satisfy the exigencies of a full blown ethical system. But what is more important is that this minimal core allows for a smooth derivation of a complete ethics which otherwise, as is often the case, would remain suspended in the stratosphere of the human 'spirit', in disconnection if not in contradiction (recognized or not) to the empirical conditions of human existence.

The ethics comprised in economic rationality is merely the precondition, a necessary condition of a wider ethics of rationality, which this chapter sketches. Whether it is also a sufficient condition, is of lesser consequence and, for now, will remain an open question. The important facts regarding the ethics of rationality grounded in economic action are the following: it follows from predicaments concerning human nature valid in the light of current science; it is an open system, allowing for integration without contradiction of maximalist ethical injunctions of a certain class, namely individualist virtue (excellence) ethical injunctions; this class of wider ethical maxims is consistent with findings of philosophers throughout the Western philosophical corpus; and, finally, it is the least normative ethical system conceivable, in that it does not rely on enforcement and/or coercion (recognized or not) in backing its predicaments.

In order to achieve its results, the chapter is structured in three main sections. The first section is analytical, providing a new perspective upon the maximizing behaviour. The second section, drawing upon evolutionary theory, offers the empirical support for the analytical results, and makes economic theory and evolutionary theory meet. The third section indicates the general outlook of a complete ethical system derived from the minimal core and formulates a set of basic propositions concerning the ethics of rationality.[1]

DIFFERENTIAL MAXIMIZATION OF FITNESS

In this section, I shall delineate the territory of rationality indirectly, by specifying what irrationality, as commonly understood, is. Which is no easy task. More than 300 years ago, Spinoza made this observation:

> Most of those who have written about ... human conduct seem to be dealing not with natural phenomena that follow the common laws of nature but with phenomena outside Nature ... They assign the cause of human weakness and frailty not to the power of Nature in general, but to some defect in human nature ... They will doubtless find it surprising that I should attempt to treat of the faults and follies of mankind in the geometric manner, and that I should propose to bring logical reasoning to bear on what they proclaim is opposed to reason, and is vain, absurd and horrifying. (Spinoza, 1992, Part III, Preface: 103)

One of the reasons for this difficulty may be the fact that human sciences, as they are epistemologically constituted today, proceed from the metaphysical assumption that humans can/will/should act rationally. In other words, the said sciences have a normative component already present, since a large part of human behaviour, from emotions such as hatred or malice to complex actions involving whole societies, such as warfare, is left out of the descriptive picture.[2] The economic science does not make an exception, and the fact has been observed by prominent economists, such as H. A. Simon:

> Economics is the human science which celebrates human rationality in all the forms in which it manifests in human behaviour and in the workings of human societies... Economics ... draws a romantic, almost heroic a portrait of the human spirit. (Simon, 1991 : 53)

That staunch defender of capitalism, economic freedom, rationality and individualist ethics which was Ayn Rand gave an exasperated expression to this difficult issue when, in a letter to Isabel Paterson she wrote: 'It is actually impossible for man to be irrational' (Rand, 1997b :182). The same sensitivity transpires from Mises's almost identical phrasing which also signals the limits of his praxeology, of human action identified as economic action *per se*: 'Human action is necessarily always rational' (Mises, von, 1966: 19).

For reasons which will become clear during the exposition to follow, economics is the only science in which this built-in normative component, the premise of rationality, and its offspring, the central concept of the rational maximizing individual, is justified. But there remains the fact that economics covers only a part of generic human action, the rational part.[3]

In order to capture the essence of irrational processes, a simple, threefold epistemological procedure ought to be followed. The first step is to group behaviour around a central concept of *individual fitness*: behaviour, thus, is centred and organized around the requirement of maximizing the fitness of the individual.[4] This simple observation is consonant with both economic and biological theory. Individuals are indeed (for evolutionary reasons, not merely because of greed, acquisitiveness, or insatiable appetites) maximizers of fitness. The second step is to understand the concept of fitness maximization not in absolute terms, as in classic, metaphysically bound economics, but in relative terms. Even if an external system of reference within which the economist, the philosopher or God could measure fitness in quasi-absolute terms exists, this is not directly available to individuals. Fitness is always relative to the environment, more specifically, to the social environment: individuals measure their fitness by comparison with other individuals, interpersonal comparison serving as the universal instrument for the assessment of fitness positions. Thirdly, given the fact that fitness is assessed relatively, the measurement of fitness is not given by an absolute value, but by *the magnitude of the fitness differential δFt* between an individual x and variables capturing the fitness of other individuals (number of cars by relation to neighbour y but also fitness position by relation to average peer group income, and so on).

Putting the three steps together, what individuals are maximizers *of*, is the fitness differential. The biological concept of fitness has been operationalized in economics in a sense congruent with the present analysis in Garry S. Becker's and Jack Hirshleifer's works, and, in an interdisciplinary political science / economics / biology nexus concordant with the present analysis on more than one point, by Paul Rubin (Becker 1962, 1976, 1993; Hirshleifer, 1977, 1978, 1985; Rubin, 2002). The only treatment of fitness maximization in relative terms I know of is an isolated and neglected (even at the time of its publication) paper of Alchian.[5] It is the understanding of the fact that relative maximization of fitness is maximization of fitness differentials that represents the original contribution of this paper.[6]

There exist two possible forms of variation of the fitness differential, given any two relative fitness positions, Ft_x and Ft_y. Considering Ft_x larger than Ft_y, the differential δFt increases in favour of x; Ft_x is larger than Ft_y, and δFt of x by relation to y decreases, which is to say, δFt increases in favour of y, while Ft_x remains the larger.[7] The two forms of variation of the fitness differential define two equilibrium points, indicated by their limit: that of maximal differential fitness (fitness differential tends to infinity), and that of equality of fitness (fitness differential tends to zero). The two equilibrium points have different characteristics, but this aspect will be developed in a different study.[8]

There exist two possible strategies for the correction of the fitness position to one's advantage (δFt Max strategies), only the first having become the object of study for economics and, indeed, defining it as science. On the one hand, individuals may increase their self-exertion, which is to say their productivity and efficiency. In a given population, this leads to known anti-entropic beneficial effects of systemic growth, diversification and increase of complexity via the known processes of division of labour and market exchanges (catallactics). In game theoretical terms, the essential mechanism of growth is represented by the games with positive sum. In the terminology proposed in this chapter, these are games whereby the fitness position of all the actors increases in a quasi-absolute sense, by relation to past moments in time or by relation to other social systems, which can be assessed by theoretical science but not directly by individuals themselves.

On the other hand, individuals can just as well increase the fitness differential to their advantage by whatever loss of fitness they can infringe unto another. Since the reduction of the fitness differential is that which matters, and since an absolute fitness of the individual arbitrarily defined is of no relevance, this strategy is not concerned with the cost to the individual performing it. Insofar as the result achieved is a no-matter-how-small reduction of the fitness differential, the strategy will be played and the action counts as maximizing behaviour, even if the cost paid by the individual is very large. The crucial factor governing this strategy is not absolute gain or cost, but a difference, independent of the quantities involved. The process at work still needs to be described with the same precision as that of the division of labour and catallactics, but it essentially must involve their opposites. The mechanism by which it takes place is that of negative sum games. In a given population, if this strategy is played above a critical frequency, it will necessarily lead to entropic processes of decreasing value-content, complexity and diversity: to 'negative economic growth', devolution and system decomplexification, in a word, to primitivism.[9] The fitness positions of all individuals will diminish by relation to past moments in time or by relation to other social systems, and personal historical memory sometimes can assess that. But, as paradoxical as this may sound, this strategy is fitness maximizing, in that the fitness positions of the individuals playing it may improve by relation to one another.

It is in this apparent paradox that lies the essence of 'irrationality': irrationality along the logical dimension, in the sense that individuals can be better off even if all of them are worse off. And 'irrational' along the dimension of habitual discursive practice, as discussed above, namely that the attribute of rationality is already normative in that it assumes constructivism, growth, creation of value. Until an economics of negative sum games is created, the economic science of today is already normative, in that it assumes that maximizing behaviour should be rational in the sense of nice positive sum players. The deductive sequence above demonstrates that individuals are indeed maximizers but not necessarily *rational* maximizers.

A third dimension, semantic-historical, will contribute to further elucidating the meaning of irrationality. The idea of self-preservation of the individual is foundational both in economics and in political science.[10] Self-preservation has been seen as consistent with actions governed by self-interest, a notion at the centre of the reconstruction of political and economic philosophy at the beginning of modern times (Hirschman, 1997). The maximization of the fitness differential by infringement of losses to another is, indeed, consistent with self-interest: as a matter of fact, self-interest is nothing but maximization of fitness, whether by losses to another or by self-exertion. But, in the strict sense, it is *not* self-preservationist, by the fact that it presupposes a penalty in the form of the potential cost of fitness associated with it. Differential fitness can, and indeed sometimes will, be reduced with extremely high costs, provided that at the end the fitness differential is smaller than at the onset.[11] These costs are not of the type associated with 'higher gains', as in the maxim 'there is a price to pay for anything.'[12] There is no gain to be achieved by the individual in the absolute sense of making himself/herself better off: s/he merely makes another worse off and, thus, indirectly, him/herself better off in pure, content-less, relational terms.

In brief, the strategy of fitness maximization by infringing losses to another is destructive and, also, potentially self-destructive. And it is this readiness for self-destructiveness which gives its mere adjectival qualification as 'irrational' an unmistakable emotional confirmation. The strategy becomes self-preservationist only upon the reduction of the potential cost to be paid when harming another, the easiest such condition being achieved by 'compounded power' and by 'combining with others' (Hobbes), that is, by ganging up in groups and by gregarious association.[13]

The difference between the two strategies of fitness maximization has been captured speculatively by Albert Jay Nock, following a distinction proposed by Franz Oppenheimer, as the difference between the economic means and the political means for self-preservation (Oppenheimer, 1997; Nock, 1935). Paying due historical tribute, the strategy of differential fitness maximization by self-exertion will be called fitness maximization Type E (δFt Max Type E), and the opposite one fitness maximization Type P (δFt Max Type P). Figure 6.1 summarizes the discussion above.

● **Type E** ● Increase of fitness differentials by self-exertion and increase of productivity; concerned with **self**; defines the Economic means for self-preservation.

● **Type P** ● Increase of fitness differentials by destruction of fitness of another; concerned with **others**; defines the Political means of self-preservation.

Figure 6.1 Fitness differential maximization, δFt Max

Rationality, as commonly understood, is maximization of fitness by self-exertion, that is, the faculty permitting participation in positive sum games. Maximization of fitness differentials of type E maximizes both absolute fitness and relative fitness. While maximization of fitness differentials of type P may maximize relative fitness, the one which is directly assessable by individuals, while reducing absolute fitness. The appearance of irrationality which δFt Max Type P takes is determined by this discrepancy: apparently, there is 'more' to be had from strategies of type E. But, as will become clearer from the next section, 'more' is not what the empirical nature of man is about.

Economics is chiefly the science of positive sum games, the science par excellence of the rationality in man, as Herbert Simon had it. But the constitution of its domain is that which gives also its normative dimension. It now appears that this normative dimension is in fact a moral dimension, since what is left out is precisely the opposite of morality, namely destructiveness and loss/harm done unto another. The maximizing individual is a genus, while the rational maximizing individual is a mere species: it describes only one class of modalities of self-preservation, the only class studied by economics.

DIFFERENTIAL FITNESS MAXIMIZATION: BIOLOGY, ANTHROPOLOGY, POLITICAL ECONOMY

Individuals are very poor evaluators of fitness in absolute or quasi-absolute terms. The injunction 'when I was your age I did not even have...' frequently uttered by a bitter parent, seldom succeeded in mobilizing gratitude or, even less, fitness satisfaction in a reckless child. At a different conceptual level, but working in the same sense, the notion that capitalism generates a larger economic pie and by that a larger portion even for the poor, comparatively to equalitarian economic systems where everyone has the same share albeit from a much smaller pie, has failed to impress countless economists, not to speak of the common folk. What these casual observations amount to is the notion that the perception of fitness in absolute or quasi-absolute terms is counter-factual. Common-sense is not sufficient a tool for recording this type of information, information not pertaining to the immediate, diachronic/historical and synchronic/topological, context of the individuals. This is to say, individuals are not equipped, evolutionarily speaking, for the recording of system-wide information and for the automatic extraction from it of rules of thumb to guide their action.[14] In other words, in order for system-wide information to input into decision-making mechanisms, it has to override their defaults which *are* evolutionarily built-in and, as such, have the imperious character of a drive or instinct.

On the other hand, there exist all the indications that the major regulator of behaviour (action) is the recording of the fitness differentials (relative assessment of fitness positions by interpersonal comparison, 'catching up with the Joneses'). Whether the brain possesses a homeostatic device for fitness level, the type of data that this device uses pertains to fitness differentials: which is to say, *fitness level is measured by fitness position*. Individuals respond to perceived differential fitness by swings in general psychological tonicity, mood, emotions, rationalizations: and this happens independently of whatever information they possess regarding their actual level of absolute fitness (larger than that of the parents or, as with Adam Smith, larger than that of an African king).[15] Psychological correlates of large fitness differentials in one's favour are serotoninergic: in what concerns the self, happiness, joy, elation, and in what concerns otherness, good will, generosity, regard for another, assistential compassion. The psychological correlates of negative fitness differentials are malice, envy, hatred, or, in milder forms, Schadenfreude, happiness at the unhappiness of another. The emotional correlates of large fitness differentials of any sign are best captured by the Greek notion of *hubris*, which combines spite with self-assertiveness.[16] Some of these emotional responses have already come to the attention of evolutionary psychologists.[17]

Equally, in the two possible strategies of correcting the perceived fitness differentials, there is no symmetry between δFt Max Type E and δFt Max Type P. Maximization of fitness differentials by self-exertion, increased fitness efficacy by productivity and/or creativity have the following conditional attributes: to begin with, work (disutility) taking the specific form of learning or training effort; secondly, this produces results only in time, and consequently to an initial investment – which is to say, it is a teleological strategy; thirdly, there exists only probabilistic certainty of the result and the involved probabilities are difficult to assess computationally – they presuppose information about the wider system state (such as the structure of the market when choosing an operational niche for oneself); finally, reward, besides being uncertain, always takes the form of delayed gratification – which is to say, extremely stressful on the brain reward mechanisms involved in coordinating action in view of fitness maximization. Being a teleological strategy, distal, abstract causes ought to operate upon the biological machinery of behaviour (attention, motivation, energy expenditure). The above considerations make the strategy of Type E a *weak strategy* contributing a low input in the decision-making, behavioural steering mechanisms.

But the most stringent condition placed upon strategies of Type E is that, due to specialization (division of labour), they require the participation of numerous other individuals (Hayek's 'extended order'; Mises's 'catallactics'). The more advanced the system thus generated, the more limitative the conditions placed upon these others. Not only their number increases, but also their anonymity and speciality (rarity). Productive associations become more random, scarce and highly anonymous. The extremely specialized and conditional nature of the cooperation is reflected by the need of its formalization as contract and by the complexity of these contracts; that is to say, the implementation of the strategy is a matter of design and conscious intentionality. The lability of the entire structure is reflected by the need of coercive clauses and agencies for its enforcement. In brief, strategies of δFt Max Type E, participation in positive sum games, are highly conditional and subject to a dynamical growth highly sensitive to noise (factors which can destroy it). In a word, they are complex (included in the technical usage of the concept of complexity is the attribute of fragility).

Few of these conditional attributes apply to the strategy of differential maximization of Type P. The strategy is, in a word, robust and simple. It does not require specialization and, by that, is very little selective as to the particular characteristics of the participants. It has a very steep learning curve, if any, and seldom requires formalization (when formalization occurs, contracts between cooperators in strategies of Type P, are replaced by oaths and rituals of allegiance, and by lethal threat in case of defection). The strategy is a strategy of proximity: anyone at hand can potentially participate. Being a strategy of opportunity, it can produce results immediately. Being a strategy of proximity, biologically evolved competence in assessment of other individuals (physical strength assessment whereby size matters foremost, facial expression, mind reading, cheating detection) spontaneously kicks in and provides a basis of 'instinctive certainty'. Proximity and opportunity added together mean that the strategy is triggered by proximal and concrete causes (the purse of the neighbour). Finally, reward, even if uncertain, is always an immediate gratification. The strategy has all the characteristics of automatisms. All of the above make of the strategy type P a *strong strategy*, contributing massively to the behaviour steering mechanisms.

Summing up, the asymmetries between the *δFt* Max strategy Type E and the *δFt* Max strategy Type P strongly indicate that differential fitness maximization type P is a built-in, inborn strategy and, thus, relying upon Darwinian evolved mechanisms. Meanwhile differential fitness maximization Type E, even though by necessity making use of some genetically evolved behavioural mechanisms, is a derivative, acquired strategy.

In the evolutionary theory of social behaviour, there exists a form of behaviour whose theoretical description matches point by point the analytical and the phenomenological structure of the differential fitness maximization type P. The behaviour under consideration is termed, using the common noun, 'spite'.

It is hereby postulated that spite represents the genetically evolved infrastructure of the differential fitness maximization strategy by loss or harm done to another member of the species.

- δFt Max Type **E**: * teleological strategy * complex
* selective * formal * anonymous * designed
* delayed gratification * acquired (learned)
    => optional, conditional & context dependent
- δFt Max Type **P**: * opportunistic strategy * robust
* indiscriminate * informal * personalized * opportunistic
* immediate gratification * innate
    => mandatory, unconditional, context independent
- δFt Max Type **P** = Darwinian δFt Max
- Biological infrastructure of δFt Max Type P = spite

Figure 6.2 The P/E asymmetry. δFt Max Type P

In the case of humans, spite is the biological infrastructure of the 'political means' of self-preservation. The results of the discussion above are captured in Figure 6.2.

The foundational theory of spite has been laid down by W. D. Hamilton and E. O. Wilson (Figure 6.3), and is just underneath the surface of the analysis carried by R. D. Alexander of the biological basis of moral behaviour.[18]

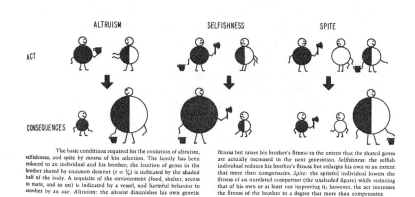

The basic conditions required for the evolution of altruism, selfishness, and spite by means of kin selection. The family has been reduced to an individual and his brother; the fraction of genes in the brother shared by common descent ($r = \frac{1}{2}$) is indicated by the shaded half of the body. A requisite of the environment (food, shelter, access to mate, and so on) is indicated by a vessel, and harmful behavior to another by an axe. *Altruism*: the altruist diminishes his own genetic fitness but raises his brother's fitness to the extent that the shared genes are actually increased in the next generation. *Selfishness*: the selfish individual reduces his brother's fitness but enlarges his own to an extent that more than compensates. *Spite*: the spiteful individual lowers the fitness of an unrelated competitor (the unshaded figure) while reducing that of his own or at least not improving it; however, the act increases the fitness of the brother to a degree that more than compensates.

Source: Wilson (2000: 119, fig. 5-9).

Figure 6.3 Spite according to E. O. Wilson

Spite has been hypothesized because of technical theoretical considerations, but also because of a need also shared by the present paper: namely to provide a foundation for what apparently is purposeless, irrational, reckless destructive behaviour, but which is too ubiquitous and pervasive not to be accounted for independently. Technically, spite is the precise opposite of altruism.

Altruism is the behavioural capacity of increasing the fitness of another with a cost to one's own fitness. Altruism is made possible by genetic relatedness, which is to say, by the presence of the genes of the donor in the recipient: whatever increment of phenotypic fitness occurs for the recipient, it represents an apparent loss of fitness only at the phenotypic level for the donor, for it is an increase of his/her genotypic fitness. Whatever forms of altruism exist outside the boundaries of genetic relatedness, they obey rules of cost-benefit familiar to the economist. Indiscriminate altruism is inexistent. Discriminate altruism is either paid back in the form of reciprocation (exchange), including delayed and indirect reciprocation (for example, in the case of humans, good reputation) or, otherwise, obeys the rule of coincidental differential marginal utility.[19]

As the opposite of altruism, spite is the behavioural capacity to produce a loss of fitness to another, even with a cost to oneself.

Evidence of spiteful behaviour in species of lower complexity is sparse. Spite does appear to be neither homologous, nor analogous (convergent).[20] It seems that the species capable of genuine spite are humans and the chimpanzees (Figure 6.4).

Source: *The Dark Side of the Chimp*, National Geographic Channel, © Granada Bristol, 2004; *Alexis Zorbas*, Michael Cacoyannis, 20th Century Fox, 1964, based on Kazantsakis, N., *Zorba the Greek*, 1946.

Figure 6.4 Spite in Chimpanzees and Humans

By way of theoretical integration, we are now in the position of making visible a series of identities, which bring together sociobiology and economic theory. On the one hand, spite and negative sum games describe in two different vocabularies the same thing, namely a strategy of differential fitness maximization based on loss to another (δFt Max Type P). On the other hand, cooperation, a term used in both economics and sociobiology, identical to positive sum games, corresponds to the strategy of differential fitness maximization by self-exertion (δFt Max Type E).[21] While the selfishness-altruism pair corresponds to zero-sum games, which basically represent a mixed strategy, whereby the gains and the losses alternate, cancelling each other, and subject to the aleatory of contingencies.[22] δFt Max Type E is *the rational* maximization of fitness; mixed strategies, as in zero-sum games, can be rational, but are not maximizing; while δFt Max Type P is maximizing, but not rationally so. These strategic alternatives are summarized in figure 6.4.

The anthropological emotional correlates of interpersonal comparison in view of a reduction of the fitness differential are described, according to various angles, as envy, malice, ill will, hatred, harmful intent and, with a particular import for political economy, equalitarianism.[23] All of these varied behavioural nuances have as their lowest common denominator the drive to reduce the fitness differential by losses infringed upon another. They differ, among other variables, by the degree of the actualization of the spiteful drive: that is to say, by the degree to which spite impacts upon the final output of the behavioural machinery.

Color Legend: Positive-Sum Games Zero-Sum Games Negative-Sum Games		A C T O R A	
		+	-
A C T O R B	+	Cooperation δFt **Max Type E** Rational, Maximal	Altruism δFt **Max Mixed** Not Maximal
	-	Selfishness δFt **Max Mixed** Not Maximal	Spite δFt **Max Type P** Irrational

Figure 6.5 Spite: sociobiology and game theory

This allows for a phenomenological classification of spiteful behaviour, as overt spite (as in fighting or warfare), mitigated spite (in which the concern for cost reduction makes room for ample deception, as in plotting, scheming, intrigue), and subdued spite (spiteful emotions, spiteful moralistic aggression, spiteful missrepresentation of another or spiteful cognitive dissonance, preliminary to and punctuated by outbursts of violence). Mitigated and subdued spite characterizes a large section of common intercourse between humans, sometimes explored in anthropology and sociology,[24] while their milder forms are ubiquitous in human life. Satirized by novelists and playwrights such as Molière, Balzac, Ionesco, by social philosophers such as Mandeville, and by moralists of all ages, mild spite takes the form of 'decorum', social pretence and hypocrisy.

In an attempt at avoiding the incorrectly formed question regarding human nature, whether it is 'good' or 'bad', one should be able to specify the conditions which preside over the rapport δFt Max E/δFt Max P determining the prevalence of one over another, while always keeping in mind their asymmetry.

The first condition refers to as yet undescribable conditions of innateness and hard-wired brain structures, in particular, the strength of the prefrontal-limbic inhibitory connections. Given the quick pace of current fMRI studies, one can soon expect insights into the substratum of spiteful versus constructive behaviour.[25] Without getting into details, it is arguable that an index of prefrontalization conveniently devised (PFC Index) would reflect the basic functioning of this substratum.[26]

The second condition for strategies of self-actualization and self-exertion is, to state the obvious, their possibility. They are excluded from the onset if external limiting conditions exist, at the system level or at the interpersonal level. Of foremost importance are system-wide external coercive limitations altering behaviour by the use of threat or of force: that is, the legal-political system, foremost in their effect on the market, the topology whereby fitness maximization by self-exertion expresses itself *par excellence*.

The third condition, which actually is the consequence of the former, refers to the relative frequency of spiteful versus constructive strategies in the population. We can safely state that the frequency of δFt Max E will be larger if their open possibility exists, that is, in non-regulatory, non-interferential economic systems.

The fourth condition refers to facilitating or inhibiting conditions of a non-coercive kind comprised by, in sequence, the immediate and the wider socializing environment, education, culture: ethical formation included.

- Inborn factors (PFC Index)
- Environment: constraints impacting   autonomy and individual entitlements = type of political regime in its relation to the market => Overall population relative frequency δFt Max E/δFt Max P
- Acquired factors: learning from social action and active observation of the social space => formation of quasi-reflex (habitual) social responses => activation/inhibition of Darwinian evolved responses (automatic)

Figure 6.6 Factors affecting δFt Max strategy frequency

Apart from currently indeterminable factors of innateness and learning factors, which should be the territory of absolute discretion of the private freedom of individuals, critical in determining the rapport δFt Max E/P is the political legal system, in particular by relation to the economic environment. This hardly represents news, since the relation between the nature of the state and the moral character of the individuals, firstly treated in Plato's *Republic*, has been known at least since the work of Bentham and Montesquieu.[27] Laws do not affect the urge of individuals to maximize their fitness, but merely the strategies, the paths they can adopt for the purpose. *In nuce*, social systems which protect and promote individual autonomy will see less spiteful, irrational, destructive (and self-destructive) behaviour (albeit, the expression of the less frequent spiteful behaviour may be biased towards overt spite). The political economy which best described such worlds is that of Locke; while literary, their most accomplished description appears in the work of Ayn Rand. Social systems which are interfering, controlling, regulating or otherwise limiting the individual drive to rational fitness maximization (and, by that, obtaining, in terms of level of fitness, a homogenized, or a 'compact' social structure) are increasing the frequency of spiteful behaviour in all its forms, but especially in the area of mitigated and subdued spite. Theoretically, such worlds derive from a Hobbesian political economy. Phenomenologically, such worlds have made the topic of copious literary investigation, with probably a culmination in the work of Franz Kafka (hence the adjective 'Kafkaesque'). According to the notational convention adopted, if we term the first type of worlds, E Worlds or Lockean-Randian worlds, and the second type of worlds, P worlds or Hobbesian-Kafkaesque worlds, their structure at the most fundamental level is captured in Figure 6.7.

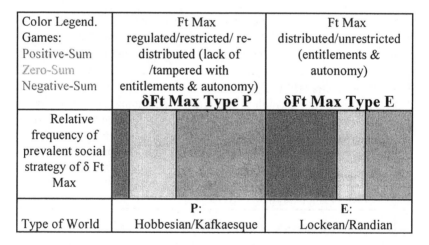

Color Legend. Games: Positive-Sum Zero-Sum Negative-Sum	Ft Max regulated/restricted/ re-distributed (lack of /tampered with entitlements & autonomy) **δFt Max Type P**	Ft Max distributed/unrestricted (entitlements & autonomy) **δFt Max Type E**
Relative frequency of prevalent social strategy of δ Ft Max		
Type of World	P: Hobbesian/Kafkaesque	E: Lockean/Randian

Figure 6.7 δFt Max Strategy/Type distribution

While a detailed discussion of the relative characteristics of P Worlds versus E Worlds would be illuminating, considerations of space rather than appropriateness confine us to a synthetic presentation, sketched in Table 6.1. In a nutshell, the crucial differences between P Worlds and E Worlds stem from the status of the individual's autonomy and entitlements. Due to their rooting in rational conditions of self-preservation, E Worlds conform to a blueprint whose specifications can be found in classical natural rights philosophies; while P Worlds, due to the irrational component, correspond to a blueprint kindred to the contractarian-positive right philosophies of late modern times.

P Worlds	E Worlds
Status of autonomy/entitlements: arbitrary => positive-rights worlds	Status of autonomy/entitlements: self-preservation based => natural-right worlds
Prevalence of kin-cooperation => tribal-like order	Prevalence of extended (Hayekian) cooperation => extended order
Access to resources based on extraction of fitness from con-specifics = sacrificial appropriation => restricted (non) market worlds	Access to resources based on exchange = catallactic (Misesian) appropriation => free market worlds
Pervasiveness of organized spite (alliances, factionalism); stable blocks of cooperation	Predominance of punctual spite (inter-individuals); flexible networks of cooperation
Massive use of social coercive power, formal or informal, based on numbers or not	Limited use of social coercive power, constitutionally stipulated
Massive role of legitimizing discourse; ideology relying on sentiment, with collectivistic/sacrificial central component	Reduced role of legitimizing discourse; ideology relying on argument, with an individualistic/hedonic central component
Low-growth/stagnation/involution of complexity	Growth and increase of complexity
Massification and homogeneity; intolerance; corporatism	Diversification and alterity; tolerance; individualism

Table 6.1 Some characteristics of worlds by relation to prevalence of δFt Max strategy/type

By way of conclusion, the essence of the last section is to be captured in the following theorem: the larger the system of political/social/cultural constraints regulating the pursuit of fitness maximization, the larger the reliance and the prevalence of spite and its socio-psychological, existential and moral correlates. Spinoza (1992: 165) confirms this finding: 'The more every man endeavours and is able to seek his own advantage, that is, to preserve his own being, the more he is endowed with virtue'.

THE ETHICS OF RATIONALITY

It follows, from the above considerations, that a set of normative prescriptions which obtains a limitation of the natural spiteful responses is an ethics of rationality. The said recommendations would concern all the factors contributing to and favouring positive sum games and constructive maximizing intercourse. Thus, such an ethics will have two domains: a transcendental domain, which concerns the individual him/herself as sovereign entity; and a frequency-dependent domain, which concerns the structure of a system of political and economic constraints upon which the first domain depends. The major characteristics of the ethics of rationality would be the following: insofar as concerned with the empirical (economic) happiness of the individuals, it will be a hedonist (eudaimonic) ethics; insofar as it concerns rationality, its maxims will aim at moulding natural, biological "appetites" and drives and its result would be virtue understood as *arete* (*Ἀρετή*), cultivation of reason, the specific excellence of humans; insofar as these processes aim at the individual him/herself, it will be an ethics of independence, autonomy being its objective-legal dimension, autarchy its subjective-existential dimension. The ethics of rationality is the individualist ethics *par excellence*: individuals' primary moral duty is towards *themselves* and whatever occurs in the space of their interactions with others, is a consequence of this obligation and an indirect effect.

Autonomy, rationality, virtue and happiness have been linked together, by a variety of conceptual derivations in all the great moments of the Western philosophical tradition, from Plato's 'noetic' (rational) man, Aristotle's 'autarchic man', and the Stoic synthesis of reason and virtue, through the Renaissance's rediscovery of the potentialities of man, Descartes's method and Leibnitz's monadology, to the individualism of modern philosophy and political economy, having their culmination in the Enlightenment.[28] The space not allowing for detailed illustrations, Figure 6.8 synthesizes some of the analytical components of the ethics of rationality.

All things considered, ethics is defined by, and limited to, rational engagement. Being a fundamental behaviour, 'the most simple, impartial observation of the self, associated to the conclusions of [biology]' will reveal spite as component of all human action (Schopenhauer, 2005: 448). Spitelessness being out of the question,[29] an ethics of rational engagement is an ethics of controlled, limited spite. There cannot be an ethical intercourse when confronted with irrational actions of oneself or of another.

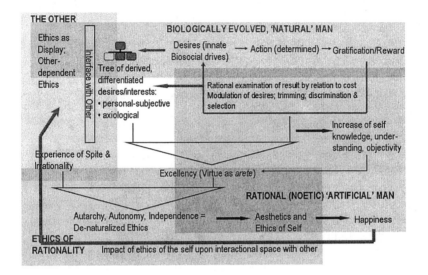

Figure 6.8 Analytical decomposition of the ethics of rationality

In normative/practical terms, this general principle takes the form of three rules of the type:

- A rational individual cannot engage ethically in actions directed against his/her rational self-preservation (non-spiteful self-preservation).
- A rational individual cannot engage ethically with any but another rational individual.
- A rational individual will remain within the boundaries of ethics when responding rationally to the actions of a non-rational individual.

The first rule prescribes the reflexive ethical relation of individuals with themselves. It can also be expressed in the form: it is immoral for an individual to perform actions whose result is a diminishment of his/her fitness (such as self-enslavement), or condone actions of others with the same result (coercive restrictions of his actual or potential actions in view of fitness maximization). In accordance with the first maxim (and also consistent with the methodological meta-rule of minimalism), individuals cannot be under any obligation to maximize the fitness of another with costs to themselves: to the contrary, they are under the ethical obligation to stop exerting themselves, were the results of their efforts to be spitefully appropriated by third parties, for their own use, or for the benefit of yet another fourth party. Were they not to stop exerting themselves, they would create the preconditions of coercive reduction of their own drive to fitness maximization: therefore, they would help the destructive action of others directed at them.[30]

Anecdotally, this is no mere abstract theory. Post-soviet, transitional economies such as the Romanian one, offer empirical illustrations for numerous aspects pertaining to spite, among which is one relevant to this first rule. For almost two decades now, politicians and intellectuals have joined voices in accusing 'Romanians' of lack of entrepreneurial spirit, willingness to work, and 'etatistic', assisted mentality. There were absent from such accounts the spiteful, predatory practices of the Romanian state as reflected in taxation, countless restrictions of economic freedom, massive parasitic bureaucracy and political corruption and, not least, the predominant dependency of the intellectual class upon the state. Accounting for this context, Romanians did the only rational and moral thing possible, namely to refuse to work since the results of their self-exertion were coercively appropriated from them.

The second rule effectively limits ethics to relations between rational agents. It basically states that there are no ethical relations except for those occurring between rational individuals. Irrational actions exclude one from the realm of ethics: being malicious, spiteful, destructive, amount to a statement of enmity, a state of war.

This rule has already been implied by John Locke, in his *Second Treatise on Government*. On the one hand, the rational defines the right: 'God gave the World ... to the use of the Industrious and Rational (and *Labour* was to be *his* title to it); not to the Fancy or Covetousness of the Quarrelsome and Contentious.' On the other hand, the rational defines the area of moral obligation: 'Such Men are not under the ties of the Common Law of Reason, have no other Rule, but that of force and violence, and so may be treated as Beasts of Prey ...' (Locke, 1960: 291 and 279 respectively). The Lockean rule stays at the basis of the common theory of the legitimacy of self-defence and, related to it, of the later libertarian principle of the non-initiation of aggression, as sole required moral obligation.[31] The notion of spite is more encompassing and less defined than that of aggression: it is from this difference in the conceptual coverage that delicate difficulties arise, but this is not the place to discuss them.

Would an individual choose not to respond properly to spiteful actions, s/he would act unethically according to the first rule. But if s/he chooses to respond, a more subtle difficulty arises: how could s/he avoid his/her response itself be spiteful, that is, originating in hatred and vengefulness, in the will to harm? In other words, how is it possible that the response to a spiteful action remains ethical?

It is here that the third rule comes in. The third rule is a rule of retaliation. Spiteful retaliation is irrational itself and, thus, triggers 'doomsday machines' of escalation of destructiveness. Retaliation is a genus within which retaliatory punishment is a species. The genus comprises also the species of containment and the extremely prickly species of pre-emption, with specific problems which cannot be addressed here. But in general, insofar as the response remains rational, retaliation also remains within the boundaries of ethics. What does it mean for the response to remain rational?

A first indication comes from the history of modern penal reform which was intended to reduce the spiteful expression of punishment (if not its intent). Pre-modern punishment was public, spectacular, and addressing emotions in the viewer: his/her fear but also pleasure at the suffering of another.[32] Modern reform rationalizes punishment, by replacing spiteful emotions with discretion, measurement and calculus: the event is no longer public, and the punishment aims at being quantitatively proportional to the deed.[33] Therefore, calculation with one's spiteful responses is a first condition for keeping them within the boundaries of reason. However, this is only the external aspect of a process which, in its internal dimension, brings about the issue of intentionality: the intention to harm. Whether at the bottom of a spiteful retaliatory response there still lingers a 'will which remains good' and, by that, performs the function ascribed by Kant to reason, is the last stage of an ethical dynamics whereby one is left alone (Kant, 1996: 52). At the bottom level of ethical conduct, there is deliberation, not rules, axioms and principles: but an ongoing dialogue and struggle between humans as rational creatures, and the biologically evolved infrastructure of their species. The lowest limit of ethical conduct remains thus open and it is here that the transcendental domain of the ethics of rationality finds its relevance.

FINAL REMARKS

Between modern economic science, the theory of rationality and ethics there appears to exist a triangular relation in which the terms support and mutually enforce one another. Together, they produce the invisible scaffolding, the infrastructure expressed in countless anonymous opinions, beliefs, motives and values which made up the modern West, but also in the formal concept of rational maximizing individuality, central to both Western philosophy and political economy.

Between the two modalities of increasing fitness differentials, the first one, based on self-exertion and productivity is specific to economic action. During the twentieth century, 'This is just business' has been, both in highbrow culture and in popular culture, used mostly pejoratively and capitalism has been seen as rather a 'necessary evil'. The argument above intends to change this view. Economic action, when free and uninterfered with, generates one of the least spiteful and most rational and ethical social environments. It secures maximization of fitness, with a host of derived desirable social phenomena: diversity, complexity, inventiveness, creativity, non-hostile or mitigated hostile competitiveness. Whenever the free market is interfered with, that is, whenever the autonomy of individuals is coercively moulded, this fragile set-up is destroyed. Individuals will shift their dominant strategies towards the predating behaviour of others or, even worse, towards spiteful destruction. The social effects of this behavioural shift will not fail to appear: social decomplexification, destruction of diversity, homogenization, dishonesty, Byzantinism, hypocrisy, predatory and hostile competitiveness.

We can find numerous similarities between Western philosophy and other cultural world-views, Oriental philosophy for that matter. But there is nothing similar to the concept of rational individual and the ethics comprised in it. Indian philosophy has produced a morality of renunciation and detachment, the result of the helplessness of man when confronting spitefulness, evil and sufferance. Confucian philosophy has produced an ethics of controlled spite, in which sociobiological relations, the family and the hierarchies of dominance are conformistically enforced in view of their inevitability. In spite of some superficial contemporary vogue of Confucian ethics in economics (in management foremost), it has produced political bondage and forms of economic stagnation out of which the most emancipated parts of this East attempt to escape: 'If the twentieth century was a century of organization, the twenty-first century will be a century of the individual', spells out the report of the commission on Japan's goals for the twenty-first century appointed to prime minister Keizo Obuchi in the year 2000 (Obuchi, 2000). The West has produced an ethics in which individual's duty towards him/herself prevails and in which spiteful behaviour is contained and overcome by the free, unhampered expression of maximizing self-interest.

In a philosophical rumination, the physicist Richard Feynman conjectured that 'if in a cataclysm, the entire scientific knowledge would be destroyed, and only one sentence would be conveyed to future generations, ...this would be the atomic hypothesis' (Feynman, 1969: 21). Translating his musing into the realm of humanistic knowledge, I believe that this singular notion would be MAXRAT, the principle of the rational maximizing individuality.

NOTES

1. This chapter is complementary to the study 'Capitalism. Foundations of Ethical Behaviour' which approaches related issues from a more speculative angle' (Boari, 2005c) and represents a re-worked, ultra-compressed version of the study prepared for the ESSEC Workshop on the 'Moral Foundations of Management Knowledge', Cergy, France, October, 2006 (Boari, 2006).
2 . A similar observation is made by Schoek (1966) in his unique sociological investigation of envy.
3. As will be discussed later, this caveat can be eliminated if, in the continuation of the present ideas, an economics of negative sum games is developed.
4. The qualification should be added: 'whether successfully so or not, whether consciously so or not'. I make this clarification in order to emphasize the lack of pertinence, for the present discussion, of various lines of criticism against rationality (maximizing or not) carried from within economics itself by a series of authors (H. A. Simon, Kahneman and Tversky, Gigerenzer, Vernon Smith).
5. See Alchian (1950, 1952) and Penrose (1953).
6. My theory of relative fitness maximization by means of differential fitness manipulations has been developed independently and in the context of ongoing work on the foundations of political biology (Boari, 2005b). I discovered Alchian's work during the research for the present application of the theory. It came as an independent confirmation of my own views.
7. A third one, the reversal of fitness positions, captures the same possible scenarios but of opposite sign. That which was the larger fitness becomes, in relative terms, *negative fitness.*
8. Boari, M., 'Conceptual Foundations of Political Biology II. Spiteful Fitness Extraction', work in progress.
9. Compare with Rothbard (1997) and Rand (1999).
10. For a discussion of this sentence, see Boari (2005a, 2005b).
11. Indeed, for evolutionary reasons, this cost may be the individual's life itself. The risk of death during a spiteful engagement is reduced if the aggressor is in a group (down to 12.5% if in an association of 4).
12. The 'gain' appears only at the genetic level, namely by an increase of the population frequency of the genes carried by the 'irrational' (spiteful, as will be introduced in the next section) individual. This is also the likely mechanism by which 'irrational conduct' (spite) has evolved.
13. By definition, aiming precisely at this, namely harming another with low cost to self and/or even with no cost to self.
14. For a detailed evolutionary discussion of this point, see Rubin (2003). Rubin considers zero-sum games as the evolved strategy.

15. See Smith (1981, vol. 1: 24).
16. Demosthenes (2004), 'Against Konon; Against Meidias'; Aristotle (1924: 1378b): 'Now slighting is the actively entertained opinion of something as obviously of no importance... There are three kinds of slighting: contempt, spite and insolence ...'
17. On Schadenfreude, see Pinker (1997: 367) and Buss (2000).
18. See Alexander (1974, 1987), Hamilton (1970, 1972, 1975), Wilson (1993, 2000), Hamilton's spite reviewed in Foster et al. (2001). Recent applications of spite theory to humans came to my attention while preparing the original workshop material for print, for instance Gardner and West (2004); West, Gardner et al. (2006).
19. A qualification of the above definitional domain may be brought by an innate condition named 'aboulia' and which can be read precisely as a deficit of spiteful will. The condition, relevant for the discussion of fitness exchanges, will be treated in Boari, M., 'Conceptual Foundations of Political Biology IV: Fitness Exchanges' (work in progress).
20. See Foster et al. (2000), Gadagkar, (1993), Keller et al. (1994), Rozsa (2000), Wilson (2000).
21. For conceptual reasons exceeding largely the confines of this study, "cooperation" is not a fortunate notion. A more suitable one would be 'trading'. But for the sake of trans-disciplinary consistency, I preserve for now the canonized terminology.
22. A conundrum of spite theory is its differentiation from selfishness. Selfish behaviour *may* amount to a diminishment of the fitness of another, but its rationale is advantage to self; while the characteristic of spite is precisely the facultative character of the advantage.
23. Among many possible illustrations, see Schoek (1996), Rubin (2002), Nozick, (1974), Rothbard (1997), Rand (1999).
24. See Boari (2000), Foucault (1977), Cosmides et al. (2002).
25. Regarding the investigation of the spiteful drive, several examples of the use of fMRI in the study of social behaviour are: Smith et al. (2001), Decety et al. (2004), Takahashi et al. (2004), Fiddicket al. (2005).
26. See Boari (2005a; 2005b).
27. See Montesquieu (1989), Bentham (1988).
28. See Plato (1986), Aristotle (1915). For the Stoic synthesis, best illustrating the present argument, see Cicero (2004), Mirandola (1991), Descartes (1984, esp. p. 12), Leibnitz (ny), Kant (1996). For the ethical philosophy of the American founding, see Jefferson, (1999), Huntington, (1981) and Bloom (1990), in particular the chapters by T. Pangle, *The Philosophical Understanding of Human Nature Informing the Constitution*: 9–77 and by D.F. Epstein, *The Political Theory of the Constitution*: 77–142; see also Rahe (1994), esp. chapter 6, 'Virtue in the Modern Republic': 206–231 and Hegel (1956): 86-97.

29. The explorations of spitelessness, philosophical, as in the utopian literature, or in fictional form, the best illustration being Kubrick's *Clockwork Orange*, are meant to induce caution rather then enthusiasm. Spitelessness remains one of the topics worth exploring in the footsteps of the present study.
30. Compare with Rand (1997a), chapter 11, 'The Mind on Strike': 389–482, especially 398. The basic idea is the same: individuals must 'go on strike' in a morally corrupt society.
31. For example, see Rothbard (1998).
32. For example, see Foucault (1977).
33. See Bentham (1988) and Beccaria (1986). For an interesting discussion of retaliation, in connection with the distinction rational/irrational retaliation, see Nozick (1981): 363–397.

REFERENCES

Alchian, A. A., (1950), 'Uncertainty, Evolution and Economic Theory', *The Journal of Political Economy*, **50** (3), 211–221.

Alchian, A. A., (1952), 'Biological Analogies in the Theory of the Firm: Comment', *American Economic Review*, **42**, 820–832.

Alexander, R. D., (1974), 'The Evolution of Social Behaviour', *Annual Review of Ecology and Systematics*, **5**, 325–383.

Alexander R. D., (1987), *The Biology of Moral Systems*, Aldine de Gruter: Hawthorne.

Aristotle (1915), Ethica Nicomachea, in *The Works of Aristotle,* Volume IX, Oxford: Clarendon Press.

Aristotle, (1924), Rhetorica, in *The Works of Aristotle,* Volume XI, Oxford: Clarendon Press.

Bacon, F., (1872 & 1870), Novum Organum, in *The Works of Francis Bacon*, Volume I, Volume IV, New York: Garrett Press Inc.

Beccaria, C., (1986), *On Crimes and Punishments*, Indianapolis: Hackett.

Becker, G. S. (1962), 'Irrational Behaviour and Economic Theory', *Journal of Political Economy*, **70** (1), 1–13.

Becker, G. S., (1976), 'Altruism, Egoism and Genetic Fitness: Economics and Sociobiology', *Journal of Economic Literature*, **14** (3), 817–826.

Becker, G. S., (1993), 'The Economic Way of Looking at Behaviour', *The Journal of Political Economy*, **101** (3), 385–409.

Bentham, J., (1988), *The Principles of Morals and Legislation*, Amherst, New York: Prometheus Books.

Berlin, I., (1992), *Four Essays on Liberty*, Oxford: Oxford University Press.

Bloom, A. (ed) (1990), *Confronting the Constitution*, Washington: AEI Press.

Boari, M., (2000), 'Ethnic Power', *Polis*, 1, 114–154.

Boari, M., (2005a), 'Biology and Political Science. Foundational Issues of Political Biology', *WP ESSEC Research Centre*, #05006, http://ideas.repec.org /p/ ebg/essewp/ dr-05006.html.

Boari, M., (2005b), 'Fitness Extraction and the Conceptual Foundations of Political Biology', *Politics and Life Sciences*, 24 (1-2), 64–75.

Boari, M., (2005c), 'Capitalism: Foundations of Ethical Behaviour', in D. Daianu and R. Vranceanu, (eds), *Ethical Boundaries of Capitalism*, Ashgate: Aldershot, 105–127.

Boari, M., (2006), 'Rationalizing the Irrational. The Principle of Relative Maximization From Sociobiology to Economics and Its Implications for Ethics', *WP ESSEC Research Centre*, #07004, http://ideas.repec.org /p/ebg/essewp /dr-07004.html.

Buss, D., (2000), 'The Evolution of Happiness', *American Psychologist*, 55 (1), 15–23.

Cicero (2004), *On Friendship or Laelius*, Kessinger: Whitefish.

Cosmides, L., Tooby, J. and Price, M., (2002), 'Punitive Sentiment as an Anti-Free Rider Psychological Device', *Evolution and Human Behaviour*, 23, 203–231.

Decety, J., Jackson, P. L., Somerville, J. A., Chaminade, T., Meltzoff, A. N. (2004), 'The Neural Basis of Cooperation and Competition', *Neuroimage*, 23, 744–751.

Demosthenes (2004), *The Public Orations of Demosthenes*: Kessinger.

Descartes, R., (1984), Meditations on First Philosophy, in *The Philosophical Writings of Descartes,* Volume II, Cambridge: Cambridge University Press.

Feynman, R., (1969), *Fizica Moderna*, Volumul I, Bucuresti: Editura Tehnica.

Fiddick, L., Spampinato, M. V. and Grafman, J. (2005), 'Social Contracts and Precautions Activate Different Neurological Systems: An fMRI Investigation of Deontic Reasoning', *Neuroimage*, 28, 778–786.

Foster, K. R., Wenseleers, T. and Ratnieks, F. L. W., (2000), 'Spite in Social Insects', *Trends in Ecology and Evolution*, 15 (11), 469–470

Foster, K. R., Wenseleers, T. and Ratnieks, F. L. W. (2001), 'Spite. Hamilton's Unproved Theory', *Ann. Zool. Fennici*, 38, 229–238.

Foucault, M., (1977), *Discipline and Punish*, New York: Pantheon Books

Gadagkar, R., (1993), 'Can Animals Be Spiteful?', *Trends in Ecology and Evolution*, 8, 232–234.

Gardner, A., West, S. A., (2004), 'Spite and the Scale of Competition', *Journal of Evolutionary Biology*, **17**, 1195–1203.

Hamilton, W. D., (1964), 'The Genetical Evolution of Social Behaviour I & II', *Journal of Theoretical Biology*, **7**, 1–52.

Hamilton, W. D., (1970), 'Selfish and Spiteful Behaviour in an Evolutionary Model', *Nature*, **228**, 1218–1220.

Hamilton, W. D., (1972), 'Selection of Selfish and Altruistic Behaviour in Some Extreme Models', in J. F. Eisenberg and W. S. Dillon (eds), *Man and Beast: Comparative Social Behaviour*, Washington, Smithonian Press, 57–91.

Hamilton, W. D., (1975), 'Innate Social Aptitudes of Man: An Approach from Evolutionary Genetics', in R. Fox, (ed), *Biosocial Anthropology*, London, Malaby Press, 133–153.

Hamilton, W. D., (1996), *Narrow Roads to Gene Land. Collected Papers of W. D. Hamilton, Vol. 1 Evolution of Social Behaviour*, W. H. Freeman: Oxford, NY, Heidelberg.

Hegel, G. W. F., (1956), *The Philosophy of History*, Dover: NY.

Hirschman, A. O., (1997), *The Passions and the Interests. Political Arguments for Capitalism before its Tryumph*, Princeton: Princeton University Press.

Hirshleifer, J., (1977), 'Economics From a Biological Viewpoint', *Journal of Law and Economics*, **20** (1), 1–52.

Hirshleifer, J., (1978), 'Competition, Cooperation and Conflict in Economics and Biology', *American Economic Review*, **68** (2), 238–243.

Hirshleifer, J., (1985), 'The Expanding Domain of Economics', *American Economic Review*, **75** (6), 53–68.

Hobbes, T., (1996), *Leviathan*, Cambridge: Cambridge University Press

Huntington, S., (1981), *American Politics. The Promise of Disharmony*, Harvard University Press, Cambridge, Mass.

Jefferson, T., (1999), *Political Writings*, Cambridge: Cambridge University Press.

Kant, I., (1996), Groundwork for The Metaphysics of Morals, in *Practical Philosophy*, Cambridge: Cambridge University Press.

Keller, L. et al. (1994), 'Spiteful Animals Still To Be Discovered', *Trends in Ecology and Evolution*, **9**, 103.

Leibnitz (ny), *Opere Filozofice*, Vol. I, Bucharest: Editura Stiintifica.

Locke, J., (1960), *Two Treatises of Government*, Cambridge: Cambridge University Press.

Mirandola, Pico della (1991), *Despre demnitatea omului*, Bucuresti: Editura Stiintifica.

Mises, L., von (1966), *Human Action. A Treatise on Economics*, Third Revised Edition, Chicago: Contemporary Books & Yale University Press

Montesquieu, J. de S., (1989), *The Spirit of the Laws*, Cambridge: Cambridge University Press.

Nozick, R. (1974), *Anarchy, State and Utopia*, Basic Books.

Nozick, R. (1981*), Philosophical Explanations*, Cambridge: Belknap Press.

Nock, A. J., (1935), *Our Enemy the State*, New York: W. Morrow and Co.

Obuchi, K., (commission appointed to) (2000), *Individual Empowerment and Better Governance in the New Millennium*, The Commission on Japan's Goals in the 21 Century, Tokyo, http://www.kantei.go.jp/jp/21century/report/pdfs/index.html.

Oppenheimer, F., (1997), *The State*, San Francisco, Fox & Wilkes.

Penrose, E., (1953), 'Biological Analogies in the Theory of the Firm: Rejoinder', *American Economic Review*, **43** (4 Part 1), 603–609.

Pinker, S., (1997), *How the Mind Works*, New York: W. W. Norton & Co.

Plato (1986), *Republica*, Bucuresti: Editura Stiintifica si Enciclopedica.

Rahe, P., (1994), *Republics Ancient and Modern Volume III: Inventions of Prudence. Constituting the American Regime*, Chapel Hill: University of North Carolina Press.

Rand, A., (1997a), *The Journals*, Penguin Group: Plume.

Rand, A., (1997b), *Letters of Ayn Rand*, Penguin Group: Plume.

Rand, A., (1999), 'The Age of Envy', in *The Ayn Rand Reader*, Penguin Group: Plume.

Rothbard, M., (1998), *The Ethics of Liberty*, New York: New York University Press.

Rothbard, M., (1997), 'Freedom, Inequality, Primitivism and the Division of Labour', in *The Logic of Action*, Vol. II: Edward Elgar.

Rozsa, L., (2000), 'Spite, Xenophobia and Collaboration Between Hosts and Parasites', *Oikos*, **91** (2), 396–400.

Rubin, P., (2002), *Darwinian Politics. The Evolutionary Origin of Freedom*, Rutgers University Press: New Brunswick, London.

Rubin, P., (2003), 'Folk Economics', *Southern Economic Review*, **70** (157); SSRN: http://ssrn.com/abstract=320940.

Schoek, H., (1966), *Envy. A Theory of Social Behaviour*, Indianapolis: Liberty Fund.

Schopenhauer, A., (2005), *Parerga & Paralipomena*, Coda.

Simon, H. A., (1991), *Sciences des systemes, Sciences de l'artificiel*, Paris : Dumond/Budas.

Smith, A., (1981), *An Inquiry Into the Nature and Causes of the Wealth of Nations*, Indianapolis: Liberty Fund.

Smith, V. et al. (2001), 'A Functional Imaging Study of Cooperation in Two-Person Reciprocal Exchange', *Proceedings of the National Academy of Sciences*, **98** (20), 11832–11835.

Spinoza (1992), *Ethics*, Indianapolis: Hackett Publishing Co.

Takahashi, H., Yahata, N., Koeda, M., Matsuda, T., Asai, K., Okubo, Y. (2004), 'Brain Activation Associated With Evaluative Processes of Guilt and Embarrassment: An fMRI Study', *NeuroImage*, **23**, 967–974.

West, S. A., Gardner, A. et al., (2006), 'Cooperation and the Scale of Competition in Humans', *Current Biology*, **16**, 1103–1106.

Wilson, E. O., (2000), *Sociobiology. The New Synthesis*, Cambridge Mass: Harvard University Press.

Wilson, E. O. (1978), *On Human Nature*, Cambridge Mass: Harvard University Press.

Wilson, E. O., (1993), 'Is Humanity Suicidal?', *New York Times Magazine*, 30 May, 1993.

7. The Moral Layer of Contemporary Economics: A Virtue-ethics Perspective

Radu Vranceanu

It is sometimes said that economists regard it as 'natural' or 'normal', and in some sense even right, that man should be governed only by selfish motives; this opinion may however be dismissed at once as a popular error, which finds no support in the teaching or practice of the best economists. (Alfred Marshall, *Principles of Economics*, 1890: 79)

INTRODUCTION

As pointed out years ago by John Maynard Keynes, the influence of economics on the global ideology of capitalism should not be underestimated.[1] Economics, like any other social science, is built on moral foundations which shape its development, guide researchers' choice of topics, and structure their recommendations. The main goal of this chapter is to present some inquiries into the moral foundations of economics, with special focus on the recent developments in this field. As the analysis takes a virtue-based ethical perspective, the main question addressed here is whether the economic model of man is consistent with the model of a virtuous person.

Broadly speaking economics studies how societies produce and deliver goods to its members. Over time several paradigms struggled to provide a rigorous explanation for this process of resource allocation. In this text we will stick to the perspective provided by what is known as the neoclassical school of thought, which has been the dominant paradigm for over a century. From this standpoint, 'economics is the study of how societies use scarce resources to produce valuable commodities and distribute them among different people' (Samuelson and Nordhaus, 1998: 4). The tension between the scarcity of resources and the limitlessness of needs thus lies at the heart of neoclassical economic theory. This tension is an overwhelming fact of life. In many developing areas of the planet, basic human needs (food, housing, public health, and so on) are still unsatisfied. In the developed countries that no longer suffer such deficiencies, the demand of more sophisticated products is still rationed. It is beyond the scope of this chapter to provide an analysis of the other paradigms, which occupy only a small part of the contemporary landscape. In the rest of this chapter, the term 'economics' actually refers to neoclassical economics.

In the neoclassical paradigm, economics is a theory of human actions undertaken by intelligent people, who understand the world they live in, can evaluate their options, and are able to decide wisely. As a study of human interaction, economics focuses on voluntary agreements or trades between individuals. This perspective was reinforced after the collapse of socially planned economies and the communist ideology in the late 1980s, and free allocation of resources through voluntary exchange became the dominant economic model throughout the world.

As Thomas Kuhn argued, a scientific paradigm needs one set of axioms on which the specific constructs of the field are developed. One important principle of neoclassical economics is *methodological individualism*: the key element of the social nexus is the individual, and society must have the characteristics of its member individuals, rather than the reverse. Another distinctive principle is that of *rationality*: the human being is assumed to make use of reason in evaluating the various courses of action open to him, and choose the best. While economics focuses on reason-driven choices, it does not deny that sentiments and instincts can also be major drivers of human action. Yet what economists believe, and hopefully they are right, is that reason plays an important role in a substantial number of human actions. The emphasis on rational behaviour drove economics towards what Williamson (1993) called 'calculativeness', a concept that he does not define explicitly, but from his examples appears to be characterized by a strong focus on analytical thinking, formalism, measurement, and so on. A third essential principle is that of *predetermined tastes*. Economics takes human goals (tastes) as given, and, in general, would not make any value judgement about those tastes. However, economists also agree that ethical principles guide human actions at the higher level, helping individuals to define their higher goals. The economist, that theoretician of the resource allocation science, is first and foremost a human being: he can only agree that human values such as honesty, fairness, fellow-feeling, kindness, and so on must be taught and instilled in a civilized society.

This chapter is organized as follows. The next section reviews the basic principles of economics, then sketches an outline of the main contemporary developments. Section 3 introduces the ethical perspective of this chapter. Section 4 comments on the concept of rationality in contemporary economics and presents its ethical foundations. We analyse the ethical implications of the quest for efficiency in Section 5. Section 6 addresses the paradigmatic frontier of taste predetermination from an ethical perspective. The final section presents the conclusion.

WHAT IS ECONOMICS TODAY?

Economics in Historical Perspective

For many years, the main quest of positive economics was to find an explanation for the determination of prices in free-market economies. A milestone was reached with the analysis of an isolated market[2] by Alfred Marshall (1842–1924). He showed how the market price of a given commodity can be found at the intersection between an upwardly sloping supply curve characteristic of producers' decisions, and a downwardly sloping demand curve characteristic of consumers' tastes. In the context of an isolated market, *partial equilibrium* is defined as a situation where the optimal plans of all agents in the market are mutually compatible.

As supply and demand in a market naturally depend on the prices of other goods, it makes sense to analyse the simultaneous equilibrium in all markets: this is the concept of general equilibrium. In 1776, in his famous treaty *An Inquiry into the Causes of the Wealth of Nations*, Adam Smith claimed that a decentralized economy, where each economic agent pursues his own interest, can achieve a highly efficient allocation of resources, as if an 'invisible hand' carries resources to the place where they are the most highly valued. This powerful allocative efficiency is the key to prosperity for society as a whole. The facts have corroborated this intuition, in that over more than two hundred years Western economies grew extremely rapidly, while the same period has seen the birth and collapse of all planned economies. Yet it took years for economics to provide a convincing explanation for this seemingly puzzling situation. In the late nineteenth century, Léon Walras expressed the problem of resource allocation via the market mechanism in a rigorously mathematical form, providing intuition for the solution finally worked out in 1956 by Kenneth Arrow and Gérard Debreu. Their analysis highlighted the restrictions needed to guarantee the existence of the general (or Walrassian) equilibrium, a set of prices consistent with the simultaneous equilibrium of all markets. The set of restrictions required by the general equilibrium is referred to as perfect competition. It was demonstrated that under these restrictions the equilibrium (a) is single and (b) allows for extremely efficient allocation of resources.

This understanding of a hypothetical, perfectly competitive free market economy led to valuable policy recommendations. Economists observed how real-life economies or market sectors deviated from the competitive model, and calculated the welfare losses that come with firms' excessive market power or various externalities. Following their analyses, governments all over the world set up laws and institutions designed to contain market concentration, limit abuses of market power by big firms and promote competition between firms.[3]

Contemporary economic theory continues to pay great attention to these inefficiencies, which originate in the market architecture. Yet in the last thirty years, a new path of research tracking 'informational inefficiencies' has provided a catalyst for a renewal of economics through an ambitious research programme.

Contemporary Advances in Economics

As early as 1961 George Stigler pointed out that the production of information in decentralized economies is a critical process that deserves close scrutiny,[4] and tried to model the mechanism whereby people spend time and effort to find out the characteristics of a given commodity (price, quality, location, and so on). The studies carried out in this field showed that even very small informational costs may put at risk the allocative efficiency of decentralized economies as imagined by proponents of the spontaneous emergence of the Walrassian general equilibrium.[5] Although this path of research came to a standstill in the late 1980s, it very clearly indicated the need for economics to incorporate a more rigorous analysis of imperfect information, a fundamental characteristic of real-life economic systems. The analysis of 'imperfect information' required a new approach to 'expectations', since people who decide on the basis of imperfect knowledge of reality must base their choices on their subjective perception of that reality.

Making extensive use of the concept of equilibrium specific to Game Theory[6] and importing elements from statistics and probability, in the 1970s economists developed the New Theory of Expectations, built around the key concept of the rational expectation equilibrium.[7] The basic idea was that over a long period, intelligent individuals should be able to eliminate all systematic biases from their perceptions. They may still be unsettled by exceptional events: indeed, random shocks are an intrinsic feature of real-life economies (tastes, technology, terms of trade, and so on do often change in unpredictable ways). Proponents of the rational expectation principle acknowledge that individuals are moving in an uncertain environment, but argue that they are not fully ignorant of the world they live in: they will utilize all the available information in order to reduce expectation errors as far as possible.

Given these developments, economic equilibrium (that is, the rational expectation equilibrium) was reinterpreted as a situation where individuals' actions and individuals' beliefs are mutually consistent. This is not just a cosmetic change: in contrast to the Walrassian equilibrium, these types of economic equilibria are not necessarily single. The economists' understanding of expectation-based systems with multiple equilibria (where, to put it simply, there is an equal chance of either a good or a bad situation occurring) allowed them to provide relevant explanations for notorious episodes of economic instability. For instance, the financial crises that hit emerging economies in the 1990s could be explained by emphasizing how the loss of trust had exaggerated the true scale of economic difficulties, with the resulting downturn confirming such pessimistic beliefs.

The new theory of expectations revealed its full potential in analysis of asymmetric information situations, where one of the participants in a trade has more information than the other. Economists have shown that in such situations, which are quite common in real life, the better-informed agent can set up information manipulation strategies with the aim of extracting an informational rent from the less-informed agent. These attempts to manipulate information strategically can lead to significant dysfunctions in a decentralized economy.

All in all, the concepts of rational expectations and the rational expectation equilibrium endowed economics with a method for analysing the formation of beliefs. This more nuanced understanding of the interaction between actions and beliefs in turn strengthened the internal consistency of existing economic analyses, and encouraged development of new approaches. The new emphasis on beliefs and interactions fostered development of more complex models of human decision-making, which even when they do not incorporate an explicit ethical dimension have the merit of acknowledging that individuals' economic choices are subject to a wider set of constraints than is assumed in standard analysis of the Walrassian equilibrium.

CHOOSING THE APPROPRIATE ETHICAL PERSPECTIVE

Everyone would agree that, in the realm of philosophy, ethical issues provide for the most controversial topic. Textbooks often state three main approaches to morality that compete on some dimensions and are mutually complementary on others: utilitarian ethics (emphasizing consequences), deontological ethics (emphasizing goals) and virtue ethics (emphasizing character).

There is a tendency for social science scholars to evaluate economics within the paradigm of *utilitarian ethics*. In a nutshell, the utilitarian moralist would argue that an action (or rule of action) is right if it brings about the greatest balance of pleasure over pain for everyone.8 What ultimately matters are the consequences of an action: right actions are presumed to bring about pleasure, and wrong actions pain. Although there is nothing to prevent the utilitarian thinker from connecting pleasures to the achievement of higher human goals, this perspective has little to say about *how* these higher human goals emerge. The emergence and definition of these higher human goals must be a key question for the moralist. Even John Stuart Mill, a famous proponent of utilitarian ethics, appeared to accept this criticism:

> If no more be meant by the objection than that many utilitarians look on the morality of actions, as measured by the utilitarian standard, with too exclusive a regard, and do not lay sufficient stress upon the other beauties of character which go towards making a human being lovable or admirable, this may be admitted. (Mill, 1863: Ch. 2)

There is no need to argue further on why utilitarian ethics suffers from too many shortcomings to be seriously considered as a suitable moral theory. But are the moral foundations of economics utilitarian? I believe they are not.

Economists agree that when it comes to satisfying basic needs, the individual's actions are indeed guided by an assessment of costs and benefits (or pains and pleasures in the old-fashioned vocabulary). But this is not the same as saying that all human actions should in fact be driven by utilitarian considerations. In particular, few contemporary scholars in economics would deny that ultimate human goals may go far beyond the simple goal of wealth accumulation. The point was clearly made by Stanley Jevons, one of the fathers of neoclassical economics:

> The calculus of utility aims at supplying the ordinary wants of man at the least cost of labour. Each labourer, in the absence of other motives, is supposed to devote his energy to the accumulation of wealth. A higher calculus of moral right and wrong would be needed to show how he may best employ that wealth for the good of others well as himself. But when that higher calculus gives no prohibition, we need the lower calculus to gain us the utmost good in matters of moral indifference. (Jevons, 1871: 27)

In no way does the logic of utilitarian decision-making as a theory of individual choice imply that modern, neoclassical economics actually advocates utilitarian ethics.

Microeconomic theory defines the individual's preferences in an axiomatic way, given the set of choices and his ability to rank outcomes from the most to the least desirable. A utility function is a compact way of representing the individual's preferred ordering of consumption bundles, a tool that gives up some generality for the sake of analytical simplicity. Yet microeconomics does not assign any role to the *level* of utility associated with a given consumption bundle, but only to the ability to rank consumption bundles as representative of the individual's ability to make choices.

True, one branch of theoretical microeconomics, welfare economics (Bergson, 1938; Samuelson, 1947), aimed to provide a formal analysis of distributional justice, and tried – based on social justice criteria – to build a social welfare function (SWF), that is a utility function representative of 'society's preferences'. Note that such a construct could be made consistent with various degrees of inequality aversion, going from the extreme principle that social decisions must aim at improving the situation of the worst-off individual (Rawls, 1971), to pure Benthamite utilitarianism where all individuals are given equal weight. In recent years, this static approach has been generalized to take into account the fact that status can change along an individual's entire life, so problems of utility inequality are placed in a dynamic perspective (what matters for an individual and society as a whole is not only instant equality but the probability of individuals improving their position over time).[9]

Yet the validity of the concept of a social welfare function has never been fully established. First of all, all these functions involve explicit or implicit interpersonal comparisons of utility, a principle that could never receive empirical or theoretical support.[10] Further scepticism on the meaningfulness of social welfare functions was contributed by Arrow (1950) who proved that given a few almost common-sense restrictions, it is mathematically impossible to determine a democratic procedure able to aggregate individual preferences so that the preferred ordering of alternatives is respected for all individuals; in other words, given alternatives $\{x, y, z, w, ...\}$, if all individuals prefer x to y (but do not all prefer x to z or w) there is no social choice mechanism involving that x is clearly preferred over y.[11]

When it comes to welfare analysis, studies outside the field of genuine welfare economics generally take the most elementary stance and resort to a elementary utilitarian social welfare function. But, in all these papers the main focus is on efficiency, or how to obtain the best allocation of resources. The choice of a utilitarian SWF is probably driven by parsimony rather than a strong belief in the positive virtues of this construct. When social choice is brought into the picture, economists very often become cautious in their recommendations, since they do not trust simple SWFs, have no idea of what the actual SWF might be, and doubt that the actual social decision process can be captured by any SWF.

To sum up, economics aims at removing inefficiencies, which is quite straightforward in situations where economic advice can improve the situation of at least one person without harming everyone else. When policy choices involve trade-offs, economists can point out the consequences for various groups, but will be cautious about advocating one solution, even though they can agree that choices involving social trade-offs should build on higher ethical values. This does not imply that economists, as members of society, do not have a personal position with respect to ethics. Taking a random sample of studies from a large database in economics (such as *EconLit*), we see that economists tend to follow the Rawlsian, rather than Benthamite, distributional principle: they will on the whole advocate decisions that protect the least favoured group of people (the unemployed rather than employers or insiders; consumers rather than large firms; small competitive firms rather than the monopoly; developing countries rather than developed countries, and so on).

If the foundations of contemporary economics are not utilitarian, are they then virtue-based? Virtue ethics places full emphasis on character; it acknowledges that outcomes and actions cannot be dissociated from the person him/herself. The origin of this approach can be traced back to Aristotle (384–322 BC) who, in his *Nicomanchean Ethics*, argued that since virtuous people can take only good action, ethics is primarily about defining virtues, those traits of character which allow the person to respond appropriately to the situation. In general, a virtue is characterized by moderation; the same trait of character pushed to extremes becomes a vice. (For instance, courage is a virtue, while cowardice and temerity are both vices.) [12]

Over the years, many lists of significant virtues have been drawn up by various thinkers, from Aristotle and St Thomas Aquinas to Jane Austen. In the realm of economic life, certain virtues come under the spotlight. Solomon (1993) argued that in modern market economies, basic business virtues are honesty, fairness, trust and toughness which should be accompanied by friendliness, honour, loyalty, a sense of shame, competition, care and compassion.

What should be emphasized here is that the virtuous person will be educated in and cultivate *all* virtues (honesty, for example, may require courage and helps develop fairness, and so on), while it is enough to give way to a single vice to become a bad person.

The main thesis developed in this chapter is that economics trains people to oppose several vices, in particular *silliness* (unreasoned actions) and *prodigality* (wasteful spending of resources). No economic analysis would advise people to steal, lie or manipulate others in order to get rich. On the contrary, since contemporary economics is above all an inquiry into voluntary exchange, it will quite naturally call for transparency, honesty and loyalty in future trades. There is no guarantee that behaving in keeping with the principles of economics is sufficient to become a good person, but ignoring those principles raises the chances of behaving wrongly.

ETHICS AND THE PRINCIPLE OF RATIONALITY

Reason as a Virtue

The Greek philosophers taught us that what distinguishes humans from animals, and thus defines the human species, is rationality. In his comprehensive analysis of rationality, Robert Nozick states:

> Copernicus, Darwin, and Freud taught us that human beings do not occupy a special place in the universe, they are not special in their origin and are not always guided by rational or even consciously known motives. What continued to give humanity some special status, though, is its capacity for rationality. Perhaps we do not consistently exercise this valuable attribute; yet it set us apart. Rationality provides us with the (potential) power to investigate and discover anything and everything; it enables us to control and direct our behaviour through reason and the utilization of principles. (Nozick, 1993: 1P).

We also know that in Aristotle's view, acting with reason is a fundamental virtue. He wrote: 'For the good man judges in every instance correctly, and in every instance the notion conveyed to his mind is the true one'. (Aristotle, *Nicomanchean Ethics*, Book III: 42). In this respect, Athannassoulis (2004) makes an important remark:

> Aristotle then observes that where a thing has a function the good of the thing is when it performs its function well. For example, the knife has a function, to cut, and it performs its function well when it cuts well. This argument is applied to man; man has a function and the good man is the man who performs his function well. Man's function is what is peculiar to him and sets him aside from other beings, and that activity is reason. Therefore, the function of man is reason and the life that is distinctive of humans is the life in accordance with reason. If the function of man is reason, then the good man is the man who functions well, i.e. reasons well, this is the life of excellence, the life of *eudaimonia*. This means that *eudaimonia* is the life of virtue, as virtue is activity in accordance with reason, man's highest function.

Economics builds on the postulate that people do think, in other words, they do exercise their fundamental virtue of reason. In this, economics is deeply in line with the concept of a virtuous person (in the Aristotelian tradition). What economics teaches us is that people reason when making choices: they weigh up the alternatives and decide as well as possible. Contrary to the popular interpretation, calculation is not the result of selfish behaviour, but of the natural decision process of a good person.

Of course, acting with reason is a necessary but not sufficient criterion for behaving well. A person with vices may be rational: the criminal may rationally choose the best method to carry out his immoral plans. All we want to emphasize here is that a person driven by the highest interest cannot be considered a virtuous person if he behaves irrationally, that is in a foolish way. The virtuous person cultivates all the virtues, and one of those virtues is well learned through economics: to act with reason.

The Model of Man in Economics: Ethical Implications

Nozick (1993) argues that the requirement of most efficient decision-making, what he calls 'instrumental rationality', is the overwhelming guide to human action at a basic level.[13] Economics has developed its full range of analyses on the basis of decisions taken by people under the banner of instrumental rationality. Although these mental processes are important, they do not apparently provide us with a comprehensive theory of human action. Emotions and instincts may also play an important role. The fact that economics studies a limited set of human actions does not however mean that understanding this reality is a meaningless exercise.[14] Furthermore, if economics acknowledges that the individual is an optimizer, it does not mean that the goals of the individual should be simplistic or basic. Finally, while economics accepts the idea that a person evaluates actions and consequences according to his own references in order to maximize something called 'utility', it does not claim that the individual is or should be selfish, and that utility is strictly related to a personal gain. The concept of utility is very abstract and can accommodate very different partial goals.[15] Economics can therefore deal with multiple objectives, including altruism, social status, cultural factors, environmental protection, and so on. (Becker, 1976, 1996; Hirshleifer, 1977; Altman, 2005). An individual may be a good, generous person, and, because of this, make good use of resources by making choices based on rational calculations.

Some experiments in behavioural economics have fuelled a debate on the merits or otherwise of economics teaching. Frank et al. (1993) claim that people educated in economics tend to be less cooperative in social dilemmas (strategic interactions), which might have morally adverse consequences. It is too early as yet to tell whether their result is robust. Yezer et al. (1996) contribute some evidence that it is not.

One important topic in economics is: what is the most appropriate way to describe the mental processes and goals of flesh-and-blood human beings? Jensen and Meckling (2005) consider this issue within a comparative analysis of competing contemporary models of human behaviour. Two of them are relevant to our analysis: the Resourceful, Evaluative, Maximizing Model

(REMM) and the model known as the Economic Model.[16] The REMM model describes the individual as an intelligent, creative being, who pursues a wide range of goals in the most efficient way possible. The authors argue that individuals evaluate and make trade-offs within a very broad range of 'goods', such as 'oranges, water, air, housing, honesty or safety'. Many economic analyses however depict the individual as caring only about 'money', or more precisely a monetary evaluation of the utility to be achieved from given actions. The Economic Model (or money maximizing model) therefore appears as a reductive version of REMM; Jensen and Meckling (2005: 90) deplore the fact that 'while economists profess fidelity to REMM, their loyalty is neither universal nor constant'.

The Economic Model is clearly not consistent with the virtue ethics approach, whereas REMM is. The fact that individuals can trade off 'a little of almost anything we care to name, even reputation and morality, for a sufficiently large quantity of other desired things' tells us nothing about the sizes of the marginal substitution rates. What the practice of virtue may teach the individual is that he should not give up the pursuit of higher goals, whatever the short-term benefit may be. The relative weights assigned to various objectives are what makes the difference between the virtuous and the non-virtuous man.

Rationality and Imperfect Information

A previous section underlines the revolution in economics brought about by new analyses of information. In this context, the concept of rationality utilized in contemporary economics by no means assumes that people are in possession of perfect information when they decide on their desired course of action. According to the new theory of expectations (the rational expectation hypothesis), people are assumed to do their best to form their expectations. This does not mean they can never be wrong. In fact since life is full of random events people will be wrong most of the time, but clever people will strive to make these errors as small as possible and try to eliminate all systematic biases (Sheffrin, 1983). Hence the new perspective on rationality in economics comes with a more nuanced image of the acting man, who struggles to understand the world where he lives, and succeeds in this endeavour. This is no doubt a humanist perspective on the human being, since man is assumed to be able to take charge of his life through reasoning.

The new perspective on rationality was accompanied by a renewed logic of strategic human interactions which built on advances in Game Theory. Combined with the logic of imperfect information, these analyses can provide powerful explanations for contracting situations, rivalries and races, which all build on non-cooperative attitudes, but also ways to increase sharing within a cooperative framework. In so doing, economics acknowledges that while the individual is solely responsible for his own decisions, he may be aware of the consequences of his decisions for his fellow beings, and the reaction of others to his own actions. This opened up a path of research into analysis of trust, honesty, loyalty, and reputation-building which highlights the role of human values in shaping human interactions.

In general, economists carrying out analyses of trust, honesty, fairness and altruism have worked within the framework of the standard model for decision-making under uncertainty. According to this model, set up by John von Neumann and Oscar Morgenstern in the 1940s, an individual who must make a decision without knowing the exact outcome but who is able to assess the probabilities of various possible outcomes, is supposed to choose the action which will bring about the highest *expected* utility. Economists thus applied this logic in assessing the benefits of telling the truth, or helping others, or comparing their status with a control group.

In recent years, behavioural economics has pointed out several contradictions between the standard (von Neumann-Morgenstern) model of decision-making under uncertainty, and actual individual choices (in very particular cases). Some researchers concluded rather hastily that the concept of rationality so dear to neoclassical economists is meaningless; others inferred that the standard decision model should be generalized in order to account for these idiosyncratic reactions. As Smith (2005) notes, the first conclusion seems to be inconsistent with the observed domination of the planet by the human species over several millennia; he embraces the second view, and suggests that economists should pay more attention to the role of contexts in mental processes as shortcuts for decision-making. There is no doubt that ethical values have an important role in context definition and selection and thus should have a bearing on the choice of the course of action.

One of the major strengths of neoclassical economics is its ability to incorporate valuable concepts from other sciences (Vranceanu, 2005). As Altman argues (2005: 752), 'conventional economic theory can easily accommodate altruistic, ethical, and moral behaviour as part of its standard rational agent maximizing framework, when such behaviour has no impact on the survival of the firm'. If ethical considerations become more prominent in practice, there is no doubt that economics will be able to provide valuable insights. In other words, if the business world becomes more ethical, economics will reflect this change in its analyses.

ETHICS AND THE QUEST FOR EFFICIENCY

We have defined economics as the social science that analyses how scarce resources are allocated. In this setup, the immediate goal of economics itself is to guide human action so as to eliminate inefficiencies in the resource allocation process. Contemporary economics puts additional emphasis on the informational origin of various inefficiencies, while traditional economics deals essentially with material inefficiencies related to the market architecture.

Yet waste and inefficiencies are abstract concepts. In practical terms, economists have long been concerned about such issues as growth and development, fighting poverty, reducing unemployment, stabilizing the macroeconomic and financial environment, or improving consumer welfare by containing firms' market power. The moral foundation underlying their quest is deeply humanist − it is the duty of the social scientists to help people live as well as possible.

The important practical contribution of economics to the development of the Western World in the last two centuries cannot be denied. Either directly, or transposed into user-friendly advice by management scholars, applied economic wisdom has helped eradicate waste in many sectors and activities and therefore sustained the economic development of the West. What should be emphasized here is that output growth comes with many moral and political benefits, clearly presented by Benjamin Friedman in a recent book. He writes:

> Economic growth − meaning a rising standard of living for the clear majority of citizens − more often than not fosters greater opportunity, tolerance of diversity, social mobility, commitment to fairness, and dedication to democracy. (Friedman, 2005: 4)

The flourishing of moral values is no doubt stimulated in an environment where basic needs are satisfied. Many human conflicts are built on quarrels over an extremely scarce resource.[17] Arrow (1974: 26) states that 'among properties of many societies whose economic development is backward is a lack of mutual trust'.

So economics' chief concern with growth and development goes far beyond a narrow-minded goal of wealth accumulation. While economics promotes growth as an immediate objective, this does not imply that the ultimate goal of economics is growth itself. All good economists take a broad perspective on human well-being. What responsible person would seriously argue that wealth accumulation is the only thing that matters for happiness? Yet the problem of growth itself cannot be overemphasized. Robert Lucas, observing that some countries tend to grow much faster than the others for reasons not yet clearly understood, wrote (in 1988):

Is there some action a government of India could take that would lead the Indian economy to grow like Indonesia's or Egypt's? If so, what exactly? If not, what is it about the 'nature of India' that makes it so? The consequences for human welfare involved in questions like these are simply staggering: once one starts to think about them, it is hard to think about anything else. (Lucas, 1988: 5)

Economics is at its most useful when it has to deal with situations where the policy decision can make (at least) one person better off while not deteriorating anybody else's well-being. Yet in many real-life situations, the solution to economic dilemmas involves trade-offs; some persons will be better off, and others worse off as a result. In general (neoclassical) economics redistribution is considered as a second order problem; one should first bake the pie, then share it. The dramatic experience of centrally-planned economies is relevant in that respect: in those countries, the focus on fair (read egalitarian) redistribution of an ever-shrinking pie did not bring people satisfaction, and in the end all these regimes collapsed under a tide of strong public unrest. Economists agree that redistributive decisions should be taken at a higher decision level, where social trade-offs can be exercised in keeping with the agreed social rules.

In his *Nicomanchean Ethics*, Aristotle praised the liberal person, the man who knows how to give his wealth rightly: to the right people, in the right proportions and at the right times. By providing a rigorous theory of prices, economics sheds light on what constitutes 'right' or 'excessive' proportions. For instance, in a competitive market, the price is the right reward for the supplier; in other market structures, more careful analysis is needed in order to find out whether an abnormal producer's margin is the 'right' price for innovation and risk-taking, or is representative of an abuse of market power.

The good person who behaves virtuously must avoid wasting resources when pursuing his (higher) goals. Society highly values such a person, as illustrated by a modern-day example. In 2000 the founder of Microsoft, Bill Gates, and his wife Melinda created a charity foundation. In 2006, Bill Gates decided to dedicate all his time to running this organization. The surprise lay in the huge flow of external resources attracted by the organization in the same year (about 10.5 billion dollars): the generous donors said that if Bill Gates, one of the most successful entrepreneurs of the past century, was running the foundation, they were sure the funds would be utilized in the most efficient way, to the highest benefit of those who need aid. We trust efficient persons in all matters, including for helping the most disadvantaged persons. Economics makes a positive contribution to human development, since it teaches us how to manage resources in an efficient way. Again this is by no means an indication that efficiency alone is sufficient to define virtuous behaviour. All we are saying is that prodigality, or careless spending, is a vice that should be opposed by educating people to behave efficiently.

ETHICS AND THE PRINCIPLE OF PREDETERMINED TASTES

In the eighteenth century, economics and ethics were closely related. Classical economists, to mention only Adam Smith, John Stuart Mill and David Hume, were at least as concerned about how people should behave within the economic interactions as about how these interactions were actually organized.[18] This normative focus required judgment regarding the fairness of distribution, and more generally the ultimate goals of society.

Yet the dominant paradigm of neoclassical economics takes individuals' tastes as given, in the sense that it makes no judgement on why people choose one goal or another (Hirshleifer, 1977; Sen, 1987). This choice was probably motivated by a concern for efficiency in their own analyses: economists were not yet comfortable with models where constraints and goals interact, given the high complexity of such structures. Since goals probably change only slowly over time, while constraints and incentives may vary rapidly, economists opted for simplification, considering goals as predetermined. Yuengert (2002: 331) argues that this separation between ethics and economics may come with a risk: 'If the researcher's ends are separated completely from the higher ends which direct it, he will either substitute the goals of economics for those higher ends, or risk conducting research that has no intelligible principle guiding it.'

One important question is whether the object of research in economics is determined by the method (assumed to be invariable), or whether the method itself can evolve so as to increase its analytical power over a given subject. If economics is about studying human choice for given tastes, the former applies, because in that case the method defines the science and not the reverse. But in the introduction we defined economics as a theory of rational human action. Changing tastes should then be seen as a worthwhile generalization of the given tastes paradigm.

This idea is given stronger emphasis when placed within a virtue ethics perspective. As observed by Aristotle centuries ago, in the long run human action also has a bearing on human character. A person's character (preferences) is the engine but also the result of the ongoing battle against scarcity. In other words, choices may also have a bearing on tastes, and not only the other way round.

In recent years it has become only too obvious that the predetermined taste paradigm has reached its limits. Buchanan (1992) foresees that in the world of economic reality where people discover their preferences through their choices, the static (predetermined tastes) general equilibrium model will become less popular as a research programme, and its normative implications might well fade away.

In order to renew their analyses, economists should become more open to ethical dilemmas, and try to keep in mind that proposed solutions should by no means support the development of unethical behaviour. They should pay more attention to situations where the goals themselves may change, depending on actions and beliefs. The call for such a research programme within the neoclassical paradigm is not new, and can be traced back at least to the writings of Albert Hirschman in the 1970s. Today, there is some optimism that neoclassical economics will address these issues adequately (Altman, 2005; Hausman and McPherson, 2006). The embryos of such studies include analyses of addictive behaviour (*inter alia*, von Weizsäcker, 1971; Pollak, 1971; Cowen, 1989) on the interactions between social status and individual welfare (*inter alia*, Frank, 1985; Scitovsky, 1992; Cole et al., 1992; Corneo and Jeanne, 1998; Oxoby, 2004).

CONCLUSION

In the last thirty years, the science of economics has been totally restructured, driven by the implementation of a research programme in the economics of (imperfect) information. The renaissance in economics was facilitated by the progress made in its tools and methods. In particular, advances in Game Theory and statistics made it possible to extend and generalize the principle of rationality, for more rigorous examination of decision-making under uncertainty and imperfect information.

Yet contemporary economics does not only consist of broader topics and better techniques. One outstanding feature of contemporary economics is a return to the ethical quest of the early neoclassical writers: with their modern awareness of how to analyse imperfect information situations, economists are beginning to focus once more on fighting waste, in order to contribute to improving the welfare of individuals and society. The raging ideological conflicts of the 1970s have almost vanished, since all economists now agree that imperfect information lies at the origins of most disruptions in decentralized economies, and that fluctuations are a built-in feature of such systems.

By focusing on informational inefficiencies within a comprehensive research programme, economics has provided helpful policy recommendations, able to stabilize and support growth in both developed and developing economies. In turn, as Friedman (2005) notes, economic development is an important factor for moral development.

By emphasizing rational decision-making, economics promotes a model of man acting wisely. In this context, calculative behaviour should not be seen as representative of a selfish person, but a responsible and prudent one. Responsibility and prudence are important virtues in the Aristotelian ethical perspective. Of course, this is only one side of the story, as efficiency is a necessary but not sufficient requirement for appropriate action. The choice of the broader goals that guide one's action is another important factor.

Although economics has so far said little about how human goals are defined, it certainly does not advocate selfish and aggressive behaviour. On the contrary, most economists would agree that human values like trust, loyalty, honesty, fairness in dealings and truthfulness are very much needed to oil the wheels of the market-based economic system, and that reneging on those ethical values would entail major economic costs in the free economy.[19] What narrow-minded economist would argue against this idea? It is clear to everybody that unethical behaviour brings about significant long-term costs, starting with the loss of reputation, an important asset in the free economy.

By taking human goals as given, economics has been able to make and is still making substantial progress in analysing human action. Yet human character and actions are interdependent. A major challenge for twenty-first century economics is therefore to take into account the possibility of changing tastes, while maintaining the requirement of rationality.

NOTES

1. Keynes wrote: '...the ideas of economists and political philosophers, both when they are right and when they are wrong, are more powerful than is commonly understood. Indeed the world is ruled by little else. Practical men, who believe themselves to be quite exempt from any intellectual influences, are usually the slave of some defunct economist. Madmen in authority, who hear voices in the air, are distilling their frenzy from some academic scribbler of a few years back.' (Keynes, 1936: 383).
2. The analysis of an 'isolated market' abstracts from interactions between this market and the other markets.
3. Economics advocates competition between firms, and not, as is sometimes claimed by uninformed critics, between individuals.
4 . Before Stigler, Friedrich Hayek also emphasized the role of market interactions as an efficient way of producing and conveying information.

5. Diamond (1971) produced a fundamental paper in this field. He shows that by introducing a small search cost into a seemingly competitive economy, firms become able to impose the abnormally high monopsony price on consumers.

6. Game theory analyses individual strategic choices in view of the reaction of competitors. In a game theoretical framework, equilibrium is often seen as a situation of no regret. In equilibrium, the individual has no incentive to deviate, and would not regret his past choices.

7. The new principles were first applied in the work of macroeconomists as Robert Lucas, Robert Barro, Edward Prescott, Finn Kydland, Thomas Sargent, and so on. or microeconomists such as Joseph Stiglitz, Bruce Greenwald, George Akerlof, Michael Spence, etc.

8. It should be emphasised here that many utilitarian philosophers give a much more nuanced account of what should be understood by pleasure, pain and utility than Jeremy Bentham (see Mill, 1863). See also Solomon (1993, Chapter 9) on Mill's broad conception of utilitarianism.

9. Not all the existing theories of distributional justice are consistent with a formalized SWF. For instance, Nozick (1974) argues that the market economy is just because it rewards the most able and the hard worker.

10. Long ago, Stanley Jevons (1871, I20) wrote: 'The reader will find, again, that there is never, in any single instance, an attempt made to compare the amount of feeling in one mind with that in another. I see no means by which such comparison can be accomplished. The susceptibility of one mind may, for what we know, be a thousand times greater than that of another.'

11. There must be more than two alternatives. One important restriction is that social preferences between any two alternatives depend only on the individual preferences between the same two alternatives (independence of irrelevant alternatives).

12. Philosophy's interest in Aristotle's view of ethics is rather recent compared to the established utilitarian and deontological ethical perspectives. Special credit should be assigned to the work of Anscombe (1958) and MacIntyre (1981). These scholars pointed out that the quest of both utilitarian and deontological theorists for universal rules of action might be void, since no rule can be consistent with the huge variety of real-life situations. Several scholars have argued that virtue ethics might provide the most suitable lens for analysing ethical issues pertaining to business situations, since it is able to strike a subtle balance between determinism (the external constraints on the individual's behaviour) and human character (Koehn, 1995; Murphy, 1999; Solomon, 1993, 2003).

13. He does not rule out that a higher level of rationality can guide individuals in their more substantive actions, and that there are bridges between the two levels of rationality.

14. Hirschman (1981) called for a research programme where emotions become part and parcel of economic analyses. The task proved to be extremely difficult. See Rabin (1993) for a decision model that incorporates some form of emotions.
15. See also Hausman and McPherson (2006).
16. The three others are the Sociological (or Social Victim) Model, the Psychological (or Hierarchy of Needs) Model and the Political (or Perfect Agent) Model.
17. Empirical analyses suggest that crime is often concentrated among those living in poverty (Oxoby, 2004).
18. For instance, during that period Adam Smith became famous for his *Theory of Moral Sentiments* (1759) well before writing the celebrated *The Wealth of Nations* (1776).
19. See Arrow (1974), McKean (1975), Becker (1976), Noreen (1988).

REFERENCES

Anscombe, G. E., (1958), 'Modern moral philosophy', *Philosophy*, **33**, 1–19.
Altman, M., (2005), 'The ethical economy and competitive markets: reconciling altruistic, moralistic, and ethical behaviour with rational economic agent and competitive markets', *Journal of Economic Psychology*, **26**, 732–757.
Aristotle, (1998), *Nichomanchean Ethics*, Dover, Mineola, New York.
Arrow, K. J., (1974), *The Limits of Organization*, W.W. Norton, New York.
Arrow, K. J., (1950), 'A difficulty in the concept of social welfare', *Journal of Political Economy*, **58**, 328–346.
Athanassoulis, N., (2004), 'Virtue ethics', *Internet Encyclopaedia of Philosophy*, http://www.iep.utm.edu/v/virtue.htm.
Becker, G. S., (1976), 'Altruism, egoism, and genetic fitness: economics and sociobiology', *Journal of Economic Literature*, **14** (3), 817–826.
Becker, G. S., (1996), *Accounting for Tastes*, Cambridge, MA.
Bergson, A., (1938), 'A reformulation of certain aspects of welfare economics', *Quarterly Journal of Economics*, **52**, 310–334.
Buchanan, J. M., (1992), 'Economic science in the future', *Eastern Economic Journal*, **18** (4), 41–403.
Cole, H., Mailath, G. and Postelwaite, A., (1992), 'Social norms, savings behavior and growth', *Journal of Political Economy*, **100**, 1092–1125.
Corneo, G. and Jeanne O., (1988), 'Social organization status, and savings behavior', *Journal of Public Economics*, **70**, 37–51.

Cowen, T., (1989), 'Are all tastes constant and identical? A critique of Stigler and Becker', *Journal of Economic Behavior and Organization*, **11**, 127–135.

Diamond, P., (1971), 'A model of price adjustment', *Journal of Economic Theory*, **3**, 156–168.

Frank, R. H., (1985), *Choosing the Right Pond. Human Behavior and the Quest for Status*, Oxford University Press, New York.

Frank, R. H., Gilovich, T.D. and Regan, D.T., (1993), 'Does studying economics inhibit cooperation?', *Journal of Economic Perspectives*, **7**, 159–171.

Friedman, B., (2005), *The Moral Consequences of Economic Growth*, Alfred A. Knopf, New York.

Hausman, D. M. and McPherson, M., (2006), *Economic Analysis, Moral Philosophy, and Public Policy*, second edition, Cambridge University Press, Cambridge.

Hirshleifer, J., (1977), 'Economics from a biological point of view', Working Paper 87, UCLA.

Hirschman, A. O., (1981), *Essays in Trespassing: Economics to Politics and Beyond*, Cambridge University Press.

Jensen, M. C. and Meckling, W. H., (2005), 'The nature of men', in D. H. Chew Jr. and S. L. Gillan, (eds), *Corporate Governance at the Crossroads*, McGraw-Hill, New York.

Jevons, S. W., ([1871], 1888), *The Theory of Political Economy*, MacMillan, London, On line edition: www.econlib.org/library/ YPDBooks/ Jevons/ jvnPE.html

Keynes, J. M., ([1936], 1973), *The General Theory of Employment, Interest and Money*, Cambridge University Press, Cambridge.

Koehn, D., (1995), 'A role for virtue ethics in the analysis of business practice', *Business Ethics Quarterly*, **5** (3), 533–539.

Lucas, R. E., (1988), 'On the mechanics of economic development', *Journal of Monetary Economics*, **22**, 3–42.

Mill, J. S., (1863), *Utilitarianism*, online: http://www.utilitarianism.com /mill1.htm.

MacIntyre, A., (1981), *After Virue*, Duckworth, London.

McKean, R. N., (1975), 'Economics of trust, altruism and corporate responsibility', in E. S. Phelps, (eds), *Altruism, Morality and Economic Theory*, Russel Sage Foundation, New York, 29–44.

Murphy, P. E., (1999), 'Character and virtue ethics in international marketing: an agenda for managers, researchers and educators', *Journal of Business Ethics*, **18**, 107–124.

Noreen, E., (1988), 'The economics of ethics: a new perspective on agency theory', *Accounting, Organisations and Society*, **13**, (4), 359–369.

Nozick, R., (1974), *Anarchy, State, and Utopia*, Basic Books, New York.

Nozick, R., (1993), *The Nature of Rationality*, Princeton University Press, Princeton.

Oxoby, R. J., (2004), 'Cognitive dissonance, status and growth of the underclass', *Economic Journal*, **114**, 727–749.

Pollak, R., (1976), 'Habit formation and long run utility functions', *Journal of Economic Theory*, **13**, 272–297.

Rabin, M., (1993), 'Incorporating fairness into game theory and economics', *American Economic Review*, **83**, (5), 1281–1302.

Rawls, John (1971), *A Theory of Justice*, Harvard University Press, Cambridge, Mass.

Samuelson, P.A., (1947), *Foundations of Economic Analysis*, Harvard University Press, Cambridge, Mass.

Samuelson, P. A. and Nordhaus. W. D., (1998), *Economics*, (sixteenth edn.), McGraw Hill, New York.

Schitovsky, T., (1992), *The Joyless Economy*, Oxford University Press, New York.

Sen, A., (1987), *On Ethics and Economics*, Basil Blackwell, Oxford.

Shleifer, A., (2004), 'Does competition destroy ethical behavior', *American Economic Review, AEA Papers and Proceedings*, **94** (2), 414–418.

Sheffrin, S., (1983), *Rational Expectations*, Cambridge University Press.

Smith, V. L., (2005), 'Behavioral economics research and the foundations of economics', *Journal of Socio-Economics*, **34**, 13–150.

Solomon, R. C., (2003), 'Victims of circumstances? A defense of virtue ethics in business', *Business Ethics Quarterly*, **13** (1), 43–62.

Solomon, R. C., (1993), *Ethics and Excellence. Cooperation and Integrity in Business*, Oxford University Press, New York.

Vranceanu, R., (2005), 'The ethical dimension of economic choices', *Business Ethics: A European Review*, **14** (2), 94–107.

Weizsäcker, von, C. C., (1971), 'Notes on endogenous changes in tastes', *Journal of Economic Theory*, **3**, 345–372.

Williamson, O. E., (1993), 'Calculativeness, trust, and economic organization', *Journal of Law and Economics*, **36**, 453–486.

Yezer, A. M., Goldfarb, R. S. and Poppen, P.J., (1996), 'Does studying economics discourage cooperation? Watch what we do, not what we say or how we play', *Journal of Economic Perspectives*, **10**, 177–186.

Yuengert, A., (2002), 'Why did the economist cross the road? The hierarchical logic of ethical and economic reasoning', *Economics and Philosophy*, **18**, 329–349.

PART III

Leadership and Team Management: Exploring
Moral Foundations

8. Leadership Virtues and Management Knowledge: Questioning the Unitary Command Perspective in Leadership Research[*]

Lucia Crevani, Monica Lindgren and Johann Packendorff

INTRODUCTION: SHARED LEADERSHIP AND MODERN MANAGEMENT KNOWLEDGE

Within the field of leadership practices, there is an emergent movement towards viewing leadership in terms of collaboration between two or more persons. Increasingly, the public debate recognizes states, corporations and organizations as led by several persons rather than by single charismatic individuals. What seems to be the claimed reason for this is that organizational leadership is nowadays a complex and exhausting job that demands too much of a single individual, and that dual leadership is a way to broaden the competence and personality bases of management and to relieve management pressures.

The basis of this is an increasing emphasis on what we may call 'sustainable leadership', that is, a search for leadership perspectives that (1) can enable people in modern society to actually work with leadership without sacrificing everything else in life, and (2) can enhance the legitimacy of leadership in a society that raises serious moral doubts concerning the content and consequences of modern management practices. Leadership has always been discussed both in terms of what leaders do/should do to lead, and in terms of what makes others confirm and make themselves subject to

[*] The research on which this chapter is based was funded by *Handelsbankens Forskningsstiftelser*. It is hereby gratefully acknowledged.

leadership. Therefore, a sustainable leadership ideal is one where leaders themselves find it possible to go on with their current way of living despite vast responsibilities, and where leaders and followers share a view of leadership practices as legitimate in terms both of effectiveness and morality. In our own earlier studies, we have seen examples of both dual and collective leadership in several entrepreneurial enterprises, and we have also seen how individuals may go beyond taken-for-granted identity bases in society (such as the single hero entrepreneur) through articulation and reflection (Lindgren and Packendorff, 2003).

At the same time, traditional literatures on entrepreneurship, leadership and organization theory are dominated almost exclusively by the perspective that leadership is something that is exercised by a single person – the idea of unitary command. Later developments in these fields have indeed emphasized cultural values, visions and leadership as an interaction between leaders and led (Bryman, 1996), but what is still rarely challenged is the notion of a single person as a leader or the notion of leadership as something that is exercised by a single person, notions that also shape leaders' identities in society. The idea of unitary command is thus still strongly contributing to the ongoing construction of leadership in society and the ongoing construction of leaders' and followers' selves. Leaders as well as followers (terms that in themselves are representatives of dualistic and dichotomous identity constructions) incorporate such taken-for-granted assumptions in society and make them a part of themselves and their ongoing interaction with others. One has almost automatically assumed unitary command as a natural perspective on leadership, in the same way as entrepreneurship research has assumed the notion of single individuals as the natural perspective on entrepreneurship.

Several of the most acknowledged studies on leadership have explicitly taken this perspective, such as Carlson (1951) and Mintzberg (1973) who both followed the days of single CEOs in order to understand what leaders do and what leadership is all about. The same perspective can also be found in formal and informal regulations and practices in society, in the notion that only a single person can be held accountable for a defined economic area of responsibility – a notion that has far-reaching consequences for who will be seen as leaders and what is seen as leadership in the modern corporate world (Öman, 2005).

Although management research is thus often discussed in practical terms, that is, in terms of finding the most suitable managerial ideals given certain tasks and environments, this discussion has also led to the construction of often hidden assumptions guiding much of the ongoing theory development. And insofar as contemporary management research can be seen as an important influence on the ongoing construction of managerial ideals and practices in society, the question of what basic assumptions guide this research should be more than only of theoretical interest. Our view of the leadership field is that the study of practicalities has led to the formulation of stable and non-disputable assumptions about leadership – such as the unitary command perspective. If ever questioned, these assumptions are strongly defended. If practitioners of leadership try to deviate from them, strong reactions are evoked. Basic assumptions in leadership research thus do not only serve as institutionalized, neutral, scientific facts defining the field, they have also developed into a set of virtues of leadership (Gustafsson, 1994). Thereby, leadership research does not only put forward a practical agenda of effective leadership, it also promotes a moral agenda of virtuous leadership.

In this chapter, we will start by discussing the moral foundations of leadership research in terms of virtues and basic assumptions. Then, the theoretical roots of the unitary command perspective are outlined. Following that, we will instead argue that all leadership can be seen as processes of interaction between several individuals – by shifting perspective from viewing leadership as a single-person activity to viewing it as collective construction processes, we will see new patterns in how decisions are made, how issues are raised and handled, how crises are responded to and so on.

In epistemological terms, leadership is regarded as ongoing construction processes where leaders, expectations on leaders, idea generation, decision-making and arenas for leadership are continuously negotiated and reformulated over time (Smircich and Morgan, 1982; Fletcher, 2004). A discussion towards future research agendas where the articulation and questioning of the moral and ideological foundations of leadership practices and leadership research are central to the development of sustainable leadership ideals concludes the chapter.

THE MORAL FOUNDATIONS OF LEADERSHIP RESEARCH AND PRACTICE

An important point of departure for this chapter is that leadership research is not only about the scientific formulation of practical and normative knowledge on the handling of managerial situations. Even though most leadership research is explicitly or implicitly focused on such knowledge, it is at the same time also shaping and reshaping basic assumptions on the nature of leadership, both in theory and in practice. And when these assumptions are then used to distinguish good leadership from bad leadership, wasteful management from lean management, egoistic leaders from responsible leaders – then they also become the basis on which managerial virtues are built. In short, when a field develops strong and taken-for-granted assumptions on their subject of study, it also starts to formulate its internal virtues and thus a moral foundation of its own.

At the core of the moral foundation of leadership is the Western tradition of viewing work as a painful inevitability, but also as a virtue, a moral duty and as something that refines and educates those who indulge in it (Jackall, 1988; Gustafsson, 1994). This view draws upon Protestant ethics, Puritanism, Marxism and several other streams of thought, and it becomes most apparent in the most advanced form of rational work – the modern organization. By means of specialization and coordination, modern organizations are supposed to contribute as much as possible to the common good, and the leaders who are entrusted with the difficult task of making this happen are required to live by certain normative virtues. Gustafsson (1994: 50) formulates these virtues in terms of thriftiness, diligence, sensibleness and responsibleness – virtues on which all management education are built. While this strong normative moral message often remains an underlying assumption in most management literature, its practical consequences – such as models and techniques for planning and control or generalized knowledge on the need for unitary command and carefully calculated spans of control – can be found anywhere. The perspective of unitary command is in this respect a consequence of underlying managerial virtues – the leader shall be in control in order to take responsibility, and organize work according to what has historically been seen as rational and sensible. The organization's best comes first, no matter what humanitarian ideals that are violated (Nylén, 1995).

There is also a second source from which the perspective of unitary command claims its moral necessity – the idea of the leader as an omnipotent hero. In a Weberian sense, the hero should be regarded as a pre-modern archetype that was to be replaced by modern managers, selected on the basis of formal merits and suitability for the job. But the idea of heroes has lived on, not least in the world of political and corporate leaders (Fletcher, 2004). As Jackall (1988) puts it, the modern corporation actually combines modernist monocratic bureaucratic ideals and re-created medieval patrimony in its governance structures – resulting in a view of the leader as a lonely expert with an almost God-given authority, a hero with superior expertise. What differentiates the hero from the non-hero is not necessarily his acts, but rather the virtues by which he lives – courage, vision, honesty, the duty to take responsibility for something larger than himself. And, more importantly – he is a single individual, a lonely man. If we free ourselves from the assumption of singularity and individuality, we will have no heroes – and, consequently, no leaders.

THE INSTITUTIONALIZATION OF THE UNITARY COMMAND PERSPECTIVE

Modern leadership theory started to emerge during the decades of the Industrial Revolution when leadership was first given attention by economists (Pearce and Conger, 2003). At that time, the concept of leadership was centred on command and control. With the beginning of the new century, the principles of Scientific Management (Taylor, 1911) became dominant in the management and leadership field. The idea of distinguishing between managerial and worker responsibilities implied that the command-and-control idea was reinforced, with management giving orders and providing instructions, and workers following them. The contribution of Fayol and Weber in Europe can also be considered important for strengthening the image of a top-down leadership based on command-and-control (Pearce and Conger, 2003).

General management theory then expanded from its base in Scientific Management through the inclusion of psychological and sociological theory and through new understandings of the environment in which managerial activities were performed, and so did leadership theory. Early explanations of leadership effectiveness were based on the notion that leaders possess certain psychological traits and personal characteristics that distinguish them from ordinary people. These theories are all individualistic in the sense that they focused on the individual leader, the 'Great Man' (Reicher et al., 2005), and they thereby supported the taken-for-granted assumption that leadership is a single-person task.

Later developments came to emphasize effective leadership as a question of leadership behaviour in relation to specific situations (Pearce and Conger, 2003). Moving focus from individual characteristics to what leaders actually did in different contexts and situations, new insights were gained that pointed at the importance of choosing the right leader for the situation at hand. Thereby, researchers could also distinguish between different leadership styles in terms of effectiveness. Often, these styles are described as composed by focus on task, focus on maintaining a good social climate in the group, and the focus on change and development.

During recent decades, there has been an increasing interest in viewing leadership as a social process, where leaders emerge from groups over time as they come to personify what it means to be a member of that group at that point of time (Pearce and Conger, 2003). As is often the case in management theory, this development is based both on theoretical advancements and on changed values and practices in organizations. A processual view of leadership is thus not only a consequence of a search for new and better conceptual and methodological tools for the understanding of leadership, but also of the new knowledge-intensive economy where neither people nor information can or should be controlled in the way they used to be. In this brave new world of 'visionary', 'idea-based' or 'charismatic' leadership, the notion of individual leaders still seems to persist. The leader is now not only the one who leads and give orders, but also a symbol and source of inspiration. As Henry Mintzberg (1999) puts it, 'we seem to be moving beyond leaders who merely lead; today heroes save. Soon heroes will only save; then gods will redeem.'

'New Leadership' is one term that has been used to group these recent approaches to the study of leadership (Bryman, 1996). The leader is the manager of meaning, the one who defines organizational reality by means of articulating a vision for the organization. Bryman describes such approaches as having a tendency to be too focused on the study of top leaders, on heroic leaders and on individuals rather than groups.

These leaders are often depicted as heroes also in the mass media, even though some researchers have started to question the real impact of such leaders on organizations and on their success (Czarniawska, 2005). Writing about major corporations such as Apple or American Express, which have been identified with their leaders, Henry Mintzberg (1999) uses these words:

> Then consider this proposition: maybe really good management is boring. Maybe the press is the problem, alongside the so-called gurus, since they are the ones who personalize success and deify leaders (before they defile them). After all, corporations are large and complicated; it takes a lot of effort to find out what has really been going on. It is so much easier to assume that the great one did it all. Makes for better stories too. (Mintzberg, 1999)

Hatch et al. (2006) have studied interviews with influential CEOs published in the *Harvard Business Review*, which has a significant impact on the managerial culture, in order to analyse the role played by aesthetics in leadership. Looking at the kind of stories told by leaders they found out that the large majority were epic stories, stories where a heroic individual succeeded in achieving a desirable goal despite all the obstacles along the way.

As well in the literature as in the organizational practice, it thus seems to be impossible to speak of leadership without speaking of leaders. Whether leadership functions really need to be performed by formal leaders seems to be an unexplored question. Accepting the need for leadership has meant accepting the need for one leader, which directly implies a differentiation between leaders and followers on a power dimension (Vanderslice, 1988). As Gronn (2002: 428) points out, the main difficulty with the taken-for-granted dichotomies leader-follower and leadership-followership in organization theory is that 'they *pre*scribe, rather than *de*scribe, a division of labor'.

Moreover, leadership is typically described as a good and desirable thing – we need leadership, as becomes evident by juxtaposing the term leadership to the term seduction (Calás and Smircich, 1991). As the two researchers write, 'to seduce is to lead wrongly, and it seems that to lead is to seduce rightly' (Calás and Smircich, 1991: 573).

If leadership theory seems to take the unitary command perspective for granted, the same can be said where general organization theory is concerned. Despite the search for new, post-bureaucratic organizational forms that acknowledge both the pace of change in the marketplace and the new values held by the young generations, managerial posts are still always treated as single-person assignments. People must know who is in charge, and whom to hold accountable.

Such a conception is also supported, at least in Sweden, by the legislation concerning different business areas. Even if, in most cases, these rules do not represent an absolute ban on two persons sharing, for example, a managerial position, it appears clear that one single person is preferred. Clearly identifiable responsibilities, more uniform practices, a simple command structure are some of the arguments used in favour of the single-person post (Öman, 2005).

To sum up, the unitary command perspective lives on in good health, although it has never been scientifically proved that it is always the most effective form. Individual leaders are still used to personify companies and countries, and most new management books treat leadership as something that is exercised by single individuals. In the same vein, the theoretical language of the field seem to incorporate the new environment for leadership activities through re-using old concepts rather than inventing new ones, thereby affirming the notion of heroic, individualist leadership. One prominent example of this is the recent stream of literature on 'charismatic leadership' (Conger, 1999), where an old Weberian concept for exceptional, radiant leaders is used to portray today's relational, democratic and trustful leadership styles. At the same time, in the practical world, we can see a development where leaders in all sectors are met with scepticism and contempt, and where young talents pursue other career forms than the managerial ladder.

SHARED LEADERSHIP: HOW AND WHY?

Historically, the fact that leadership is shared is not something new. Rome, for example, had two consuls in ancient times and, during one period, also a triumvirate (Lambert-Olsson, 2004; Sally, 2002). The reason for these collective institutions was mainly to avoid concentrating power in only one person's hands. In the same way, in some countries, as for example the USA, the legislative, executive and judiciary power are divided and assigned to different institutions. This is however not the main reason for sharing leadership in an organisation. It is anyway interesting to reflect on the fact that an idea (that of sharing leadership) that most of us almost spontaneously tend to reject has indeed already been applied in different historical contexts. In Table 8.1, the main arguments for shared leadership are summarized.

Two different personalities or competence areas completing each other are common for those forms of leadership that are not formally regulated but that are shared in practice. For example, tight collaboration between a CEO and the chairman of the board or the CEO and the COO in a corporation, or between a coach and his collaborator in a football team, like the Swedish couple Sven-Göran Eriksson and Tord Grip who managed the UK national football team for several years. Likewise, the cultural and media sectors are full of dual leadership models with one administrative and one professional leader (de Voogt, 2005; Lambert-Olsson, 2004). An 'emotional leader' and a 'task leader' has been an arrangement used by well-known international corporations such as Microsoft, HP, Boeing and Intel (O'Toole et al., 2003). Shared leadership is also described as a better alternative than a single leader when 'the challenges a corporation faces are so complex that they require a set of skills too broad to be possessed by any one individual' (O'Toole et al., 2003: 254) or when companies are dealing with very complex technologies that make the communication between technical and non-technical persons difficult. If two co-leaders could work together a period of time, they could develop a common language and understanding (Sally, 2002). Team work in projects and discourses of team members' empowerment seem also to set the premises for sharing leadership within groups. Some research (quantitative) has been done on particular types of teams, as product development or change management teams and the degree of shared leadership has been claimed to be related to team effectiveness (Pearce and Sims, 2002).

Despite these premises, there are not many organizations explicitly implementing forms of shared leadership today. Recent surveys made in Sweden among managers showed that most of them were positive to the idea of introducing shared leadership and that about 40 per cent of them already share leadership in some way (Holmberg and Söderlind, 2004; Döös et al., 2005). This seems to suggest that interest in this new model is large, but up to now the number of formal co-leaders is still very limited and the new model has not yet had the big impact it was expected to have.

Organizational perspective (shared leadership as a way of enhancing leadership effectiveness)	• Single-person leadership cannot reflect and handle today's environmental complexity – several different competences / skills / roles are required • Co-leaders can have a larger span of control together, they have more time for their co-workers and for reflecting on the strategy and the basic values for their unit • Shared leadership means that different organizational parts, interests and/or professions can be represented at the same time at managerial level. • By presenting leadership as a less challenging and stressful task, young ambitious employees can be retained. • Both stability and change can be represented by a dual leadership, thereby facilitating organizational change. • Less vulnerability in case of leader absence or resignation • Lower risk for sub-optimal solutions if the leadership of an organisation is truly shared by the management team	Holmberg and Söderlind (2004), Pearce and Conger (2003), Sally (2002), de Voogt (2005), Denis et al. (2001), Yang and Shao (1996), Bradford and Cohen (1998)
Co-worker perspective (shared leadership as a way of enhancing the correspondence between employee values and actual organizational practices)	• The young generations are used to working in teams with some degree of shared leadership. When they rise to higher organisational levels, they are more likely to continue to share leadership and to resist traditional solo command. • Expectation for co-leadership created by the experience of living in modern (at least Western) family models, where both parents have the same participation in decision-making, reinforced by experiences of working in teams • Young employees expect more 'democratic' leadership in modern organisations	Sally (2002), Bradford and Cohen (1998)
Individual perspective (shared leadership as a way of enhancing managers' lives)	• Solo leadership 'consumes' people and there is a risk for high level of stress and anxiety. • Balance of work requirements and personal responsibilities/private life. • Better sense of security and stability in decision making and implementation • Enhanced opportunities to learn having the co-leader as an example and as a feed-back giver • More fun	Holmberg and Söderlind (2004), Sally (2002), Fletcher (2004), Döös et al (2005)
Societal perspective (maintaining and increasing the legitimacy of leadership)	• When power is too concentrated, it may result in immoral and/or illegal actions taken by individual leaders struck by hubris • Shared leadership increases the possibility of including minorities in managerial positions, thereby increasing the legitimacy of leadership	Lambert-Olsson (2004)

Table 8.1 Summary of arguments in favour of shared leadership practices

One possible reason could be that the understanding of leadership as an individual trait and activity is so well rooted in our culture: every one of us has in his/her mind clear images of famous leaders such as Mohandas Gandhi or Martin Luther King, Jr, but we tend to ignore the team of people on whom they relied (O'Toole et al., 2003).

Large corporations in the business world are also identified by the personality of their leaders, on whom the focus is concentrated. Moreover, as the same authors also underline, people in Western cultures seem to need to identify one single individual as responsible for the performance of a group. We are instinctively reluctant to accept that two persons can share this responsibility, in the same way that we can be sceptical on the capability of two or more persons to make quick and clear decisions together when necessary. Even those who have shared a leadership position with another person seem to have a need to specify that in certain situations a single-person leadership is probably more appropriate, as for example in the army or during the coaching of a football team (Lambert-Olsson, 2004). On the other hand, there are also co-leaders witnessing that the opposite can happen. Having co-leaders seriously and deeply discuss visions for their group, basic understandings of their role and approaches to their activity, decisions can be made more quickly and are better grounded (Holmberg and Söderlind, 2004; Döös et al., 2003). Moreover, the fact that the decision is made together with another person can give more confidence to both leaders and allow them to shorten the time of reflection (they have already reflected and agreed on basic values and ideas). So, there are some positive experiences, even if the great majority of organizations have not yet tried any explicit form of shared leadership.

THEORIZING SHARED LEADERSHIP: POST-HEROIC IDEALS

In the introduction to this chapter, we viewed the issue of sustainability in terms of leadership ideals that (1) enable people in modern society to actually work with leadership without sacrificing everything else in life, and (2) can enhance the legitimacy of leadership in a society that raises serious moral doubts concerning the content and consequences of modern management practices. In other words, that leadership should become a natural part of many people's lives rather than a hard and lonely temporary situation for a chosen few.

During recent years, there has been an emerging debate on what has been called post-heroic leadership, which seems most important to the issue of sustainability. According to Eicher (2006), the old heroic ideal is a lone leader who feel that his leadership is based on superior knowledge and information (omnipotence), who fears failure more than anything (rightness), who keeps up appearances at any cost including blaming others (face-saving), and who views his subordinates as inferior creatures in constant need of assistance and rescue (co-dependency). Against this, Eicher poses the post-heroic ideal, where the leader wants others to take responsibility and gain knowledge (empowerment), encourages innovation and participation even in ambiguous situations (risk-taking), seeks input and aims for consensus in decision-making (participation), and wants others to grow and learn even at the expense of himself becoming dispensable (development). To us, the heroic ideal creates both unhappy and stressed leaders and also problems of legitimating leaders and leadership in the eyes of employees and citizens. The post-heroic ideal represents both individual situations and societal norms that enable people, organizations and societies to live on and develop.

Fletcher (2004) examines the power and gender implications of this new understanding of leadership. According to her, 'doing leadership', 'doing gender' and 'doing power' are related to each other and not being aware of these connections means a risk of failing in introducing shared leadership in organizations. Shared vertical leadership does not imply eliminating all formal leaders, but recognizing that the 'visible positional "heroes" are supported by a network of personal leadership practices distributed through the organization' (Fletcher, 2004: 648). One example of metaphor used to represent this 'collaborative subtext' (Fletcher, 2004: 648) that supports the visible leaders is that of the iceberg (McIntosh, 1989), with its larger part invisible to the eyes. The individual-focused perspective is changed with a view of leading and following as 'two sides of the same set of relational skills that everyone in an organisation needs in order to work in a context of interdependence' (Fletcher, 2004: 648). This means that, even if formal positions remain unaltered, who will take the role of the leader depends on the situation and individuals are required to move fluidly between the two roles. In such a context, the classical notion of self as an independent entity could be replaced by the self-in-relation notion, where interdependence is instead the basis.

Describing shared leadership in this way, we assign it many traits that are traditionally seen as feminine, that is traits that have been 'socially ascribed' to women, as for example 'empathy, vulnerability, and skills of inquiry and collaboration' (Fletcher, 2004: 650). On the other hand, traditional forms of leadership are more characterized by masculine traits, such as 'individualism, control, assertiveness, and skills of advocacy and domination' (Fletcher, 2004: 650). This does not mean that every man has all the masculine traits and all women all the feminine. These are social constructions that influence our identities and that are continuously reconstructed/deconstructed. Fletcher also speaks of the 'logic of effectiveness' that underlies heroic vs post-heroic leadership. Heroic leadership relies on a masculine logic of effectiveness, on 'how to produce things' in working life, while post-heroic leadership relies on a feminine logic of effectiveness on 'how to grow people' in domestic life (Fletcher, 2004: 650–651). The two spheres are socially constructed as dichotomies ('separate and adversarial', linked to men vs women, and evaluated in different ways: skills and complexity vs innate nature). This may not be the case in 'real life' where both sexes participate in both spheres, but, 'at the level of discourse', they influence our gender identities.

Here we could find one possible explanation as to why post-heroic leadership ideals are mostly invisible in companies. When leaders tell about their leadership, they still use the classical hero individual-focused narrative. If we consider that we construct our identity each time we have an interaction with another person and that a relevant part of our identity is our gender identity, we can see that also when working we are 'doing gender'. The fact that working life has long been dominated by men suggests that 'doing work' is linked to 'doing masculinity'. So, since practices related to post-heroic leadership are unconsciously associated with femininity and powerlessness, this new form of leadership violates gender and power assumptions about leadership. These gender and power-related questions make the change to the new leadership model more difficult and delicate, since we are speaking of highly charged aspects.

A possibility, at the individual level, is to adopt the 'self-in-relation' stance instead of the usual individualistic 'self'. The 'self-in-relation' concept was proposed by the Stone Center (Fletcher and Käufer, 2003) and was developed within a model of human growth. While traditionally growth is seen as a process of separation from others and of achieving autonomy, the Stone Center maintains that growth occurs as a process of connection. 'The ability to connect oneself in ways that foster mutual development and learning is what characterises growth' (Fletcher and Käufer, 2003: 27). In this way, interdependence is the basis and the self is seen as a relational entity. Mutual influence and co-creation through interactions are evidenced.

LEADERSHIP AS A COLLECTIVE CONSTRUCTION: FROM EMERGING PRACTICE TO RESEARCH PERSPECTIVE

Our analysis of the existing literature on shared leadership portrayed above is that it can, roughly, be divided in two related streams: (1) one that focuses on the practicalities of why and how managerial duties and positions should be assigned to more than one person, and (2) one that assumes a basic perspective on all leadership as being collective construction processes with several people involved. Although these two traditions do not exclude each other, they imply quite different research agendas.

In the first tradition, which has been described above, we find several reasons why and how managerial tasks should be divided between several individuals. Concepts like 'post-heroic leadership' are used to discuss the inhumane workload of the modern manager and the need to enable him (and sometimes also her) to live a balanced life (Sally, 2002; Pearce and Manz, 2005). Modern decentralized ways of organizing – through high-performing teams rather than through bureaucratic command structures – are also used as arguments (Walker, 2001; Lambert, 2002; Pearce, 2004), and also the observation that an increasingly complex world requires top management competence profiles broader than can possibly be expected to be found in one single person (O'Toole et al., 2003; Waldersee and Ealgeson, 2002; Pearce, 2004). By reference to established theories on group composition and role complementarity it is also usual to describe managerial tasks as requiring several different individual roles at one and the same time (Yang and Shao, 1996; Denis et al., 2001). Sometimes we also meet arguments linked to the general legitimacy of leadership, such as that organizational and societal change processes may be facilitated by having several different perspectives and/or interest groups represented in the managerial function at the same time (Denis et al., 2001; Sally, 2002; Ensley et al., 2003). In cases where this literature refers to actual empirical experiences, it is usually in the form of successful instances of shared leadership (usually from top management settings) and practical advice on how the co-working leaders should distribute tasks, roles and information in order to make things work (O'Toole el al., 2003). Some authors still also maintain the continued need for traditional vertical unitary command in many situations; shared leadership is primarily suitable for tasks characterized by reciprocal interaction, creativity and complexity (that is, advanced teamwork situations).

One problem of this perspective is that it views shared leadership as an exception to 'usual' leadership, an exception to be practised in extraordinary situations. Shared leadership is also defined according to the number of involved individuals, rather than according to the individuals' experiences of whether exercised leadership was actually shared or not – that is, a focus on formal organizational arrangements rather than on practical everyday organizing. The alternative, as we see it, is to apply a basic perspective on leadership as something that individuals construct together in social interaction (Gronn, 2002; Smircich and Morgan, 1982). Gronn discuss this in terms of level of analysis, that is, that the level of analysis should be the exercised leadership rather than the single individual leader. Accordingly, Vanderslice (1988) invites us to separate the concept of leadership from that of leaders. Meindl (1995) and Reicher et al. (2005) claim that traditional leadership models contribute to the institutionalization of a dualism of identity between leaders and followers in society – a dualism that may be challenged through studies of leadership identity construction. A dualism that also raises moral questions as if it is possible to explain how leaders transform other people's thinking, for example, and at the same time not to deny these people their own ability to think. Or to celebrate charismatic leaders without encouraging tyranny.

Fletcher (2004) takes this line of reasoning one step further in her discussion of post-heroic leadership in terms of collective, interactive learning processes. She does think that such a theoretic development will run into difficulties, and that those difficulties may better be understood from a gender perspective. The traditional images of leadership are strongly masculinized, she says, and the femininization that is inherent in the post-heroic perspective will challenge several deeply rooted notions of leadership. Among these Fletcher finds the taken-for-granted individualization of society (reinforcing unitary command as the only viable solution), and also the contemporary idea that problems of gender inequality are finally being solved (implying that any basic redefinition of leadership would be unnecessary since we have already found the most suitable forms) (Vecchio, 2002). A social constructionist research agenda where leadership, leader identities and masculinization/femininization as constantly constructed and reconstructed (Lindgren and Packendorff, 2006) should thus be central to advancing both leadership theory and leadership practices in the direction of sustainable leadership.

The point of departure of this chapter was the moral foundation of leadership research and practice that views leadership in terms of unitary command. This perspective has here been questioned by means of the current research debate on shared leadership and post-heroic leadership ideals. Viewing leadership in terms of collective constructions would imply that leadership is created by many people in interaction and that not all responsibilities need to be placed on one single person. The consequences of that can be most important to many organizations. It will, for example, imply that different individual roles are seen as important to leadership, that the notion of role-complementarity may become even more important in the composition of managerial teams, and that single individuals may be relieved of unrealistic and harmful workloads. In addition, this might also result in new views on how the daily operations of the company can be organized; if employees are recognized as responsible and accountable co-leaders rather than as untrustworthy subordinates, they should be entrusted to make decisions not only on operative matters but also on governance matters. The principle of inverted delegation (that is, that tasks are delegated upwards rather than downwards) is one possible outcome of this, and it also may become natural that the composition and role structure in a management team is a matter for the team's subordinates to decide upon. This is not to say that hierarchies will not exist, but rather that hierarchies should be seen as systems of relations that are open for construction and re-construction by all of their members. That builds on the assumption that the members are responsible people who view their organization as a common interest that must be maintained into the future. By this, modern leadership practices might become both less harmful to individuals and more legitimate in the eyes of its beholders – that is, increasingly sustainable.

Theoretically, viewing leadership as collectively constructed implies several things that should be of importance to future research. Moving the focus from leaders to leadership activities (Gronn, 2002) is one such. Thereby, it may be possible to follow the construction processes where power, organizational roles, and definitions of reality are negotiated in social interaction (Smircich and Morgan, 1982), viewing these processes as leadership even though they may not result in clear decisions, unitary action strategies and so on. In that way, moving the focus from leaders to leadership activities is also a way of moving focus from leadership outcomes to the processes of leadership.

By advocating a sustainable leadership perspective, we argue that studies within the field of leadership need to take one step further towards the inclusion of axiological or ideological perspectives. Leadership activities are thus not only interesting as processes of social construction, they are also interesting in the sense that they are important manifestations of hidden and/or taken-for-granted ideological and moral norms in society. Like several other fields within general management research, the leadership field maintains a mainstream perspective where the object of study is essentially a positive thing with desirable outcomes. If these desirable outcomes are indeed delivered, the processes preceding them are rarely questioned. When critical researchers and/or voices in society demand ethical perspectives or humanistic perspectives, or indulge in criticism of psychopathic leaders, greed and other modern phenomena (Jackall, 1988) they actually advocate a leadership research where not only the processes and outcomes of leadership should be studied, but also the hidden ideological and moral meanings on which modern leadership practices and theories are based. Post-heroic leadership is to us one such way towards leadership theorizing where the articulation and questioning of moral foundations is central to theory development.

In this chapter, we have focused our discussion on one central – but often hidden and taken-for-granted – aspect of leadership: the unitary command perspective. By discussing the roots of unitary command and the recent challenges to this perspective in leadership literature, we have portrayed a development where both established leadership practices and leadership norms are questioned, both in terms of what they do to people in organizations and what they do to the general views of leadership in society. While questioning the forms and consequences of unitary command and also actively promoting the perspective that leadership is something people create together, it is not easy to discard all traditions in the field. Not least because companies operate in a society that expects single, powerful, hard-working, masculine leaders that deliver decisions and strategies and who can control their organizations and be held accountable for everything that happens there. In that sense, questioning the unitary command perspective is one way of articulating and questioning the moral foundations of modern leadership knowledge, which we see as the necessary first steps towards the formulation of sustainable leadership ideals – in single organizations and in society as a whole.

REFERENCES

Bradford, D. L. and Cohen, A. R., (1998), *Power Up: Transforming Organizations through Shared Leadership*, Wiley, Chichester.

Bryman, A., (1996), 'Leadership in organizations', in S. R. Clegg, C. Hardy and W. R. Nord, (eds), *Handbook of Organization Studies*, Sage, London.

Calás, M. B. and Smircich, L., (1991), 'Voicing seduction to silence leadership', *Organization Studies,* **12** (4), 567–602.

Carlson, S., (1951), *Executive Behaviour*, Strömbergs, Stockholm.

Conger, J. A., (1999), 'Charismatic and transformational leadership in organizations: an insider's perspective on these developing streams of research', *The Leadership Quarterly,* **10** (2), 145–179.

Czarniawska, B., (2005), *En Teori om Organisering*, Studentlitteratur, Lund.

Denis, J-L., Lamothe, L. and Langley, A., (2001), 'The dynamics of collective leadership and strategic change in pluralistic organizations', *Academy of Management Journal,* **44** (4), 809–837.

Döös, M., Wilhelmson, L. and Hemborg, Å., (2003), 'Smittande makt: samledarskap som påverkansprocess', *Ledmotiv,* **3**, 58–71.

Döös, M., Hanson, M., Backström, T., Wilhelmson, L. and Hemborg, Å. (2005). *Delat ledarskap i svenskt arbetsliv – kartläggning av förekomst och chefers inställning (Shared leadership in Swedish working life – an overview of its occurence and managers' attitudes to it)*, Stockholm: Arbetslivsinstitutet.

Eicher, J. P., (2006), *Post-heroic Leadership: Managing the Virtual Organization*, retrieved August 25, 2006, from http://www.pignc-ispi.com/articles/management/post-heroic.htm

Ensley, M. D., Pearson, A. and Pearce, C. L., (2003), 'Top management team process, shared leadership, and new venture performance', *Human Resource Management Review*, **13**, 329–346.

Fletcher, J. K., (2004), 'The paradox of postheroic leadership: an essay on gender, power, and transformational change', *Leadership Quarterly*, **15**, 647–661.

Fletcher, J. K. and Käufer, K., (2003), 'Shared leadership: paradox and possibilities', in C. L. Pearce and J. A. Conger, (eds), *Shared Leadership: Reframing the Hows and Whys of Leadership*, Sage, London.

Gronn, P., (2002), 'Distributed leadership as a unit of analysis', *Leadership Quarterly*, **13**, 423–451.

Gustafsson, C., (1994), *Produktion av allvar: Om det ekonomiska förnuftets metafysik*. Nerenius & Santérus, Stockholm.

Hatch, M. J., Kostera, M. and Kozminski, A. K., (2006), 'The three faces of leadership: manager, artist, priest', *Organizational Dynamics*, **35** (1), 49–68.

Holmberg, K. and Söderlind, E., (2004), *Leda genom att dela: Om delat ledarskap i praktiken*, Lidingö: Navigator Dialog.

Jackall, R., (1988), *Moral Mazes: the World of Corporate Managers*, Oxford University Press, New York.

Lambert, L., (2002), 'A framework for shared leadership', *Educational Leadership*, **59** (8), 37–40.

Lambert-Olsson, H., (2004), *Delat ledarskap – om äkta och oäkta dubbelkommandon*, Svenska Förlaget, Stockholm.

Lindgren, M. and Packendorff, J., (2003), 'A project-based view of entrepreneurship: towards action-orientation, seriality and collectivity', in C. Steyaert and D. Hjorth (eds), *Entrepreneurship: New Movements*, Edward Elgar, Cheltenham.

Lindgren, M. and Packendorff, J., (2006), 'What's new in new forms of organizing? On the construction of gender in project-based work', *Journal of Management Studies*, **43** (4), 841–866.

McIntosh, P., (1989), 'Feeling like a Fraud, Part 2', Working Paper No. 37, Centers for Women, Wellesley College.

Meindl, J. R., (1995), 'The romance of leadership as a follower-centric theory', *Leadership Quarterly*, **6** (3), 329–341.

Mintzberg, H., (1973), *The Nature of Managerial Work*, Harper &Row, New York.

Mintzberg, H., (1999), 'Managing quietly', *Leader to leader*, **12**, 24–30. Retrieved March, 2007, from www.leadertoleader.org/ knowledgecenter/ L2L/ spring99/mintzberg.html

Nylén, U., (1995), 'Humanitarian versus organizational morality: a survey of attitudes concerning business ethics among managing directors', *Journal of Business Ethics*, **14**, 977–986.

O'Toole, J., Galbraith, J., and Lawler III, E. E., (2003), 'The promise and pitfalls of shared leadership: when two (or more) heads are better than one', in Pearce, C. L. and Conger, J. A., (eds.), *Shared Leadership: Reframing the Hows and Whys of Leadership*, Sage, London.

Pearce, C. L., (2004), 'The future of leadership: combining vertical and shared leadership to transform knowledge work', *Academy of Management Executive*, **18** (1), 47–57.

Pearce, C. L. and Conger, J. A., (2003), 'All those years ago: the historical underpinnings of shared leadership', in C. L. Pearce and J. A. Conger, (eds), *Shared Leadership: Reframing the Hows and Whys of Leadership*, Sage, London.

Pearce, C. L. and Manz, C. C., (2005), 'The new silver bullets of leadership', *Organizational Dynamics*, **34** (2), 130–140.

Pearce, C. L. and Sims, H. P. Jr., (2002), 'Vertical versus shared leadership as predictors of the effectiveness of change management teams', *Group Dynamics: Theory, Research, and Practice*, **6** (2), 172–197.

Reicher, S., Haslam, S. A. and Hopkins, N., (2005), 'Social identity and the dynamics of leadership: leaders and followers as collaborative agents in the transformation of social reality', *The Leadership Quarterly*, **16**, 547–568.

Sally, D., (2002), 'Co-leadership: lessons from republican Rome', *California Management Review*, **44** (4), 84–99.

Smircich, L. and Morgan, G., (1982), 'Leadership: the management of meaning', *Journal of Applied Behavioral Science*, **18** (3), 257–273.

Taylor, F. W., (1911), *Scientific Management*, Harper & Bros, New York.

Vanderslice, V. J., (1988), 'Separating leadership from leaders: an assessment of the effect of leader and follower roles in organizations', *Human Relations*, **9**, 677–696.

Vecchio, R. P., (2002), 'Leadership and gender advantage', *The Leadership Quarterly*, **13**, 643–671.

de Voogt, A., (2005), *Dual Leadership as a Problem-Solving Tool in Arts Organizations*, paper presented at the 8th International Conference of Arts and Cultural Management, Montréal, Canada.

Waldersee, R. and Eagleson, G., (2002), 'Shared leadership in the implementation of re-orientations', *Leadership and Organization Development Journal*, **23** (7), 400–407.

Walker, J., (2001), 'Developing a shared leadership model at the unit level', *Journal of Perinatal and Neonatal Nursing*, **15** (1), 26–39.

Yang, O. and Shao, Y. E., (1996), 'Shared leadership in self-managed teams: A competing values approach', *Total Quality Management*, **7** (5), 521–534.

Öman, S., (2005), *Juridiska aspekter på samledarskap – Hinder och möjligheter för delat ledarskap*, Arbetslivsrapport nr 2005: 29, Arbetslivsinstitutet, Stockholm.

9. The Psychological Dimension of Love as Foundational for Transformational Leadership Theory

Mary Miller

INTRODUCTION

An interdisciplinary approach will be used in this chapter as the field of psychology will inform some aspects of the moral foundations of management theory, specifically Burns's (1978) transformational leadership theory. The relevance of transforming leadership theory to management theory is based on one simple fact. This fact is that organizations that desire to implement dimensions of transformational leadership do so from a completely pragmatic motive: it is arguably the most effective form of leadership (Bailey, 2001).

The discussion to follow in the next section will identify how love can be defined within psychological theory as one of the underlying foundations of transformational leadership theory. The specific focus will be limited to identification of the parallels in theorizing between some transformational leadership theories and some psychological theories with respect to the psychological dimension of love as a choice understood to be 'empathy with action', love as a form of power, and love as a method of influence. The non-abusive process that is consequent to the use of love as a basis of power within an organizational context is one of the aspects necessary in creating an ethical environment.

The field of psychology seeks to understand underlying dimensions, so psychology is often used in seeking to understand leadership processes. Psychology's defining contribution to the world of academia is to identify and as a consequence understand what underlies behaviour that is observable. The underlying psychological dimension of love will be examined in this chapter to provide a conceptual idea of love within an organizational context. This conceptualizing provides the framework necessary to identify one aspect of the moral/ethical foundations that underlie the theory of transformational leadership as initially articulated by Burns.

Section 3 will identify two of the debates surrounding transforming leaders, also identified as moral leaders. First, some theorists define transforming leaders as those leaders able to make others (employees/colleagues) work sacrificially within their organization (Bass, 1985; Bass, 1995; Bass, 1996; Bass et al. 1997; Bass, 1998), unlike Burns's definition quoted below (Burns, 1978). The discussion will identify the moral concerns that are being raised with this specific theorizing, and the need to evaluate both the end goals as well as the process of transforming leaders. Second, there is a brief overview of an ongoing discussion; how do perceived personal qualities of transforming leaders impact their decision-making? The transforming leader's perceived personal qualities are not necessarily a guarantee that moral decisions will be based on those perceived personal qualities.

'EMPATHY WITH ACTION' WITHIN AN ORGANIZATIONAL CONTEXT

Definition of Transforming Leadership

> The transforming leader looks for potential motives in followers, seeks to satisfy higher needs, and engages the full person of the follower. The result of transforming leadership is a relationship of mutual stimulation and elevation that converts followers into leaders and may convert leaders into moral agents. (Burns, 1978: 4)

The aforementioned definition of what it means to be transforming as a leader came out of qualitative historical analysis of leaders across cultures (Burns, 1978). Burns drew from the leaders' speeches and texts, some autobiographies, biographies, major works on leaders, as well as an array of social, psychological, historical, and political theorists. He also instituted a peer review process to evaluate his conceptions and ideas as he wrote.

The starting point for the research in understanding transforming leaders was Burns's (1978) in-depth historical analysis identifying transforming leaders as a unique phenomenon or theory within the field of leadership research. Burns's conceptualizing of transforming leaders thrust this paradigm into prominence. Burns's definition, quoted above, will be used in this chapter to provide understanding of what constitutes transforming leadership.

Burns's definition does not mention or use the word 'love'. The discussion of love in leadership theory will be informed by Boulding's (1989) analysis of the types of power used by leaders. Boulding theorized that love is one type of power used by leaders. Boulding identifies the influence process used by leaders who use love as a power base as 'integrating power'. Burns does not state what specific behaviours are used to enable the end goals of 'mutual stimulation and elevation' to occur. Boulding's theory of love as integrating power in relationship to Burns's transforming leadership definition provides reasoning for understanding how the focus and process of the transforming leader has the consequence of mutuality and power sharing.

Before discussing Burns's definition and its relationship with Boulding's theorizing, the psychological definition of love as a choice, or as 'empathy with action' will lay the framework from which to conceive of love as a choice that has legitimate expression within an organizational context. Some psychologists have identified love as an underlying dimension that is others-oriented and has elements of choice. Fromm (1963), Frankl (1984), and Allport (1983) all wrote about love as a choice. Allport (1983) described a process of steps that are used in making this choice (these choices) occur(s). These theorists acknowledged that love has elements of the metaphysical, but they focused on the knowable aspects of love as cognitive[1] processes chosen with deliberation.

Framing Love as a Choice in Psychology

Fromm provided an understanding of love as a function (as action) instead of love being identified as emotive construal. Fromm described love as 'not primarily a relationship to a specific person; it is an attitude, an orientation of character which determines the relatedness of a person to the world as a whole, not toward one "object" of love' (Fromm, 1963: 38).

The 'attitude' and 'orientation' is a result of placing love as a primary approach in relating to the world. The 'attitude' and the 'orientation' that Fromm describes come from a choice to deliberately demonstrate the 'attitude', to deliberately have an 'orientation'. Fromm speaks of the 'relatedness' of the person. The 'attitude' and the 'orientation' that are chosen with deliberation have the consequence of the person relating to the world in expressions of love. The 'relatedness' was consequent to the 'orientation' or decision to love. The 'orientation of character' that Fromm describes came first as a choice; the consequent 'relatedness' is the person's interaction on multiple levels, including cognitive choices that result in concrete actions.

In further theorizing, Fromm made the seminal distinction that the focus of love's attention was as a 'function', not in an object. Fromm uses the word 'function' to identify an ongoing process that is activated by a choice to love, and then finds expression in all that the individual does. The word 'function' denotes a level of integration that goes beyond simply having an object that one loves.

The integration that Fromm has identified means that the person has real impact that is consequent with their orientation to love. This orientation to love in how the person functions involves continually making choices for the highest benefit to others that evidence the orientation to love. This is an integrated approach of love towards others, because it involves continuity and learning.

The concept of function is far reaching in the life of the person because it is an underlying dimension in the person's behaviour towards the world. Fromm identified that love as function can be enacted with choices in such a way that love becomes an art. There is a learning process largely based on motivation and action. Fromm states, 'Love is an activity, not a passive effect' (Fromm, 1963: 18). This statement shows that Fromm understood that love could be chosen with deliberation. Fromm's identification of love was that one can make the choice to love, and this choice then needs to be demonstrated in concrete actions. The emotive construal might be ancillary to the choice to love, but it is not the primary focus in learning to love.

Frankl (1984) had a similar perspective of love. Frankl, like Fromm, saw love as an orientation that was chosen with deliberation. Frankl described love as a value that one chooses, with consequent actions. Frankl states, 'The salvation of man is through love and in love' (Frankl, 1984: 57). Frankl connected the verb 'to love' with actions towards others. It was also actions of love towards oneself.

Frankl's psychological theorizing on a person's ability to love as a choice came as a result of his concentration camp experiences. In his concentration camp experience, Frankl found himself in a laboratory context that unwittingly tested the prevailing psychological theories of man. He found that there were people in the camp that held to their values in the face of being denied basic human needs. He found that there were people who did not seek to exert power over others, but sought to love others, even in the gruesome reality of the concentration camp.

Frankl identified some individuals who chose to love, chose to hold on to the meaning that had been part of their lives prior to the concentration camp throughout the entire concentration camp experience. As a consequence, Frankl discounted Freud's 'will to pleasure' as the ultimate understanding and value of individuals. Frankl discounted the will to power with its attendant desire for superiority of Adlerian psychology as ultimate understanding of humankind. Adler and Freud did not provide a psychological framework that adequately explained the responses that Frankl witnessed first-hand.

Both Fromm's theorizing and Frankl's logotherapy identified the concept of individuals being able to select values, and choose to act on the basis of those values, in a realistic manner with knowledge of self. This process involves knowing oneself well enough to determine what values one wants to consciously hold as central to one's identity. 'Logotherapy ... considers man as a being whose main concern consists in fulfilling a meaning and in actualizing values, rather than in the mere gratification and satisfaction of drives and instincts,' (Frankl, 1984: 164).

Frankl identified the idea of love as a value that was chosen with impact on others, as well as impacting oneself. The choice to love was crucial in understanding oneself. It was the actualizing of values that enabled meaning to occur. It is as love is chosen that meaning results.

Burns is not a psychologist, so he was not seeking to identify underlying psychological dimensions, he was identifying an approach or process that he considered to be the most important force in how a leader is shaped. That important force is learning. Burns's psychological perspective of transforming leaders involves his own concept of self-actualizing; which identifies a leader's proactive choice to be a learner.

> I suggest that the most marked characteristic of self-actualizers as potential leaders goes beyond Maslow's[2] self-actualization; it is their capacity to learn from others and the environment – the capacity to be taught. That capacity calls for an ability to listen and be guided by others without being threatened by them, to be dependent on others but not overly dependent, to judge other persons with both affection and discrimination, to posses enough autonomy to be creative without rejecting the external influences that make for growth and relevance. Self-actualization ultimately means the ability to lead by being led. It is this kind of self-actualization that enables leaders to comprehend the needs of potential employee/colleagues, to enter into their perspectives. (Burns, 1978: 117)

One of Burns's identifiers of transforming leaders is as those who deliberately make choices to learn from others. The leader makes deliberate choices to receive from others and to be led. The leader can be taught. There is a reciprocity that seeks to validate others by receiving from them. This process of exchange involves choosing specific behaviours that enable the leader to place him/herself in the position of the employee/colleague. Please note that this concept of the leader's placing themselves in the position of the employee/colleague will be discussed further in this chapter when the distinction is drawn between consideration, love, and empathy.

While there is a basis in Fromm and Frankl's theoretical frameworks in psychology (for the concept of love as a choice), the metaphysical aspect of love is not dismissed; it is not discussed either. It is clear that love has a metaphysical aspect. The motivation to love has elements of the metaphysical. The perceptions of behaviour are likely to have a metaphysical aspect. It is possible and even likely that the metaphysical aspect of love (why anyone would want to make the choice to love in the first place) may be its driving force.

If love can be chosen with deliberation, then those choices can be perceived by others. It is this particular aspect of love that it is suggested has relevance for transforming leader theory. Love as action is significant to employee/colleague perception, and can be identified outside of the emotive aspects that also may be present. The consequences of the motivation to love can be analysed by specific perceptions of behaviour. The concepts or dimensions of love being analysed are the behaviours that are evidenced as a result of a choice to love that involves the dyad relationship of employee/colleague and leader in a work context. This is a narrow and limited focus.

Issues of the Heart, Habits of the Mind

The difficulty in identifying love within a work environment has always been how to empirically measure this dimension. Allport (1983) and then Argyris (1993) identify reasoning and methodology for empirical analysis to be able to be performed by examining the steps involved in the process of implementation of values.

Allport (1983) advocated a continual development model of personality, where the person is not static but continues to develop over time. This process is ongoing throughout the life of the person. The 'proprium' is the place where assimilation of personality takes place. He believed that individuals will seek to act out of their value system, whatever that may be, even if they do not completely attain what their value system espouses. This concept of continual assimilation will be a basis for understanding and examining love as a choice.

Allport's (1983) basis for the aforementioned perspective has the theoretical postulation that three important changes occur in the course of transformation. The first is that what is perceived externally as valued by the individual begins the transformational process by first being internalized or recognized as a value the individual wants as their own. The second step in this process is that the inhibitions that might prohibit implementation of the value system of the person are resolved by experiences, 'of preference, self-respect, and "ought"' (Allport, 1983: 73). There is proactive implementation on the part of the person seeking to incorporate these values into their lives. There is a cognitive process in this second step that identifies the issues that need to be addressed in order to implement the value. The third step in this transformation is that, 'generic self-guidance, that is to say, to broad schemata of values that convey direction upon conduct' (Allport, 1983: 73) kick in. This third step is given expression in concrete behaviours that represent the value. These three steps give a rough outline of how it is possible to identify the steps that go into making the choice to love.

Burns's aforementioned description (of transforming leaders going beyond self-actualizing by being learners) also fits with Allport's transformation process. Burns's learning process can be understood within Allport's description of transformation. The second step of Allport's process of identification of issues fits with Burns's description of the leader who is able to be influenced by others. The second and third steps of Allport's process also fits with Burns's outcome of transforming leaders comprehending employee/colleagues because of their ability to be influenced by others.

Allport describes the process that one uses to incorporate a value into one's life as a transformational process. When the value that one wants to incorporate is love then the second stage of the transformational process seeks to identify what the best case scenario would be in order to effectively activate the value of love. Within a work context in the relationship between the leader and employee/colleague, step two would involve examining what choices would reflect the best for the employee/colleague. Love seeks the best for the other. The third step in his description of transformation indicates that action is consequent to the examination of best choices available. Thus love seeks 'choices to will the highest good', or choices to do the highest good.

These are issues of the heart in combination with habits of the mind. The values are the issues of the heart. The cognitive choices are the habits of the mind. An individual can begin a choice to love as an action of choice in response to a heart desire or value, and then have it become a normal (preferred) aspect of conduct. The actual desire to implement the value has a metaphysical component. The process of implementation of that value has a component that is measurable.

Allport's additional point is that the person might not find total expression all of the time of what has been identified as a key value. What is essential, however, is for the target of implementation of the value to be validated, for actions to occur consistently. As this process of implementation occurs, the values themselves will dictate a major part of the person's behaviour. Allport puts it best that, 'in agreement with such schemata he selects his perceptions, consults his conscience, inhibits irrelevant or contrary lines of conduct, drops and forms subsystems of habits according as they are dissonant or harmonious with his commitments' (Allport, 1983: 76). The fact is that one hundred per cent predictability is not possible, but the overarching point is that there will be a significant level of prediction based on the values chosen.

The definition of love as a 'choice' and to 'will the highest good' comes from Frankl, Fromm, and Allport's psychological theories. The definition of love as 'choice to will the highest good' is being used with the understanding that the individual makes one choice at a time per situation. Each situation might involve numerous choices. Obviously, an array of choices is made over numerous situations. An equally valid definition would be love as 'choices to will the highest good', which implies that this is an ongoing process across multiple situations that occurs with regularity.

Argyris's 'Ladder of Inference'

The main focus of Argyris's research has been interpersonal relationships within organizations, specifically the relationship between employees, colleagues, leader-employee, and leader-colleague. The behaviour between these dyad relationships within an organizational context was the context for his research. He worked in collaboration with a corporation in seeking to determine the applicability of his models.

Argyris (1993) sought to discover the 'what' that is involved in arriving at the choices leaders and others make. He identified specific steps that are involved in the process used to draw conclusions. Argyris described these as forming the 'ladder of inference'. He sought to unravel some of the complexity that is involved in making choices within an organizational context.

To describe what has become known as Argyris's (1993) 'ladder of inference', an imaginary ladder is drawn and at the bottom rung of the ladder is the 'observed data and experience'. Nothing has been added so far because initially what data will be selected is left totally open to the perception of the perceiver. From the entire array of available data and experience available to the individual, the individual moves up one rung on the ladder to 'data'.

Data is what is selected from what is observed. No one can select every piece of data available. Choices are made to select one piece of data over another and this is a process that we all attend to. The next rung of the ladder are the 'meanings'.

Meaning is the personal and cultural construal of the data that we have selected. Now based on the meaning that we have attached to the data that has been observed; we move up to the next rung and add our own 'assumptions'.

Assumptions are put onto the meanings we have made. We assume specific things about the meanings we have made. From the assumptions we place on the meanings we have made from the data we have observed comes the next rung of the ladder, which are the 'conclusions'.

Conclusions are drawn specifically from the assumptions. From these conclusions we have drawn comes the next rung on the ladder, and that is 'beliefs'.

Beliefs are adopted about the world, factoring in the conclusions that are drawn from the assumptions that were made from the meanings that were drawn from the data we observed. Finally we have reached the top of the ladder, 'actions'.

Actions come out of the beliefs that are drawn from the conclusions we made from assumptions placed on meanings from the data we observed. The entire process then loops back to impact what we select from observing data to begin to climb the ladder again.

Argyris distinguishes between the espoused theory of action as exemplified by the person's espoused values, and the, 'theory in use', (Argyris, 1993: 51). The 'theory in use' evidences the actual behaviour and process used. If there is a disconnection between what the person says and what s/he does, the real 'theory in use', than there are hidden values that are overriding the espoused values.

Argyris's identification of this cognitive process enables some identification of learning processes between leaders and others within organizations. Argyris's process identifies how assumptions can be tested. This line of reasoning fits research that observed 'self-reflection is related to the growth of leadership skills and subsequent leader performance' (Strange and Mumford, 2002: 348). It is an expansion of Burns's concept of transforming leaders having a primary focus on learning.

Learning through self-reflection can take place, and this process is possibly the integration component of the action of love as a 'choice and to will the highest good'. This learning will be observed by others, because it is interactive learning. When assumptions are tested and changes need to be made, these are observable actions by others. The learning of the leader has tangible consequences that are observable. These tangible, observable learning processes can be identified as specific behaviours that have impact between the employee/colleague and leader. This is the basis for being able to create psychometric instruments that seek to profile leadership. Because the learning is identifiable, employee/colleague evaluation of the leader's impact can be obtained.

From a leader's perspective, if there is a desire and a motivation to love, then the observed data is the starting point, and attention is paid to see if the data that is being observed corresponds, or actively facilitates, the choice to love. If it does not then different and new data is taken in, and the process of learning to implement choices to love continues. The cognitive process as 'choice to will the highest good' is an ongoing development that is chosen with deliberation by the leader. The learning along the 'ladder of inference' for a leader (who chooses to learn) will be a continual process along all the various dimensions (data, meaning, assumptions, conclusions, beliefs). This process will be observable, because of the actions that are consequent to the learning.

The employee/colleague is the recipient of this learning process that is undertaken by the leader, within the interpersonal relationship behaviours between leader and employee/colleague. It is being presumed that the employee/colleague can identify the salient aspect of this learning process, because of the actions that have resulted from the leader's decisions. These behaviours can be identified by employees/colleagues. These behaviours should reflect choices that employees/colleagues perceive as 'choice to will the highest good' within an organizational context in the relationship with the leader. The identified behaviours are the actions of love that Fromm said could be chosen and become an art.

Consideration, Empathy, and Love

Prior to Miller's (2005) research, love had not been examined in the leadership research literature. A number of other psychological dimensions, closely related to love, have received some attention. The conceptual differences between consideration, empathy, and love are briefly reviewed here.

Consideration has been identified as an important aspect of leadership for decades (Stogdill and Coons, 1957). The concept of love as 'choice(s) to will the highest good', and empathy are different from consideration, although there will be some overlap of meaning. The dimensions of consideration, empathy, and love may all come out of the underlying desire to esteem others, but the behaviours that are evidenced, and the cognitive approach that is taken towards employees/colleagues, has significant differences and involves different abilities.

Empathy is different from consideration. Consideration is being considerate towards another individual with aspects of kindness. Recent research described consideration as among leader behaviours that are, 'friendly, supportive, and concerned' (Kellett et al., 2002: 527). Empathy is defined as, 'the ability to comprehend another's feelings and to re-experience them oneself' (Kellett et al., 2002, citing Salovey and Mayer, 1990: 194). Kellett et al. (2002) make the point that a leader can have consideration without empathy, because empathy involves a component of understanding the employee/colleague, and consideration does not necessarily have this dimension of understanding.

Love as 'choice(s) to will the highest good' is different from consideration. The leader who is friendly, supportive, and concerned is displaying a range of emotions and behaviours that express being basically considerate. The actions of the leader who is considerate, and how these actions impact the employee/colleague, may not be for the ultimate or highest benefit of the employee/colleague; more importantly from a definition and construct perspective, there is no indication that the leader is prepared to make decisions on the basis of consideration.

Having an emotional orientation does not necessarily mean that actions will result from this emotional orientation. It is possible to have a sympathetic disposition towards employees/colleagues and not be acting in their interest. Both consideration and love value employees/colleagues, but how these orientations directly affect the employee/colleague are different conceptually. 'Choice(s) to will the highest good' has implications of cognitive (behaviour) choices that directly benefit the employee/colleague whereas consideration has implications of emotional orientation towards the employee/colleague.

Both empathy and love go beyond consideration, so consideration is a dimension of both of these. The empathetic individual will show friendliness, support and concern, as will the individual who seeks to love as 'choice(s) to will the highest good'. The additional factors, of having the emotional ability to understand in empathy, and to make choices in the construct of love, go beyond being considerate.

The psychologist Lewin, in seeking to understand value systems, points out that the decision to act must be part of the process (beyond motivation) if the underlying dimension or value is to actualize (Lewin [1948], 2000). It is not enough simply to be motivated. The aspect of empathy or genuine understanding of the employee/colleague does not necessarily mean that the empathetic leader will use her/his empathy to benefit the employee/colleague. It is also possible to use empathy to manipulate, as evidenced in some sales situations and abundantly in television advertising. Leadership researcher, Ciulla, makes the point that empathy must be a necessary part of a successful organization, not an optional extra; but she includes the caveat that empathy has to be applied in a way that is non-manipulative and ultimately beneficial (Ciulla, 1998).

It is possible that appropriate use of empathy is a part of the process of love as 'choice(s) to will the highest good'. It would be logical for empathy to go hand in hand with love. It would seem probable that the leader who is making a cognitive choice to love is able to experience or develop empathy to some degree. In making determinations for another concerning what might be in the other's best interest, empathy plays a part in being able to understand what the other individual might desire as their highest good.

Empathy understands the employee/colleague, while love seeks to understand. Researchers suggest that empathy involves both, 'personal involvement and imagination' (Kellett et al., 2002: 526). Seeking the highest good for another requires some level of personal involvement and imagination to be able to determine what the highest good might be. It is possible that in making a choice to love, empathy is developed or is utilized.

With this line of reasoning, a possible definition of love in an organizational context between leader and employee/colleague can be 'empathy with action'.

Mutuality and Power Sharing as Influence Processes

Boulding's theory of love as power can help identify the underlying dimension of love used by transforming leaders, by examining the specific influence processes leaders use towards employees/colleagues. The definition Burns gives of transforming leadership fit the descriptors of Boulding's non-abusive and integrative power.

The use of power for the transforming leader is not reverence for the leader, but as will be identified further in this section, a space is held open for the employee/colleague to form a personal identity within the organization in a non-abusive manner. In Burns's articulation of transformational leadership, the value base within the power base has a positive impact on individuals and community (Burns, 1978). The specific behaviours or outcomes are elevation of the employee/colleague and mutual stimulation. All of these points identify Burns's definition as a theoretical fit with Boulding's descriptors of a power base of love for the leader.

The psychological benefits described in Burns's definition of transforming leaders find concordance with Boulding's (1989) theory of love as integrating power. There are clear psychological benefits to the employee/colleague in Burns's definition, which are not based on inappropriate paternalistic or hierarchical control, because the result of the relationship is mutual stimulation and mutual elevation. Examination of Boulding's theory indicates that mutual stimulation and elevation are evidence of a dimension of love as power underlying the transforming leader's behaviour.

Boulding's Theory of Love

Boulding identified specific types of power that are used by leaders within society, and identifies love as a type of power that is used by leaders. He defines power as, 'in the human sense, power is a concept without meaning in the absence of human valuations and human decision … its widest meaning is that of a potential for change' (Boulding, 1989: 15). It is evident that power cannot exist in a vacuum, so power always has a value base. Leadership always has an attendant power base. Boulding brought the two concepts together, identifying value bases for power in leadership.

Boulding's concept of love (as a form of power in a leader within an organization) has a number of distinctive expressions. Boulding points out that love is the only form of power that is not abusive (Boulding, 1989). A leader who operates out of a power base of love avoids the abusive elements that so often pervade power, and this has to do with the fact that using love as a power base is integrative power.

Boulding states, 'the most fundamental form of integrative power is the power of love' (Boulding, 1989: 110), and suggests, 'integrative power as the ultimate power' (Boulding, 1989: 109). Boulding describes integrative power in a number of different ways in seeking to conceptualize how integration functions within an organization. Boulding defines power as the, 'potential for change' (Boulding, 1989: 15). Boulding identifies the structure of integrating power as a 'complex network of communication and learning' (Boulding, 1989: 117), which is a method of enabling change to occur. He also states that integrative power is the enabling force within productive power (what is being produced) in organizations.

Boulding, referring to the structure of integrative power, stated that, 'the extent and the power of this network depends a great deal on the development of what might be called a "learning identity" and a culture that puts a high value on learning' (Boulding, 1989: 118). He suggests that a reciprocal dynamic is an important aspect of integrative power; that the exchange must come in both directions: leaders and others. The high value placed on learning enables stimulation of creativity, ideas, and implementation of vision from both leaders and employees/colleagues. Importantly, this process provides an environment where there can be mutuality between leaders and employees/colleagues within organizations.

Boulding's concept of love is tangible, not emotive, although undoubtedly there will always be an emotive element associated with love. Boulding is describing love as action in identifying that love is not abusive, and that love as a power base integrates. He states that this integration is the key to success within organizations because it enables the individual to have a 'personal identity' within the organization (Boulding, 1989: 61). He does not identify the leader as the one with whom the individual must have a personal identity. Integration is the space that is held open for the individual to form their own identity within the organization, in whatever shape or form is important to them.

Mutuality and Power Sharing

The transforming leader empowers, but Burns's definition also alludes to a mutual stimulation that elevates both employee/colleague and the leader. The aspect of mutual stimulation can be seen as the mutuality of the leader and employee/colleague relationship. Burns prefers the term 'transforming' to the term 'transformational' in describing the leader because 'transforming' captures this dimension of mutual interaction, with the implication of both leader and employee/colleague simultaneously being transformed (Bailey,

2001). The dimension of mutuality is an important aspect of transformational leadership.

Mutuality is also addressed in Boulding's thinking on power. As stated previously, Boulding defines power as the 'potential for change' (Boulding, 1989: 15), and the possibility of change must be present for mutuality in the leader and employee/colleague dyad. Mutuality takes place within the structure of integrating power as a 'complex network of communication and learning' (Boulding, 1989: 117), with the aforementioned learning identity within the organization being consequent. This structuring of a learning identity creates a reciprocal dynamic between the leader and others; enabling the mutuality referred to in Burns's definition. Boulding hypothesises that it might be possible to learn to have integrative power. According to Burns transformational leadership is not an innate process but can be learned (Bailey, 2001).

A possible way to illustrate the transformational leader's approach inclusive of the mutuality of exchange in the leader and employee/colleague relationship is given in figure 9.1. The figure identifies the transformational leader's focus, process, and goals, in relationship to mutuality of exchange.

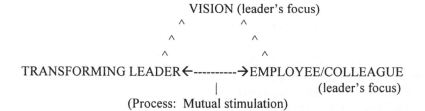

VISION (leader's focus)

TRANSFORMING LEADER←----------→EMPLOYEE/COLLEAGUE
                    | (leader's focus)
        (Process: Mutual stimulation)

Figure 9.1: Transformational leader

There are two foci for the transforming leader, the employee/colleague and the vision. These are distinct and somewhat complementary foci. But the distinctive here is seminal because the vision is to develop the employee/colleague not only as a means to an end (getting the vision accomplished), but also as an end in itself. The leader is not doing this development of the employee/colleague out of a sense of expediency, but because it is part of his/her vision.

The process of the leader points to an understanding of the self-schemas of the leader. The openness, which the transforming leader extends to the employee/colleague, which encourages and fosters mutual stimulation, can only happen because of the leader's self-schema. Self-aggrandisement can not come into the picture here because self-aggrandisement prohibits the type of free exchange that allows mutual stimulation to occur. In order to have an environment that fosters mutual stimulation, the power differential cannot be the focus of the relationship. Boulding (1989) was aware of this, and undoubtedly this is one of the reasons he posited that integrative power and integrative leadership has its basis in love.

Because love can be viewed from a base of power perspective, love can be seen as integrative; consequently fostering transformation as an aspect of a learning environment in the relationship between leader and employee/colleague. This led to a discussion of the implications of how a learning environment is created with deliberation by the transforming leader as a consequence of having a self-schema that includes love as one of its underlying dimensions. This section showed a possible way to illustrate the mutuality of exchange in the dyad relationship between the transforming leader and others. There is an adequate theoretical basis within the fields of psychology and leadership theory for research to be undertaken in examining love as a basis of power or as 'empathy with action' in an organizational context.

TRANSFORMING LEADERS AS MORAL LEADERS

Transforming Leadership as Moral Leadership

There is ongoing discussion involving the legitimacy of moral leadership as an aspect of transforming leadership theory; specifically in relationship to a stream of leadership theorists who would define transforming leadership as leadership that enables the employee/colleague to work sacrificially for the organization. These theorists identify transformational leaders as those who, among other things, get the employee/colleague to be sacrificial on behalf of the organization, and to put the needs of the organization above the employee/colleague's own needs (Bass, 1985; Bass, 1995; Bass, 1996; Bass et al., 1997; Bass, 1998; Pielstick, 1998).

The ethical implications of this perspective, that employee/colleagues need to evidence being 'sacrificial' and that true transformational leaders are focused on ensuring that employee/colleagues are 'sacrificial' in the workplace, are a concern. The concern is potential abuse of the employee/colleague within the organization. With this perspective, the organization is elevated, as are the needs within the organization, and the dynamics of empowering behaviours towards the employee/colleague to actualize the organization's goals are certainly in evidence. Leadership behaviours are examined in the light of the profession or business to determine what works, what is effective, and what promotes positive change for the organization. This is legitimate and even vital. The organization needs to prosper and the organization prospering is an aspect of transformation, but this describes transformation for the organization (Colvin, 1999), not necessarily for the employee/colleague. Importantly the moral issues of concern are when these leadership behaviours are inclusive of forcing the employee/colleague to be sacrificial to self in order to evidence commitment to the organization.

Ciulla (1998) raises the issue of forced empowerment of employee/colleagues as a legitimate concern, especially examined from the power differential in the work environment. When a worker knows s/he must evidence a certain degree of sacrifice to get into the good books of the leader, then this is not necessarily indicating a heartfelt buy-in to the organization. It might indicate a keen instinct to survive in that organization. Ultimately, at what price to worker satisfaction and benefit should the organization profit? If employees/colleagues have to work in order to live, and organizations are expecting their employees/colleagues to buy into the values and mission of the organization on a heart-felt level; then how does the organization go about determining the sincerity of the employee/colleague in relation to the buy in of values and mission; and how ethical is it to expect a heart felt buy in for a job someone needs in order to live? Argyle's (1992) research indicates that leisure is more important to many people than work. Can the fact that the workers are being sacrificial to an organization really be an indicator of transforming leadership within that organization?

Bass's conceptualizing of the leader impacting the employee/colleague to be sacrificial is a subject of debate in the literature. Bass observed that Burns does state that transforming leaders can have the effect of enabling employees/colleagues to extend themselves beyond their self-interest for the good of the group. For Burns's thinking to be a conceptual parallel to Bass's thinking, there would need to be reciprocity throughout all areas of the organization with everyone within the organization being called to this level of sacrifice. This would involve the CEO, the entire leadership within the organization, the stakeholders involved, the Board, and so on.

Bass has responded to critics by stating, 'to be truly transformational, leadership must be grounded in moral foundations', and anyone who is not is a 'pseudotransformational' leader (Bass and Steidlmeier, 1999: 181). He stresses that the identifiers of what constitutes transforming leaders are to have authentic moral foundations, a concern for the common good beyond the organization into society and community, and development of employees/colleagues into leaders. Bass and Steidlmeier (1999) have suggested that the indicator of a real transformational leader is the presence of a strong moral basis to leadership, and that without aspects of integrity, honesty, and a strong positive moral code, the leadership would be described as pseudo-transformational. But the question remains; are personal qualities sufficient to ensure that the leader is in fact a transformational leader?

Burns does emphasize the moral nature of transformational leadership, identifying the fact that understanding this paradigm requires a broad examination of the leader's life that includes morality (Burns 1978; Bailey, 2001). Theoretically, moral leadership is part of Burns's descriptor of transforming leaders. Alimo-Metcalfe and Alban-Metcalfe suggest that transformational leadership has some conceptual parity with the servant-leadership model (Greenleaf, 1977), with the attendant descriptor of desiring to serve as the motivation for being a leader (Alimo-Metcalfe and Alban-Metcalfe, 2001).

Identifying Transforming Leaders

To add to the confusion in understanding transforming leadership theory, authors have sometimes labelled leaders as 'transformational leaders' because those leaders had significant success in making their companies more profitable. Success is not the ultimate criterion that defines a leader as transformational. More to the point, success leaves the larger moral frame unaddressed.

Examples of labelling 'successful' leaders as transformational leaders abound. In Ticky and Devanna's (1986) chronicling of CEOs who have been successful in transforming their organizations. Those leaders were described as transformational leaders who did what it took to make the organization profitable; so the focus was on increased financial profitability, often meaning that the company was reduced in size, with large numbers of employees out of work. It seems that the ability to do what it took was the component of transformational leadership in this analysis. This describes success and there is no question that the organization was transformed. Tichy and Devanna (1986) do cite Burns's (1978) descriptor of the outcome of transformational leaders in the life of employee/colleagues, but do not evaluate transforming leaders on this basis.

Part of the answer to the question of what forms the broader criteria in identification of transforming leaders might lie in distinguishing between evaluating end goals and evaluating process. The focus of many organizations is evaluation of end goals, not necessarily the method of obtaining those goals. Similarly, the identification of transforming leaders can be focused more on end goals than process, and possibly there is a perception that the process itself is not an end goal. Evaluation of a leader who is potentially transforming must involve examining end goals and the ability to lead, as well as process and how those end goals were achieved. Evaluation of the process needs to be brought into the analysis as a legitimate end goal in itself. Without evaluating process, it is impossible to identify transforming leaders.

'Empathy with Action' and Moral Leadership

Moral leadership is often equated with perceptions of the transforming leader's personally held values or qualities, with the assumption that those personally held qualities will be adequate to ensure the leader is a moral leader. The personal qualities of the leader that are perceived and possibly valued by others include but are not limited to qualities such as trust, loyalty, honesty, and confidence. However, personal qualities are only one aspect of moral leadership.

'Empathy with action' is yet one other aspect of moral leadership. Love as 'empathy with action' is not completely divorced from individuals' perceptions of their leader's personal qualities. However, evaluating a leader's personal qualities is distinct from evaluating his/her expressions of 'empathy with action'. The evaluation of love as 'empathy with action' is identification of a specific leadership process. Action is consequent to the empathy. This is different from evaluating the leader's innate or chosen personal qualities. Personal qualities and 'empathy with actions' are equally valuable aspects of moral leadership, and are not mutually exclusive.

'Empathy with action' involves identifying the desired outcomes of the employees/colleagues within the organization of very specific leader behaviour(s). The employees/colleagues would be in a good position to assess the leader's actions in the area of 'empathy with action' because this represents the narrow focus of a dyad relationship. Employees/colleagues could evaluate how well the leader is doing in exercising 'empathy with action'.

Evaluating the leader's personal qualities is complex because the assessment by its very nature utilizes a more emotive process, some of which is disconnected from specific actions that can be assessed cleanly or clearly. Personal qualities are often simply felt or sensed by others. Each person uses their own individual sense-making in forming the determination of which personal qualities their leader may or may not have.

The choices transforming leaders make within their organization may or may not be reflective of their perceived personal qualities. It is possible for a leader to be perceived as having high ratings in personal qualities that reflect what one would consider a strong moral component, and yet have ultimate loyalty in decision-making to the organization, instead of seeking to strike a balance that indicates equity for both organization and employees. The leader's personal qualities or values might not be sufficient in ensuring abuse by the leader does not occur in some situations where the leader's personally held values are in conflict with broader moral values.

> Explicitly stated, the theory of authentic transformational leadership misses the fact that leaders sometimes behave immorally precisely because they are blinded by these values. Virtuous though these leaders may be, their distinctive understandings of the collective good and of the morality of the processes necessary to achieve it must be evaluated against generally applicable moral requirements. For these requirements do not originate with them as individual leaders but, rather, as part of a much larger social and moral framework that binds the behavior of all actors. Burns (1978: 75) is correct, then, that '[a] test of adherence to values is the willingness to apply principles or standards to oneself as well as to others'. However, the more critical test may be one of adherence to morality. Leaders must be willing to sacrifice their other-regarding values when generally applicable moral requirements make legitimate demands that they do so. (Price, 2002: 79)

Can the leader abuse the employee's/colleague's trust by adhering to personal values not described in the sum of the personal qualities valued within a work context? Is the leader who is faithful, honest, trustworthy and the like, blinded to the larger moral picture, because of a preoccupation to make the organization successful no matter what the cost to individuals or the larger community outside of the organization? Is the leader's loyalty first and foremost to the organization and corporation, above the individual, or the other way around? These are some of the larger ethical questions, which need to be asked in order to identify if the transforming leader is potentially abusing the trust of the employee/colleague. The issue of the ethics of the transforming leader are still being debated, and much of the core of the discussion involves the personally held values of the leader having congruence with morality (Ciulla, 1998; Price, 2002).

CONCLUDING REMARKS

Theory suggests that the power base of love plays a key role in transformation in organizations. Love as 'empathy with action' can be chosen with deliberation and results in choices that affect transformation within organizations. Because love can be viewed from a base of power perspective, love can be seen as integrative. The integration aspect of love results in fostering transformation as an aspect of a deliberately cultivated learning environment in the relationship between leader and employee/colleague. Both leaders and employees/colleagues take part in the transformational process.

The metaphysical and emotive aspects of love have not been addressed. Even so, application of the cognitive aspects of love have substantive ramifications for relationships within organization, as well as in the organization as a whole. There is a dearth of research on this topic.

There is a relationship between a leader's personal qualities and the broader question of morality. Some personal qualities can be clearly identified because they are observable in the life of the leader; however how these values impact the decision-making of the leader has yet to be satisfactorily determined. In identifying the moral foundations of any management or leadership theory, the process to attain the end goal is what constitutes the moral foundation as well as the theory. So it is essential that the process be identified and evaluated. Process is a significant feature of transformational leadership, and the leader's process in obtaining the end goals needs to be evaluated. Ultimately, the decisions the leader makes will themselves blaze a trail over time, and be an indicator if the transforming leader's perceived personal qualities have concordance with morality.

NOTES

1. 'The term cognition is used in a variety of different ways in the literature (e.g. Rummelhart and Ortony, 1977; Bartlett, 1932; Schank and Abelson, 1977). Here, "cognition" is used to refer to the mental models, or belief systems, that people use to interpret, frame, simplify, and make sense of otherwise complex problems. These mental models are referred to, variously, as cognitive maps (Tolman, 1948), scripts (Schank and Abelson, 1977), schema (Bartlett, 1932), and frames of reference (Minsky, 1975). They are built from past experiences and comprise internally represented concepts and relationships among concepts that an individual can then use to interpret new events.' (Fleck et al. 2005).
2. Maslow, a humanistic psychologist, had a different perspective on actualizing. He believed that lower needs had to be satisfied before higher needs were attended to. The important concept here is that all of the previous needs have had to have been met prior to entering the final stage of self-actualizing. The process of satisfying lower needs and moving on to satisfying higher needs is called 'Maslow's hierarchy of needs'. The five steps are; 'Physiological needs (hunger, thirst, sex), Safety (security, order, stability), Belongingness and love, Esteem (including self-respect and feelings of success), Self-actualisation' (Turner and Helms, 1995: 69).

REFERENCES

Alimo-Metcalfe, B., Alban-Metcalfe, R. J. (2001a). 'The development of a new Transformational Leadership Questionnaire', *Journal of Occupational and Organizational Psychology*, **74** (1), 1–26.

Allport, G. W. (1983), *Becoming: Basic considerations for a psychology of personality*, Chelsea, MI: BookCrafters Inc.

Argyris, C. (1993), *Knowledge for Action: A Guide to Overcoming Barriers to Organizational Change*, San Francisco, CA: Jossey-Bass.

Bailey, J. (2001), 'Leadership lessons from Mount Rushmore: An interview with James McGregor Burns', *Leadership Quarterly*, **12** (1), 113–128.

Bass, B. M. (1985), *Leadership and Performance Beyond Expectations*, New York: The Free Press.

Bass, B. M. (1995), 'Theory of transformational leadership redux', *The Leadership Quarterly*, **6** (4), 464–478.

Bass, B. M. (1996), *A new paradigm of leadership: An inquiry into transformational leadership*, Alexandria: VA: U.S. Army Research Institute for the Behavioral and Social Sciences.

Bass, B. M. (1998), *Transformational Leadership: Industry, Military, and Educational Impact*, Mahwah, NJ: Lawrence Erlbaum.

Bass, B. M., Avolio, Jung, B. (1997), *Full range Leadership Development: Manual for the Multifactor Leadership Questionnaire*, Redwood City, CA: Mind Garden.

Bass, B. M., Steidlmeier, P. (1999), Ethics, character, and authentic transformational leadership behavior. *Leadership Quarterly*, **10** (2), 181–218.

Boulding, K. E. (1998), *Three Faces of Power*, Newbury Park, CA: Sage Publications.

Burns, J. M. (1978), *Leadership*, London, UK: Harper Torchbooks.

Ciulla, J. B. (ed.) (1998), *Ethics: The Heart of Leadership*, Westport, CT: Praeger.

Ciulla, J. B. (2000), *The Working Life: The Promise and Betray of Modern Work*, New York: Three Rivers.

Colvin, R. E. (1999), 'Transformational leadership: a prescription for contemporary organizations', Doctoral Dissertation, Virginia Commonwealth University: USA.

Fleck, J., Scarbrough, H., Swann, J. (2005), 'Trainer notes: Cognitive mapping techniques', http:// omni.bus.ed.ac.uk/ opsman/ oakland/ contents. htm

Frankl, V. (1984), *Man's Search For Meaning*, revised edition, New York: Washington State Press.

Fromm, E. (1963), *The Art of Loving*, New York: Bantam.

Greenleaf, R. K. (1977), *Servant Leadership: A Journey into the Nature of Legitimate Power and Greatness*, New York: Paulist Press.

Kellett, J. B., Humphrey, R. H., Sleeth, R. G. (2002), 'Empathy and complex task performance: Two routes to leadership', *The Leadership Quarterly*, **13** (5), 534–544.

Lewin, K. ([1948] 2000a), *Field theory in social science: Selected theoretical papers* (2nd edn), Washington, DC: American Psychological Association.

Lewin, K. ([1948] 2000b), Resolving social conflicts: Selected papers on group dynamics (2nd edn), Washington: DC: American Psychological Association.

Miller M. (2005), 'The relationship between transformational leadership and love as a "choice will the highest good" using the transformational leadership questionnaire', Unpublished Dissertation, British Library, UK.

Pielstick, D. C. (1998), 'The transforming leader: A meta-ethnographic analysis', Retrieved 9/4, 2002, from http://www.findarticles.com

Price, T. L. (2002), 'The ethics of authentic transformational leadership', *Leadership Quarterly*, **14** (1), 67–81.

Stogdill, R. M., Coons, A. E. (ed.) (1957), *Leadership Behavior: Its Description and Measurement* (Vol.88), Columbus Ohio: The Bureau of Business Research.

Strange, J. M., Mumford, M. D. (2002) ,The origins of vision: Charismatic versus ideological leadership', *Leadership Quarterly*, **13** (4), 343–377.

Ticky, N. M., Devanna, M. A. (1986), *The Transformational Leader*, New York: John Wiley & Sons.

10. An Ethical Encounter with the Other: Language Introducing the New into Thought

Sara Louise Muhr

INTRODUCTION

In knowledge management as well as the entire field of organization studies, ethical issues have mainly been discussed following the line of three dominant ethical views: utility ethics, deontological ethics and virtue ethics (for reviews see for example Jones et al., 2005; Parker, 1998). Utilitarism was founded by the British philosopher John Stuart Mill. Actions in the utilitaristic view are good when they overall reduce pain and enhance pleasure; it thereby judges only the overall consequences of actions. Utilitarianism is undoubtedly easy to implement, however it holds little respect for the individual human being as it promotes the greatest good for the greatest amount of people. Deontological ethics is mainly related to the philosophy of Immanuel Kant. Kant argued that we all have to live by an absolute duty to support any person as a free and rational being. This absolute duty he called the categorical imperative and it consisted primarily of the maxims that you should always treat any other person not simply as a mean, but always as an end in itself, and you should only act in a way that you would want to become universal law. Deontological ethics in this sense judges the intentions of actions. Virtue ethics goes all the way back to the ancient Greek philosopher Aristotle, and is focused on defining virtuous characters. In this sense, the good character is defined according to the virtues of a given society.

On these views business ethics has mainly been focused on discussing whether managerial decisions have ethical consequences or intentions and whether managers can or should hold ethical virtues. Business ethics has thereby taken the form of a guideline, which shows us how to behave in an ethical manner. It ensures that if we know the right rules, we will be able to make the right moral decisions (Jones et al., 2005). Following this argument, ethics is a form of mathematical and codified knowledge in which any sign of independent thought is removed, or as du Gay (2000) more positively in favour of bureaucratic ethos said, where the agent can become impartial or distanced from the object of morality. In this chapter I will take a different perspective and investigate what it means to talk about an ethical foundation of management knowledge. In doing this I will argue that rules and guidelines have nothing to with ethics. In fact, they create moral distance (Bauman, 1993). Instead, I will draw attention to what I believe ethics is basically about: the encounter with other people. In doing this, I follow the French philosopher Emmanuel Levinas (1906–1995) and argue that ethics is beyond consequences, intentions and virtues. Ethics happens in the encounter with other people; in the encounter with the Other. Seeing another person as Other means acknowledging that person's fundamental difference and letting that person interrupt one's own world. Ethics therefore is a question of openness to interruption, and this very interruption puts 'me' into question. The encounter with the Other, therefore, holds the possibility of transforming the knower, bring novelty into thought and fostering creativity.

An ethical encounter with the Other is an encounter where responsibility – response-ability – for the Other is at centre-stage. Only through the responsible response to this Other, and with respect for the Other's otherness, can managers hope to foster an environment where differences are reflected and respected, and where creativity thereby finds space to unfold. The main focus of this chapter will therefore be on discussing the role language plays when I as a self am facing the Other. To achieve this, some fundamental notions on the philosophy of Emmanuel Levinas are essential. I will, therefore, begin the chapter with a clarification of the basic encounter with the Other – the relationship between self and the Other. This relationship leads to the argument that Levinas's ethical responsibility for the Other is prior to any human relationship and Levinas's notions on ethics as first philosophy is explained. On this basis, I proceed to the discussion of the role language plays in this ethical relation. Next, Levinasian ethics will be brought back into the creativity discussion. The main argument here is that the act of ethical saying is always intertwined in the already said, which makes the self respond to the call of the Other, who thereby interrupts the stable knowledge of the self and brings novelty into thought. Letting the Other interrupt oneself thereby fosters a different level of creativity. That is, creativity is not viewed simply as the driver of product innovation. Creativity is instead taken beyond the logic of production and introduced as the ethical interruption that transforms knowledge, transforms the knower and creates ever new identities and relations.

I will therefore not discuss whether managers live up to certain rules or guidelines, whether their actions had 'pleasurable' consequences, whether managers had 'good' intentions or whether they as persons hold ethical virtues. Instead, I will suggest a move away from the traditional universalistic perspectives on ethics and introduce the Levinasian alternative. On this view, I will propose that a personal ethical responsibility for the Other is not only the foundation for justice, it also fosters creativity. And not just any creativity: but a different form of creativity, a creativity beyond product innovation and the management of capabilities.

INTRODUCING THE CONCEPTS: SELF AND THE OTHER

The concept of the Other is central to Levinasian ethics, along with its relation to the self. Following Levinas, the self cannot survive by itself alone and cannot find meaning within an ontology of sameness. Still, there is a strong tendency within both philosophy and organization theory to attain an egocentric attitude and to think of other individuals either as different versions of oneself, or as alien objects to be manipulated. According to Levinas (1961), the Other is often understood as separate from the same or the self, however, ultimately and ideally united with it. That is, even though the self traditionally has been seen as unique, the goal has been to perform a normalizing function in order to approach a situation of sameness where people are alike. Thus, otherness or alterity has traditionally appeared as a temporary interruption, which must be attempted to eliminate as it is reduced to sameness. According to Levinas, however, these egocentric views do no justice to our original experience of the Other, since this means reducing the Other to something the Other is not – the Same. 'The identification of the same is not the void of a tautology nor a dialectical opposition to the Other, but the concreteness of egoism' (Levinas, 1961: 38). Instead of the egoism of viewing the Other as the same, the Other exists entirely beyond the understanding of the self, and ought to be perceived – and appreciated – in all its peculiarity, as it were. The Other is situated absolutely outside the self's intellectual capacity. It is not simply a mirror image of oneself.

> The Other is in no way another myself, participating with me in a common existence. The relationship with the Other is not an idyllic and harmonious relationship of communion, or a sympathy through which we put ourselves in the Other's place; we recognize the Other as resembling us, but exterior to us; the relationship with the Other is a relationship with a mystery. (Levinas, 1987: 75)

Thus, my relationship with the Other is that of co-presence. That is, I am aware that there is another person coexisting with me and of similar appearance, however we are not equal, and I will never comprehend this person completely. As I am never able to comprehend the Other completely, the Other cannot, according to Davis (1996), be a mere object to be included in one of my categories, and given a place in my world. The Other is a stranger, and I can never be certain of what this strangeness contains. Therefore, instead of placing the Other within a sterile category, to be truly ethical, I should focus on the Other's otherness, and find a world basically different from my own. This ethical recognition and acknowledgement of another person's infinite difference is exactly what the concept 'the Other' implies; and this recognition is the very starting point of ethics. Therefore, the ethical encounter with the Other as radically other is essential for any relationship. Any social relation is necessarily ethical before anything else. As Levinas (1961) argues, ethics is first philosophy, ethics precedes ontology.

ETHICS AS FIRST PHILOSOPHY

Levinas (1961) explains the before of ethics with the point that ethics is a transcendence of being. Ethics does not come as a second layer; ethics has an independent and preliminary range. Thus, the ethical self is constituted through its ability to be *for* another, as opposed to being *with* another. It is not by the preposition 'with' that the original relationship with the Other should be illustrated. 'With' belongs to, and represents ontology, and ontology does not embrace ethics. 'With' means to be aside of, thus following Levinas, 'being with', ontologically separates beings. Ethics is beyond ontology. 'Being for' is therefore ethical, being for is before being.

Levinasian ethics thereby moves beyond that of utility, intentions and virtues. In an ethics as first philosophy, there is nothing to justify the responsibility of the self, and nothing to determine whether the self is responsible. That responsibility belongs alone to the self, and this 're-personalization' of ethics is what makes it moral. As a consequence, ethics has nothing to do with rules. Ethical propositions cannot be labelled either true or false, and reason alone cannot produce a solution to a moral problem. Thus, ethical phenomena are intrinsically non-rational. They are not regular, repetitive, monotonous or predictable, and are therefore excluded from governance by the rational application of an ethical code. Morality, therefore, does not exist on the basis of a certain set of ethical rules as believed in utilitarian ethics, deontological ethics and as well as virtue ethics. Instead, morality is personal and arises in the 'face to face' encounter with the Other. To be more precise, it is the interruption called upon me by the acknowledgement of the Other's difference. The first time Levinas mentions the word ethics in his first major work *Totality and Infinity* he argues that:

Critique does not reduce the Other to the same as does ontology, but calls into question the exercise of the same. A calling into question of the same – which cannot occur within the egoist spontaneity of the same – is brought about by the Other. We name this calling into question of my spontaneity by the presence of the Other ethics ... that is as the ethics that accomplishes the critical essence of knowledge. (Levinas, 1961: 43)

Ethics is therefore not a universal measure; it cannot be measured by particular pleasurable consequences, good intentions or a certain virtuous character. Instead, ethics is the interruption of my knowledge, my willingness to be changed by the Other's critique. Levinasian ethics does therefore not start with the Other, 'alterity is possible only starting from *me*' (Levinas, 1961: 40, original italics). Rather, ethics arises in the encounter with the Other. That is, ethics is only possible when I let myself be changed; when I am willing to exchange my own perspective for that of the Other. Ethics is not about defining rules for the Other, it is about letting the Other be other and different from me, and letting this difference interrupt my thoughts.

The above willingness of being for the Other introduces the concept of responsibility. Ethics as first philosophy does not start with the self, but starts with the relationship to the Other, with responsibility. Levinasian ethics is, therefore, not about closure, but about openness and infinity. Ethics cannot be solved procedurally (Jones et al., 2005). It arises in the self as a response to the Other's face, as an indication of the infinite distance between the self and the Other. Being moral means, according to Bauman (1993), that I take responsibility no matter who takes the same duty and responsibility as I do. To sacrifice myself is moral, but as Davis (1996) explains, to say that the Other has to sacrifice himself, would be to preach human sacrifice. The ability to see the infinity of the Other's otherness, and the willingness of sacrificing my own ego to welcome this difference, is responsibility for the Other. This responsibility is moral because only I can take it. In fact, because responsibility is not due to a matter of exchange of services or favours, it is never possible to standardize responsibility and make it universal. Derrida (1992: 34–70) makes a similar distinction between gift and economy. Giving a gift with no intentions of getting something in return is a moral act, or an act of 'pure friendship'. On the other hand, giving a gift with the expectation of getting something in return can never be a moral act, but will always be an economic one. As a result, the ethical encounter with the Other is a one-sided ethics, and because of its asymmetry it cannot be turned into a general set of rules (Davis, 1996). The self is moral only because of the unique morality in the self, not benchmarked to others' actions. The moral responsibility is before being since it has no goal and no origin – it arises in the proximity of the Other's face.

THE FACE OF THE OTHER CALLING ME TO RESPONSIBILITY

According to Levinas, morality arises in the encounter with the face of the Other. The face of the Other draws me to responsibility. Importantly, however, the face is more than appearance and vision for Levinas; it holds many more facets beyond the plastic form. 'The face of the Other at each moment destroys and overflows the plastic image it leaves me, the idea existing to my own measure and to the measure of its *ideatum* – the adequate idea. It does not manifest itself by these qualities, but καθ'αύτό [is in itself]. It *expresses itself*' (Levinas, 1961: 51, original italics). The Levinasian face is therefore, and here I follow Kaulingfreks and ten Bos (2005), not a thing that can be expressed and comprehended in a stable system of knowledge. In recognizing that the Other is more than the plastic appearance, I acknowledge the Other's difference. The face's expression is a calling to be for the Other, to caress, to live with the Other, to be put into question by the Other. The face of the Other draws me to be interlocutor, and the Other to be my interlocutor. Interlocutor is in this relation a very essential concept as it means that the Other is not just an object of my monologue, the Other is a partner in the conversation, the Other takes part.

In respecting the Other's otherness, the face is therefore exposed simultaneously with a refusal to be contained. In this sense, even though it is exposed as a face, it can never be comprehended, 'neither seen nor touched' (Levinas, 1961: 194). In fact, the face enters the world of the self from an absolutely foreign sphere – from the absolutely absent: 'The Other remains infinitely transcendent, infinitely foreign, his face in which his epiphany is produced and which appeals to me breaks with the world that can be common to us, whose virtualities are inscribed in our nature and developed by our existence' (Levinas, 1961: 194). Here Levinas again emphasizes that the encounter with the Other moves me and changes me. The ethical encounter is not about changing the Other, but it breaks with my common sense, and makes me reflect over my world. The Other's otherness disturbs and interrupts my world; makes me open my eyes to see beyond the plastic face. I see the Other's otherness and not only the visible differences. The face of the Other is central, because when the Other is presented as a face, I cannot stay blind to the appeal, or forget it: the Other's face initiates my response-ability, demands my response. The 'stable' consciousness of the self is in this way challenged by the face of the Other. The face challenges me to go beyond the limits of myself and into the world of the Other. This is, according to Levinas (2003), a desire for the infinity of the Other, to the novelty the Other might bring into my world. 'It consists paradoxically, in thinking more than is thought while keeping it immeasurable with regard to thought, and entering into relation with the ungraspable while maintaining its status as ungraspable' (Levinas, 2003: 33). The desire for knowing more about the ungraspable world of the Other is thus initiated in the proximity of the face-to-face encounter.

The question that remains, then, is how this ethical relationship with the Other is accomplished. How can I coexist with the Other and still leave the Other's otherness intact? How can the self and the Other as a team 'benefit' from each other's otherness without destroying their uniqueness and reducing each other to the same? According to Levinas (especially 1974), there is only one way – and that is by language. The questioning glance of the Other seeks a meaningful response – for the self to be response-able. I can respond with a simple word, and proceed with indifference, concentrating on my own task, passing the Other by. But if an ethical relation is to be achieved, a real response, a responsible answer must be given. 'The calling into question of the I, coextensive with the manifestations of the Other in the face, we call language' (Levinas, 1961: 171). This means that I must be ready to 'put my world into words' (Wild, 1961: 14), and to expose myself and offer my vulnerability to the Other. The face presents itself in its nakedness (Levinas, 2003), stripped of all plastic form, and it is therefore an exposure of the vulnerability of the self. It is a window to one's otherness, and in this exposure there is a calling for responsibility, a calling for response.

LANGUAGE: AN ETHICAL RESPONSE

According to Levinas, language is not reducible to a system of signs doubling up beings and relations. The sign is not the shortcut of a pre-existent real presence, and it is not an exact representation of the past. Rather, language already bears sensible life – temporalization and being's essence. In fact, language constructs us as human beings. Levinas is not denying that a great part of our speaking is systematic and bound by logic of some kind. But prior to these systems we find the self, and its ethical choice to respond to the Other and to expose its world by speaking to the Other. In other words, Levinas again places ethics as first philosophy – before being. We do not become social by first being systematic, rather we become systematic by first freely making a choice for morality and responsibility. Speaking becomes serious only when the self pays attention to the Other, recognizes the strange world the Other offers, and responds to the Other. By contrast, speaking as an illuminating monologue would not qualify as ethical. Communication should not be a one-sided monologue. The Other should never become an object that is interpreted and illuminated by my superior knowledge. If we are both response-able (Eskin, 2000) – and not illuminating – we can enter an ethical communicative relationship of giving, which can evolve and contribute to both of us.

Following Levinas (1961), I as a self can either decide to remain within myself, assimilating the Other and try to make use of him, or I may take the risk of going out of my way and try to speak and to give to him. Levinas (2003) extends this argument as he points out that most analyses of language in contemporary philosophy emphasize the embodied being that expresses itself as a superior person in an attempt to assimilate or illuminate the Other. Levinas does not neglect the speaking self, but asks whether the dimension of the Other has not been forgotten? Following this line of thought, the Other is not only collaborator and recipient of our expression, but he is interlocutor – 'the one to whom expression expresses' (Levinas, 2003: 30). This relation to the Other as interlocutor originally transpires as discourse – it is essentially inquiring and vocative (Eskin, 2000). Ethical discourse, therefore, involves interlocutors, a plurality of others, whose originary purpose is not a mere mutual representation. Instead, it is a radical separation, the interlocutors' mutual strangeness, their exposure of otherness. The Other who faces me is, therefore, not included in the totality of being that is expressed. The Other arises behind all collection of being, as the one to whom I express what I express. Levinas agrees: signification for him is the infinite, and infinity does not present itself to a transcendental thought, but presents itself in the Other. When the Other faces me, he puts me in question and calls me to respond qua the infinity between us, he makes me desire infinity. 'That "something" we call signification arises in being with language because the essence of language is the relation with the Other' (Levinas, 1961: 207). That is, the face of the Other speaks to me, and the manifestation of the face is, therefore, the first discourse. There is always an expression of the face that precedes the said. Language and speaking is a way of coming from beyond one's appearance, beyond one's form; an opening of the otherwise than being – a window to the vulnerable self; to otherness. The expression of the Other's face, which originates in the unreachable otherness of the Other, puts the self into moral question (Cohen, 2003). The Other thereby interrupts the stability of the self and demands a moral obligation to respond. The ethical event of intersubjectivity is thus achieved via the Other's ability to interrupt the stability of the self, and making it open up.

For Levinas, meaning as expression follows a distinction, highlighted in one of his main works *Otherwise than Being or beyond Essence* (1974), between what is said, the content of discourse, and the more original and interhuman saying of them (Cohen, 2003), which is an ethical event exposed by the vulnerability of the response-able self. For Levinas (1974) the said is the written or spoken word, that is, the apparent communication, which proclaims this as that, whereas saying, although always intertwined in the said, always precedes the said. According to Eskin (2000), this inherent notion of transcendence informs the claim that saying underlies and conditions the said. However, just as any said depends on saying for its possibility, saying depends on the said for its witnessability. Language is in this way always constructed by both saying and said; the pre-ontological and a code intertwined. Before cultural expression, before the said, lies therefore the universal but deformalized humanism of the Other, the saying of the other as Other, as another human being (Cohen, 2003), who communicates to the Other for no other purpose other than that this Other's face demands a response. The before is therefore not an epistemological condition, but rather lies before it as the involuntarity of the pure humanism of responding to the Other's face. The face is here an unconditional ethical imperative. The saying is imposed in the immediate and imperative deformalization, breaking down common sense, and affected by the moral responsibility to the Other. It is said in the ethical obligation to respond to another human being. Saying, therefore, surfaces in the response-able self. In fact, it is a response to the appeal or call of the Other's face. Saying is a sign to the neighbour about a responsibility, which can never be contracted, and because of the lack of a contractual relationship, saying is unverifiable by the self.

My response to the Other is, therefore, an exposure of saying. Saying is communication as a condition for all communication, as exposure. To respond ethically to the Other is, therefore, to expose one's inner self. In saying, the self approaches the Other by expressing itself, in being expelled, that is as Levinas (1974) explains, 'no longer dwelling, not stomping any ground. Saying uncovers beyond nudity, what dissimulation there may be under the exposedness of a skin laid bare' (Levinas, 1974: 49). This is what Levinas (1974) calls the extreme passivity of responsibility:

> The passivity of the exposure responds to an assignation that identifies me as the unique one, not by reducing me to myself, but by stripping me of every identical quiddity, and thus of all form, all investiture, which would still slip into the assignation ... stripped to the core as in an inspiration of air, an ab-solution to the one ... a denuding beyond the skin. (Levinas, 1974: 49)

In this way, the self is 'stripped' from all identical being and is reduced to the ethical one, willing to change. Therefore, in an extreme passivity, the self is ethical in its response, without any intentions or any relations to who the self is. Exposedness is, therefore, the one in its uniqueness, stripped of all protective categories that could multiply it and make it belong to a defined group. Exposedness is the self, without prejudges towards the Other, and thus reduced to the one-in-responsibility. When the self appears in a 'denuding beyond the skin' it therefore means that it shows levels of itself, which are beyond the apparently different. And Levinas continues by clarifying that saying thereby uncovers the responding self 'in the sense that one discloses oneself by neglecting one's defences, leaving a shelter, exposing oneself to outrage, to insults and wounding' (Levinas, 1974: 49). That is, exposedness is not just to strip oneself of categorical characteristics. To expose oneself is also to take a chance, to run a risk of failure and embarrassment. In responding to the Other in a saying I reveal my inner self and offer my world to the Other. In this exposure I make myself vulnerable of critique and attacks. Saying is, therefore, following Corvellec (2005), self-denuding in the sense that I disclose myself in it. It stands for an effort and an orientation towards openness, proximity and responsibility. In saying, I approach the infinity of the Other. I make myself capable of receiving infinity from the Other. That is, in this sense I make myself ready to be changed by the Other.

INTRODUCING THE NEW INTO THOUGHT

Levinasian ethics might appropriately be called a responsive ethics rather than a communicative ethics (Waldenfels, 1995). This implies that the response primarily refers to something that has to be said or done, as opposed to something that has already been said and done. Ethics is therefore not about judging other people following a certain set of moral rules or codes. Instead, by emphasizing the response, Levinas opens up to a future; a future that is not reached by the self alone. The response creates a passage to the Other, or rather a passage for the Other to interrupt and thereby change me. In fact, saying constitutes the very uniqueness and novelty of human speaking. Saying is the non-thematizable ethical element of language that is capable of interrupting thought, and thereby enables the movement from the Same to the Other (Werhane, 1995) – the possibility of introducing the new into thought.

> Language is perhaps to be defined as the very power to break the continuity of being or of history. The knowledge that absorbs the Other is forthwith situated within the discourse I address to him. Speaking rather than 'letting be' solicits the Other. (Levinas, 1961: 195)

In other words, the exposure of myself in saying requests for Other's questioning, and through his questioning I open up to novelty, I open up for the Other to change my world. Jones et al. (2005) have pointed out that the learning experience from the encounter with the Other is central in the work of Levinas. The ethical relation with the Other involves an opening up of the subjectivity of the self, an exposure that allows the experience of the Other's otherness to change the self:

That which is outside us, and that which we acknowledge as strange, takes us beyond ourselves. Beyond our common sense. The Other transforms the one who sees the Other. (Jones, et al., 2005: 76)

To approach the Other in conversation is therefore to welcome his expression, in which at each instant he overflows from the idea a thought that would carry away from it. To approach the Other is therefore to *receive* from the Other beyond the capacity of the I, which means exactly: to have the idea of infinity. But it also means to be taught (Levinas, 1961: 51).

An ethical encounter with the Other is therefore an encounter I can learn from. It is an encounter that transforms me, changes my future. As Levinas says, the other is the future: 'The future is what is not grasped, what befalls us and lays hold of us. The Other is the future. The very relationship with the Other is the relationship with the future' (Levinas, 1987: 77). Affecting the future or creating novelty is therefore not the work of the self alone. Instead, it is the Other that opens up to a changed future. By not exposing myself, and by not opening up to what the Other might offer, I create a deadlock, where my thoughts stay rigid and the same. This would result in a situation where I try to assimilate or illuminate the Other instead of welcoming the Other, and assimilation or illumination does not bring novelty. However, if I encounter the Other in an ethical readiness to expose myself, and with a willingness to let the Other change me, I hold the chance of gaining novelty. The difference of the Other is what can change my future, and therefore the Other *is* the future. The Other and the future are similarly unknowable and ungraspable. The future, therefore, involves a relation with something that is radically Other. The very existence of a future bears otherness, and the alterity of the future then is discovered in the alterity of the other person. Rosenthal (2003) explains that it is because the responsibility for the Other is transcendent that it can change my existence. Transcendence fosters real newness, because the transcendence per definition cannot be pre-thought. The sense of the future that is opened by transcendence to the Other is another instant rather than continuity. A new instant is what allows for radical novelty, the opportunity to begin again, to let go of previous ideas constraining creativity and be inspired by the Other's presence.

For Levinas it becomes a matter of desire for what the Other's otherness can offer me:

Otherness challenges me, empties me of myself and keeps on emptying me by showing me ever new resources. I did not know I was so rich, but I don't have the right to keep anything anymore. Is the Desire for Others appetite or generosity? (Levinas, 2003: 30)

Here, Levinas not only tells us that otherness challenges the self, but also that it empties the self. However, it creates a dilemma for the self because, while opening up to the Other's world makes me richer in thought than ever, it is frustrating, since the thoughts are not mine to keep. In the ethical encounter with the Other, the Other keeps questioning my common sense and will not let me rest on my newly found knowledge. In the ethical encounter with the Other, knowledge is constantly transformed, and it is this transformation I in this chapter call creativity.

CREATIVITY AS THE TRANSFORMATION OF THE KNOWER

Sørensen (2006) argues that discussions of innovation mainly take the distinction between order and chaos as their point of departure. Following this dualistic perspective novelty proceeds from two possible starting points. It is either construed outside human control, as a 'gift from above'; proceeding from pure exteriority. Or novelty springs from turning information into knowledge. All information is already here, in the world, we just need to actualize it, or following the knowledge management tradition originating from Nonaka and Takeuchi (1995), to externalize it. That is, knowledge in this view proceeds from pure interiority, controlled and managed by the human being. Sørensen (2006) describes both these points of view as dead ends, one obsessed with chaos and the other with management. He then proposes to view innovation 'not as an entity, but as an event, a number of actual occasions, incidents, encounters ... innovation occurs when you put your event to work and multiply your crisis' (Sørensen, 2006: 137). Although Sørensen is drawing on Deleuze, his point of departure fits my argument well. In drawing on Levinas, I also view innovation as beyond this dualism described by Sørensen. In Levinasian terms everything happens in the interplay between interiority and exteriority; everything originates in the encounter with the Other, the encounter between my interiority and the Other's exteriority. I thereby also view innovation as the result of the encounter between interiority and exteriority. In addition, I take the discussion back to creativity. Innovation is the result – the product – of this encounter whereas creativity is the happening; the event itself. Creativity thereby precedes innovation, as occurring in a crisis, an encounter; it is an encounter where creativity in fact changes knowledge and results in innovation. But when drawing on Levinas, this encounter is of an ethical nature; the crisis proceeds from the interruption of the Other, and the putting into question of one's own identity.

When trying to understand creativity in teams, I find useful relations between creativity and the bond Levinas makes between expression and responsibility.

> In the welcoming of the face of the Other, the will opens up to reason. Language is not limited to maieutic awakening of thoughts common to beings. It does not accelerate the inward maturation of a reason common to all; it teaches and introduces the new into thought. The introduction of the new into a thought, the idea of infinity, is the very work of reason. The absolutely new is the Other .(Levinas, 1961: 219)

That is, the new is not something latent in the being waiting to be extracted by Socratic questioning. Instead, the absolutely new is the Other. In fact, the absolutely new – not the latent – arises from the Other's interruption, which puts me into question. The absolutely new arises from the profound creativity brought about in the ethical encounter with the Other. This is not how Levinas is normally read, however. Generally, readings of Levinas are used to emphasize, for example, a postmodern ethics as opposed to traditional approaches (Bauman, 1993), notions of affectivity (Tallon, 1995), language, responsibility and ethics (Eskin, 2000; Waldenfels, 1995; Werhane, 1995), post-humanism (Cohen, 1998; Fryer, 2004) and matters of identity (Rosenthal, 2003). Levinasian ethics is rarely used for issues of management and organization, and when it is, it is primarily used for the purpose of renewing or provoking traditional business ethics, thereby discussing the possibilities of a personal ethics in business and the interrelation between ethics, morality and justice (see, for example, Corvellec, 2005; Jones, 2003; Jones et al., 2005; Kaulingfreks and ten Bos, 2005; ten Bos and Willmott, 2001; Van de Ven, 2005).

In addition to the business ethics focus, I propose the value of using Levinasian ethics to interrupt our traditional definition of creativity and view creativity differently. That is, I argue that 'the new into thought' can be used to explain the flash of insight that teams often experience when working together. To be more specific, the flash of insight can be explained as the interruption of the Other and the ethical acknowledgement that opens me up for change and novelty. To obtain novelty, I cannot work alone as an individual. I need the creative feedback of my team members to ignite the creative process. After all, creativity is the transformation of the known, and this is why the knower must be open to interruption. The reason why Levinas is rarely used in the creativity or knowledge management debate is that he hardly ever discusses knowledge or creativity directly. In one of the rare passages, however, where Levinas directly connects his thoughts on interruption to knowledge, he states that:

Knowing becomes knowing of a fact only if it is at the same time critical, if it puts itself into question, goes back beyond its origin – in an unnatural movement to seek higher than one's own origin, a movement which evinces or describes a created freedom. This self-criticism can be understood as a discovery of one's weakness or a discovery of one's unworthiness (Levinas, 1961: 82–83).

The central element of this quote is that if one is truly to obtain knowledge, one has to move beyond one's origins, which brings us back to the encounter with the Other. The unnatural movement to seek higher is the ethical draw to the Other's face. That is, putting oneself into question and being open to interruption. Only in the sometimes dramatic, exhausting and even traumatic confrontation with otherness can we change our basic assumptions and allow for profound creativity. So it is in the notion of interruption that Levinas's central imperative of openness to the Other's otherness and exposure of one's own self becomes paramount for creativity.

By taking a Levinasian ethical perspective on knowledge, I propose that we can move beyond a categorical and stable view on knowledge, and instead reach back to the infinite creativity of the interruption of knowledge. On this view, I don't view knowledge as a stock, a capability or something which needs to be handled in order to foster innovation, but instead as something which needs to be put into question by the ethical encounter with the Other. 'Critique or philosophy is the essence of knowing' (Levinas, 1961: 85), and 'this awakening comes from the Other' (Levinas, 1961: 86). Understanding creativity in a Levinasian perspective, however, is not only the transformation of knowledge, but also the transformation of the knower. After all, the encounter with the Other, and the interruption it implies, changes me as a knower. In fact, an ethical encounter with otherness not only changes my assumptions, but it changes my identity. The identity of a person is for Levinas constantly changing in the encounters with otherness. That is, identity is a becoming in the interplay between interiority and exteriority. The encounter with radical exteriority, the Other, which is per definition always exterior to my comprehension, calls me into question and reveals and changes my interiority, my identity. That is, transforms me as a knower.

BEYOND LABOUR, BEYOND PRODUCT INNOVATION

I now proceed to link these thoughts on Levinasian creativity and the transformation of knowledge and the knower to the distinction Levinas makes between labour and the immediate relation to the Other. I intend to use this link to further support the argument of how a Levinasian ethics makes us reach a more profound level of creativity. That is, not the act of product innovation, but instead the ethical event of creating new relations.

As was established above, profound creativity is inevitably linked to the ungraspable future the ethical encounter with the Other brings. The uncertain future of the element, however, is suspended and calmed in the 'possessive grasp' of labour (Levinas, 1961: 158). That is, the things produced from labour are possessed and stabilized. Stable possessions produced by labour are therefore to be distinguished from the infinity of enjoyment created in the immediate relation with the Other, the ethical encounter. In fact, labour possesses being and suspends its element. This kind of possession neutralizes being: it 'masters, suspends, postpones the unforeseeable future of the element – its independence, its being' (Levinas, 1961: 158). Labour, construed as this possessive acquisition, is a movement towards oneself, not towards the Other. However, the immediate relation with the Other is a possession without acquisition, where I possess without taking and keeping. 'Possession is accomplished in taking-possession or labor, the destiny of the hand. The hand is the organ of grasping and taking, the first and blind grasping in the teeming mass: it relates' (Levinas, 1961: 159). Through labour the hand grasps and relates knowledge to needs. The immediate relation with the Other, on the contrary, is not related. This relation is as such immediate, carries infinity. As we learned above, following Levinas's criteria for knowledge, my newly found knowledge is not mine to keep, not to be possessed. It will continue to be put into question by encounters with otherness. Product innovation, which belongs to labour, to the production of possessions, therefore, differs from the ethical encounter with the Other, the creation of new relations. 'Labor "defines" matter without recourse to the idea of infinity' (Levinas, 1961: 160). That is, labour stabilizes and produces possessions.

In this sense we find what Jones and Spicer (2006: 197) call a 'general economy' beneath the 'productive economy'. They relate this general economy to thoughts on excess, exuberance and passion. I take it one step further and relate it to the ethical encounter with otherness; an encounter that in fact allows for and produces excess, exuberance and passion. 'Commerce with the alterity of infinity does not offend like an opinion; it does not limit a mind in a way inadmissible to a philosopher. Limitation is produced only within a totality, whereas the relation with the Other breaks the ceiling of totality' (Levinas, 1961: 171). In the immediate relation with the Other, in seeking the ethical responsibility in work, we can move beyond mere labour. I must know how to give what I possess. Only then can I situate myself absolutely above my engagement in labour, and engage in the Other. But for this I must encounter the indiscreet face of the Other that calls me into question. To allow for profound creativity, I must encounter the Other ethically, acknowledge the Other's difference in a response. I must let the Other's otherness interrupt my thought, introduce the new into my thought, and allow for that novelty to change me as a knower. Language, therefore exceeds labour, it is an action without action. It exceeds labour by its generosity of offering my world to the Other. Therefore, we should not only look at production, innovation, and outcomes, but go beyond innovation, beyond the product, beyond labour, and look at creativity as new relations and identities. The very encounter with the Other, which puts the knower into question, and brings new into thought.

Knowing often amounts to grasping knowledge out of nothing, to removing its alterity. Knowledge is categorized, managed, utilized; that is, possessed through labour. But to know ethically, to put knowledge into question, transforms knowledge, creates something. Therefore, the novelty of the future presupposes a relation with an Other that is not given to labour, but is ethically an acknowledgement of the infinite difference between me and the Other.

If philosophy consists in knowing critically, that is, in seeking a foundation for its freedom, in justifying it, it begins with conscience, to which the other is presented as the Other, and where the movement of thematization is inverted. But this inversion does not amount to 'knowing oneself' as a theme attended to by the Other, but rather in submitting oneself to an exigency, to a morality. (Levinas, 1961: 86)

Levinasian creativity is therefore not about gaining knowledge, using knowledge and possessing knowledge. It is not about knowing oneself and externalizing a potential. Creativity precedes being, it is beyond ontology. Profound creativity is therefore rather to submit to a morality, to hear the call of the Other.

CONCLUSION

Levinasian ethics brings a new perspective to the field of business ethics. In opposition to the universalistic perspectives of utilitarianism, deontology and virtue ethics, Levinasian ethics rejects measurement of ethics on scales, following rules and codes. In fact following rules and codes holds the risk of creating moral distance, and promoting immoral behaviour. Instead, Levinasian ethics moves us away from the preoccupation with the self, and indicates a neglected theme in business ethics: the Other. That is not understood as an ethics to the Other, for the Other to follow. But an ethics for the Other, on the Other's conditions – not mine. The central issue is not what the other person should do to behave ethically. On the contrary, the question is how I, as an individual, encounter another person as the Other. Ethics for Levinas is the acknowledgement of the infinite difference of the Other, of the Other's status as always incomprehensible. It is about how I open up to the Other's otherness and, in a response-able saying, expose my inner self. In this exposure, I let go of my prejudices and categories, leave my shelter and make myself vulnerable to attacks and critique. In this sense, ethics for Levinas is being ready to let the Other interrupt me, change me, and introduce the new into my thought.

Although far from extensively represented in organization theory, Levinasian ethics has slowly begun to make an entrance into the literature of business ethics. My intention in this chapter has therefore not only been to discuss Levinas in a business ethics context. It has also been the purpose to introduce a new discussion, namely, to open up for a discussion of creativity, which is based in the ethical encounter with the Other: an encounter where the Other's face calls me to response-ability. I thereby wish to advocate for perceiving the other as Other and always infinitely different from myself. Moreover, the recognition of and respect for the Other's otherness develops a willingness to be interrupted, a desire to be transformed and in the middle of all this the courage to expose one self in the encounter with the Other – with the future. The otherness of the Other is what can change my future. My openness to the Other's infinite possibilities is what creates the future. Creativity, therefore, arises in the transformation of my self, not the Other. That is an ethics for the Other is what fosters profound infinite creativity; the transformation of knowledge and of the knower.

Levinasian ethics therefore fosters creativity both as a transformation of knowledge and as the transformation of the knower. That is, creativity can be approached in the traditional sense of product innovation, but also in a more fundamental way that demands radical novelty and a change in basic assumptions: a creativity of identity and human relations. This means grappling with relations where the other is not denied to be Other, relations where I allow for the Other to change me instead of denying his otherness. This type of creativity exceeds the type of creativity usually discussed in relation to producing new commodities. It takes us beyond knowledge, and transforms the knower. In Levinasian creativity the identity of the knower itself is called into question, which allows for more than just producing new possessions. It creates new relations where the future itself is radically being called into question. The ethical encounter with the Other, therefore, takes us beyond the ontology of labour and product innovation and draws us to submit to a morality. In fact, it takes creativity beyond the foundation of knowledge, it questions this very foundation; ethics puts every foundation into question.

REFERENCES

Bauman, Z., (1993), *Postmodern Ethics*, Blackwell Publishers, Oxford.

Cohen, R. A., (1998), 'Foreword' in Levinas, E., 1998, *Otherwise than Being or beyond Essence*. Duquesne University Press, Pittsburgh, Pennsylvania.

Cohen, R. A., (2003), 'Introduction: humanism and anti-humanism - Levinas, Cassier, and Heidegger', introduction to E.Levinas, 2003, *Humanism of the Other*, University of Illinois Press, Illinois.

Corvellec, H., (2005), 'An endless responsibility for justice: for a Levinasian ppproach to managerial ethics', Paper presented at the Levinas, Business, Ethics Conference, University of Leicester, 27–29 October 2005.

Davis, C., (1996), *Levinas - An Introduction*, Polity Press, Cambridge.

Derrida, J., (1992), *Given Time*, University of Chicago Press, Chicago.

du Gay, P., (2000), *In Praise of Bureaucracy – Weber, Organization, Ethics*, Sage Publications, London.

Eskin, M., (2000), *Ethics and Dialogue – in the Works of Levinas, Bakhtin, Mandel'shtam and Celan*, Oxford University Press, Oxford.

Fryer, D. R., (2004), *The Intervention of the Other: Ethical Subjectivity in Levinas and Lacan*, Other Press, New York.

Jones, C., (2003), 'As if business ethics were possible, "within such limits"...' *Organization*, **10** (2), 223–248.

Jones, C., Parker, M., and ten Bos R., (2005), *For Business Ethics: a Critical Text*, Taylor and Francis, Andover, UK.

Jones, C. and Spicer, A., (2006), 'Entrepreneurial excess', in J. Brewis, S. Linstead, D. Boje and T.O'Shea, (eds), *The Passion of Organizing*, Copenhagen Business School Press, Copenhagen.

Kaulingfreks, R., and ten Bos R., (2005), Kate's face: on defacing and an ethics of versatility', paper presented at the Levinas, Business, Ethics Conference, University of Leicester, 27–29 October 2005.

Levinas, E., (1961), *Totality and Infinity – an Essay on Exteriority*, Duquesne University Press, Pittsburgh, Pennsylvania.

Levinas, E., (1974), *Otherwise than Being or beyond Essence*. Duquesne University Press, Pittsburgh, Pennsylvania.

Levinas, E., (1987), *Time and the Other*, Duquesne University Press.

Levinas, E., (2003), *Humanism of the Other*, University of Illinois Press, Illinois.

Nonaka, I. and Takeuchi, H., (1995), *The Knowledge-creating Company: How Japaneese Companies Create the Dynamics of Innovation*. Oxford University Press, New York.

Parker, M., (1998), *Ethics and Organizations*, Sage Publications, London.

Rosenthal, S. B., (2003), 'A time for being ethical: Levinas and pragmatism', *Journal of Speculative Philosophy*, **17** (3), 192–203.

Sørensen, B. M., (2006). 'Identity sniping: innovation, imagination and the body'. *Creativity and Innovation Management*, **15** (2), 135–142.

Tallon, A., (1995), 'Nonintentional affectivity, affective intentionality, and the ethical in Levins' philosophy', in A. T. Peperzak, (ed.), *Ethics as First Philosophy: the Significance of Emmanuel Levinas for Philosophy, Literature and Religion*, Routledge, NY.

ten Bos, R. and Willmott, H., (2001), 'Towards a post-dualistic business ethics: interweaving reason and emotion in working life', *Journal of Management Studies,* **38** (6), 769–793.

Van de Ven, B., (2005), The (im)possibility of a Levinasian business ethics: towards an interpretation of the ethical in business, paper presented at the Levinas, Business, Ethics Conference, University of Leicester, 27–29 October 2005.

Waldenfels, B., (1995), 'Response and responsibility in Levinas', in Peperzak, A. T., (ed.), *Ethics as First Philosophy - the Significance of Emmanuel Levinas for Philosophy, Literature and Religion*, Routledge, New York.

Werhane, P. H., (1995), 'Levinas's ethics: a normative perspective without metaethical constraints', in A. T. Peperzak, (ed.), *Ethics as First Philosophy - the Significance of Emmanuel Levinas for Philosophy, Literature and Religion*, Routledge, New York.

Wild, J., (1961), 'Introduction', to Levinas, E., 1961, *Totality and Infinity - an Essay on Exteriority*, Duquesne University Press, Pittsburgh, Pensylvania.

PART IV

Management Systems and Ethics: Can We Go
Beyond Hypocrisy?

11. Are Management Systems Ethical? The Reification Perspective

Annick Bourguignon

INTRODUCTION

Management systems (or instruments) are generally considered as powerful means of dealing with the complexities of organizational life and business. Generally implemented through computerized arrangements, they are increasingly found in any business function (management control – MC, Human Resource Management – HRM, marketing, logistics and so on), where they are assigned multiple objectives, either explicitly or implicitly, relating to various aspects of collective action in organizations (decision, coordination, communication, planning, legitimization and so on).

Consequently a large part of management knowledge in these various subfields focuses on management systems. Research about management systems is thus significantly spread. For a long time IS (Information System) scholars have focused on the computerized aspects of the implementation of management systems, while HRM or MC academics have developed abundant streams of research based on various paradigms (Burrell and Morgan, 1979). Critical studies have sometimes contributed to questioning the social consequences of such systems, as for instance Foucauldian accounting studies (Gendron and Baker, 2005), but as far as the present author is aware ethics have not been directly addressed in management systems research.

The perspective on ethics used in this chapter is the utilitarian one (Jeremy Bentham, John Stuart Mill and followers) according to which the ethical character of one thing should be appreciated on the basis of its consequences in terms of well-being for everyone. Drawing on the reification framework (Lukács, [1923], 1959), this chapter argues that management systems contribute to reifying the social world, which ultimately can prove detrimental to persons. As a consequence ethics could be at stake with management systems.

This chapter[1] basically offers an analytical demonstration, although some of its elements are empirically founded. An analytical approach aims at increasing the level of clarity and precision in the concepts used for analysing and understanding the social world. Such clarification is relevant if we are to understand and discuss the constitutive use of management systems in firms. On the other hand, an analytical approach may be criticized for being speculative and not being based on empirical observation. However since any explanation of empirical results cannot be found 'objectively in the world' and relies, to a certain extent, on the (always subjective) logic of the interpreter, any explanation of an empirical phenomenon is speculation to a certain extent (Wittgenstein [1921], 1961). The present author is aware that whatever the intended rigour and depth of the demonstration, it does not thoroughly describe the social phenomenon this author aims at conceptualizing. To some extent this is probably always the case in social science where any model is reductive as a result of the complexity of the social world. Nevertheless it may contribute to increased understanding of the ethical stakes involved in management systems. Such an understanding appears all the more vital since such systems, originally developed and used in firms, are increasingly diffusing throughout non-profit or public organizations.

The remainder of this chapter is structured as follows. The next section presents Lukács' reification framework ([1923], 1959) that will be further used for the analysis of management systems in terms of reification. Drawing on this framework, the following section explains how management systems achieve objectification through three processes of, respectively, categorization, inscription and quantification, resulting in the concealment of nearly all the subjectivities involved in the social world, so that finally social conflict and dispute are prevented, and existing social order and domination maintained. Section four evidences the detrimental effects of the maintained social order on its weakest constituents. A synthesis of recent research is presented, suggesting that there is a relationship between the development or renewal of management systems in a social group and various damages affecting the weakest constituents of this group. It is further explained how, according to the utilitarian perspective on ethics, these detrimental consequences raise ethical concerns about their origin, here management systems. The final and conclusive section discusses the contribution and limitations of this analysis and suggests academic perspectives as well as implications for practice.

THE REIFICATION FRAMEWORK

This section presents the reification framework (Lukács [1923], 1959), that is, a process through which the social world, which is inherently subjective, is transformed into a facade of objectivity. The concealment of subjectivity contributes to preventing social conflict and dispute and, further, to maintaining the existing social order and domination.

The concept of reification was developed by Lukács ([1923], 1959) from Marx's notion of commodity fetishism. According to Marx, modern capitalist societies are dominated by the structure of commodity, which he describes as follows:

> The mysterious character of the commodity form simply consists [...] in its reflecting towards human beings the image of the social characters of their own work, in presenting them as objective characters of the very result of their work, as natural social properties that these things would naturally possess: it thus reflects towards [human beings] the image of the social relationship of producers to global work, as an external social relationship, a relation between objects. Through this interpretation, the work products become commodities, sensitive things [become] suprasensitive, social things. (Marx, [1867], 1993: 82–83)

Thus commodity fetishism means an abstraction of human work which is objectified into goods. Lukács has reformulated Marx's concept in more general terms and defined the social process of reification as follows: 'Its basis is that a relation between persons takes on the character of a thing and thus acquires an "illusory objectivity", which has a proper, rigorous, thoroughly closed and apparently rational system of laws, so as to conceal every trace of its fundamental nature: the relation between people' (Lukács, [1923], 1959: 110, original emphasis[2]).

This transformation of genuine social relations between human beings into relations between things has various consequences. Firstly, the commodity resulting from the objectified human activity 'becomes subject to the objectivity of natural social laws, although objectivity is unknown to persons' (ibid., p. 114). Thus, Lukács explains, the rationalization of work increasingly eliminates the qualitative human and individual properties of the worker, both in fragmenting the working process and in reducing the worker to an objectively calculable amount of working time. Consequently, both the object (the commodity) and the subject (the worker) of the production are broken up. The unity of the commodity does not rise from the working process, as was the case before, but from the mere calculation of rationalized partial systems. As for the person, (s)he is 'incorporated as a mechanized part into a mechanical system which stands completed before him/her, which works thoroughly independently from him/her and the laws to which (s)he has to submit' (ibid., p. 117).

The reification process also leads to the enhancement of a reified conscience and approach to reality. Lukács argues that 'as the capitalist system continuously produces and reproduces itself at a higher economic level, the reification structure penetrates deeper and deeper, inevitably and intrinsically, into human consciousness' (ibid., p. 122). The reified world appears as the only conceivable world (ibid., p. 140).

Reification is an ideological concept in the Marxist sense of the term. In the Marxist tradition, ideology is 'a false consciousness, a distorted representation of a reality that tends to mask the working-class's actual bargaining position, and the oppression to which this class is subject' (Chiapello, 2003: 156). Indeed reification hides the true nature of human relations, which is revealed more in the original relationships (between persons) than in the reified relationships (between things) (Lukács [1923], 1959: 118). Moreover, although reification means alienation of oneself for both the dominating and the dominated classes, its alienating effects are detrimental only to the latter. Indeed, whereas alienation is the very power of the dominant class, then the confirmation of its domination, alienation means helplessness and inhuman existence for dominated people (ibid., p. 188). Thus the objectification of the working force (both through its transformation into a commodity and through the fragmentation and mechanization of work) turns daily reality into an 'insurmountable' one, in which 'personality becomes the helpless spectator of all that happens to its own existence' (ibid., p. 118). While individuals accept the laws of reification with fatalism, they experience a 'split of [their] self between what is and what should be' (ibid., p. 239). Lukács concludes that there is no individual 'contemplative and cognitive' way of breaking with the process of reification, and that only a pragmatic class consciousness can '*in practice* eradicate, in the capitalist society, the "reality" of this illusion' (ibid., pp. 252–253).

To make this concept operational, this author proposes to draw four basic elements from Lukács' concept. Reification is thus a process including: (1) a shift from subjectivity to objectivity, (2) resulting in the masking of the real subjective world and, further, its potential conflicts, (3) which prevents social dispute, (4) which finally aims at maintaining social order.

1. Reification is a process of replacement. It is about a shift from the world of human beings to the world of things, from the subjective to the objective, from the living to the inanimate. In epistemological words, it is a shift from the interpretative to the positivist position. According to the former, there is no reality outside our internal thus subjective

representations, while according to the latter, the world is external and objective (Le Moigne, 1995: 19).

2. A main consequence of this shift is the masking of the world. Reality is always subjective. Indeed, basically there is no objective reality and no un-enacted world. Moreover, in a social world, different subjectivities may conflict, so subjective reality always includes potential conflict. Substituting objectivity for subjectivity means changing the facade of things and hiding both their true subjective nature and their potential conflicts.

3. Masking subjectivity aims at preventing dispute, because dispute occurs all the more easily as divergent standpoints are evidenced. There is no point in disputing in an objective world, which is thus made irrefutable.

4. Any social order serves the interests of some participants at the expense of others. In a given social order, objectivity then is both the facade of domination (because the pseudo-objectivity is nothing more than the dominant subjectivity) and its reproduction device (objectivity prevents contesting, and thus maintains social order).

This reification framework is used further for the analysis of the reifying power of management systems. The next section will explain how management systems objectify the social world, which makes it appear irrefutable and further prevents social dispute – the three first steps of the reification process as summarized above. Another section will focus on the maintenance of social order and domination at the expense of its weakest components (the fourth and last step of reification).

MANAGEMENT SYSTEMS, OBJECTIFICATION AND IRREFUTABILITY

This section shows how management systems offer objective and further indisputable representations of the social world. Since the word 'system' is used with a variety of meanings and emphases according to fields, a tentative definition of 'management systems' is first offered. The second subsection presents the three processes of objectification realized in management systems and their consequences. The third subsection further shows how discourse associated with management systems adds to this facade of objectivity and indisputability. Various management subfields (MC, HRM and marketing) provide examples in the three subsections.

Management Systems: A Tentative Definition

What is a 'management system'? The answer will certainly be different according to whom the question is put, because meanings of both 'management' and 'system' may vary according to persons and management subfields. For instance the word 'system' may point to data processing arrangements as well as a general set of interrelated elements.

This author's definition of a 'management system' is quite broad inasmuch as it is defined as made of formalizations and associated procedures that rely (and embody) rules. Its implementation is generally associated with computerized arrangements. A management system has various aims, either implicit or explicit, dealing with any aspect of collective action in organizations.

The words 'instrument' or 'tool' might be used instead of 'system' although in this writer's view, the latter term probably better conveys the close relationships between its various elements (formalizations, rules, computerized arrangements, procedures and so on). It is worth noting that although implementation generally and increasingly relies on computerized arrangements, there can be management systems operating outside computerization – as has been the case for decades in the accounting field (budgetary and management accounting systems) before the computer era.

Frequently a management system has various aims and some of its objectives may remain implicit. For instance investment decision systems have the explicit objective of helping to make the most efficient decision. Pezet (2000) who studied investment decisions between 1890 and 1950 in the aluminium industry has shown, however, that, according to period, the associated systems also had a political, cultural or rhetorical function. 'Collective action', as mentioned above, also has multiple aspects. Some may be related to Fayol's typology (decision, coordination, control) but political and cultural processes are also part of any collective action. Although it is common that explicit objectives generally refer to decision, information, action or control, while 'social' objectives remain implicit, there can be cases where such social aims are made explicit (for example, a new performance management system being explicitly associated with ongoing organizational change).

'Formalizations' spontaneously conjures up quantitative data, but words are also very important. For instance words such as 'performance' or 'value creation' may designate very different things according to firms and systems. The choice of words is not independent of the objective of the system and can even be as important as technical elements (for example, computation formulae) when some organizational objectives are involved.

Rules form the basis of many management systems. There are rules for computing performance measures, for employee rating, but also rules for deciding what expenses should be allocated to whom, rules of internal invoicing and so on. The rule may be more important in terms of social consequences than the system that embodies it.

Management systems give support and opportunity to individual or collective practice such as analysis (individual or collective) or meetings (collective). Some management systems explicitly include meetings, for instance personnel appraisal systems (which most generally include an annual meeting between the evaluator and the evaluatee). This is also the case of some recent performance management systems in which the performance scorecard is explicitly designed and labelled as the basis of team meetings scrutinizing performance (see for example, Bourguignon et al., 2005).

In terms of observation all of this means that analysing a management system should pay attention not only to its different components (aims, formalizations, computerized systems, rules, words, consequences), in terms of design but also in terms of how the system is run and used in practice. While design is generally aligned with the intended aims, use provides interesting insight into how the system actually works. In the conceptual approach taken in this chapter, however – the aim of which is to open up new perspectives on management systems in general – actual use (which is always contextual) will not be considered.

Management Systems and the Processes of Objectification

This subsection explains how objectification operates through three processes of, respectively, categorization, inscription and quantification, resulting in a reduction of complexity but also in the concealment of most subjectivities involved in the social world, so that finally the objective-looking world represented appears indisputable and legitimate.

Management is a social activity (it relates various social agents such as customers, suppliers, investors, employees). It is inherently subjective since its various agents are human subjects, with their own unique subjectivity. Any management system includes a representation of a particular aspect of this social activity.

Psychology postulates that there is no representation without categorization: 'Perception involves an act of categorisation ... we stimulate an organism with some appropriate input and it responds by referring the input to some class of things or events' (Bruner, 1957: 123). Categorization simplifies perceptual treatments and makes it possible to treat more information in spite of our limited capacities. The category referred to depends on both contextual and individual factors. Moreover once a stimulus has been categorized, everything which, in the stimulus, does not fit within the category traits is lost information.

What is true for human representation is also true for representation offered by management systems. Categorization realized in management systems objectifies (in the form of average representations) the inherent subjectivity of the social world – as illustrated by the two following examples.

Customer segmentation is a management system. It is used for decision-making and/or to support more complex management systems such as those dealing with customer profitability analysis. By definition customer preferences are subjective: they vary according to customers. Market segmentation is made according to the representation the marketer develops of the preferences of an average archetypical customer of each segment. Segmentation relies on categorization. When the stimulus (the perceived preferences of the customer) disappears into the category (the main characteristics of the market segment), everything which has not been categorized (the variance to the archetypical traits of the segment, that is, the unique subjectivity of each customer) is lost. Subjectivity is thus veiled under the objective-looking traits of the market segment.

The second example relates to the segmentation of the firm's activities that is the basis of activity-based costing (ABC) systems and can also be used autonomously for decision-making or rationalization programmes. Cooper et al. (1992) report observations from a case study where such segmentation was under construction. Observations show that the character of 'the customer' of the firm infuses all the debates of the team in charge of the project. The subjectivity of each customer is objectified through the use of the article ('the'), which 'sums up' all clients into an average representation. The case study also clearly exhibits the difficulties encountered by the team to reach an agreement about the final segmentation; in other words each member had a subjective perception of what was important and valuable to the customer.[3] The report is silent about power and influence games which have very probably informed the agreement process, but it suggests that the firm's objectives (that is, the subjectivity of upper management[4]) have been given an important place in debates – at least as important as the perceived archetypical customer's interests. What this example adds to the previous one is the fact that final categories are not neutral at all: they are impacted by system designers' and upper management subjectivities. In other words not only is the subjectivity of categorized agents (in both examples, customers) dissolved into an objective-looking representation, but system designers' and upper management subjectivities are totally ignored – although they have played a very important part in the system design.

The second step of objectification occurs when the categorized representation is inscribed into the management system. The two former examples provide illustrations of this process.

If service quality has been identified as valuable for a certain market segment, service quality is likely to become an 'objective' (an aim) for the firm. When the firm internalizes the customer's representation (which has previously been subjected to a first process of objectification through categorization), representation is further transformed into an 'object' likely to inform management acts (such as decision) or other management systems. Such 'objects' can be 'objectives' (as formulated in budgets or MBO practices) or performance measures. Thus inscription complements the process of objectification initiated by categorization. (And at least in English and French languages polysemy might be an active contributor to objectification – an 'objective' (an aim) is all the more likely to be perceived as 'objective' since the signifiers are the same!)

The same process takes place regarding the second example. Once the segmentation of activities is agreed on and each activity attributed a certain level of 'value creation' for the customer, those are inscribed into the ABC system. As a result both the segmentation and the value attributed to each activity appear objective: any trace of all subjectivities involved in the segmentation process is lost.

In both cases the inscription of categorized representations into management systems is a further step towards objectification.

Additionally the form of the inscription realized can contribute to foster the appearance of objectivity of the thing inscribed. Quantification, the third and final process of objectification, does not systematically occur although most management systems include quantified formalizations.

Objectification refers to the transformation into an object – which results in making the transformed thing 'objective', that is 'uninfluenced by thought or feeling; dealing with outward things, actual facts, etc uninfluenced by personal feelings or opinions' (*Oxford English Dictionary*). Then objectification gives the thing the special properties of an object. The third process involved in objectification is quantification which gives objectivity (that is, independence of affects and prejudice) to the objects represented in management systems. Quantification deals with any residual subjectivity that could remain after the two first processes of objectification (categorization and inscription).

Drawing on measurement theory, the author has proposed that performance measures be categorized into two sets, according to their form: quantitative and qualitative measures (Bourguignon, 2004). Quantitative measures follow the triple rule of equality, additivity and unit rule.[5] For instance, sales, expenses and, more generally, accounting data are quantitative performance measures, as are most non-financial performance measures computed in management control systems (time indicators such as lead time or delivery time, and rates measuring quality, breakdown, absenteeism, for example). Conversely qualitative criteria do not meet the three rules (equality, additivity and unit rule). Most of the time they are comparative: they 'tell us how an object is related, in terms of more or less, to another object' (Carnap, 1966: 52). Measures of traits, behaviours or abilities (which generally use scales) are qualitative, as well as (mainly customer or employee) satisfaction indexes. HRM systems use quantitative and qualitative criteria. While these systems 'borrow' some criteria, mainly quantitative, from MC systems, they also include qualitative criteria, which picture performance dimensions inadequately represented in the quantitative terms of MC systems (Otley, 1999).

The form of the measure has a direct impact on the evaluative judgement. With a qualitative criterion, judgement comes first (for instance the evaluated ability is perceived as high or low), and ranking on the scale only comes in a second stage. Measure is thus a consequence and a formalization of judgement – although in practice both operations take place almost simultaneously. With a quantitative criterion, measurement comes first, and then judgement arises from the comparison of the measure with the referent. Measurement and comparison may be integrated (for instance, in the form of a percentage of budget realization), but as judgement always comes last, its inherent subjectivity is moderated by the measure – which is not the case with qualitative criteria. Consequently quantification moderates the subjectivity of the evaluative judgement that is thus rendered more independent of the judge's affects and interests.

Regarding HR appraisal systems, the level of subjectivity included in evaluation has a negative impact on its legitimacy which is likely to foster dispute about the outcome of the evaluation process (Baron, and Kreps, 1999; Bourguignon and Chiapello, 2005).

The same can be said of 'objectives' that can be formulated either in quantitative or in qualitative terms,[6] although the former are generally recommended since quantification is considered to 'complement the objective' (Maitre, 1984: 52) and to provide a less disputable basis for evaluation.

In other words the inscription of management 'objects' into management systems can use the language of quantification. This language leads the reader to see the object (which is itself an inscription of an objectified representation of subjectivities) with increased objectivity, which reduces possible social dispute. The process of objectification is summarized in Figure 11.1.

The Discourse of Management Systems: A Further Step to Irrefutability

This section further shows how discourse associated with these systems sometimes adds to this facade of indisputability. Indeed before entering into the complexities (computation, rules, procedures and so on) of any management system, any observer is faced with the name of the system.

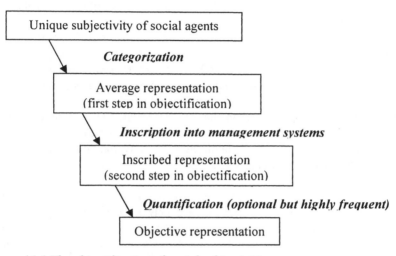

Figure 11.1 The objectification of social subjectivities

Labels are not neutral (as shown by the place given in organizational debates about how to label such new management system, or the frequent positive-sounding acronyms). The words associated with management systems are thus as worth scrutinizing as their 'technical' elements. This subsection reports works exemplifying how labels convey objective-looking representations likely to discourage social dispute, or how the formal structure of discourse (namely the use of oppositions) makes management systems indisputable.

Analyses of the polysemy of the French '*performance*' and the English 'value' have shown how those signifiers could be associated with objective representations, thus hiding the subjective political aspects of the thing represented.

From the mid-1980s on, the French word '*performance*' has been extensively and ambiguously used in relation with various management systems in almost all domains of management with various context-dependent meanings, by contrast with previous specific usage and meaning which were limited to the accounting field (Bourguignon, 1997). For much longer, however, *'performance'* also referred to machines. The use of the word thus conjures up the affect-free rationale of physical systems and, further, the idea of objectivity. However what is labelled 'performance' in firms highly depends on strategic choices, which are highly political and impacted by the subjectivity of upper managers. What 'performance' is remains highly subjective, not objective, as suggested by the label. When 'performance' locally means 'profit', the use of 'performance' instead of 'profit' is likely to reduce the level of possible social dispute about the relevance of the local definition of performance.

A similar analysis can be made about the English signifier 'value' which has been associated with various 'value creation' management systems since the early 1990s (Bourguignon, 2005). 'Value' is a very polysemic word, which has economic as well as philosophical meanings. These latter also have a variety of shadows – individual, universal, subjective, objective. Philosophers generally mention that the borderline between subjective and objective value is not clear-cut and that both meanings are not always easily distinguishable. 'Value', they claim, links the individual to the universal, and further, subjectivity and objectivity:

> Value, which invariably appears to have its origin in the individual, always outstrips the individual ... [appearing] precisely at the moment when this change starts to occur, namely when the individual who, up till then, was the judge of value, now accepts judgement by value, based on a criterion applied to all other beings as well as to him- or herself. (Lavelle, 1991: 221)

Moreover some philosophers argue that the use of the word 'value' could be intentional, thus aiming at presenting subjective value under objective appearances:

> [This use demonstrates] an effort to grasp and declare as fact an 'external quality' of things, which is *objective* [emphasis added], substantially constant within the limits of observation and scientifically measurable, and which nevertheless has its 'raison d'être' in an inclination of subjects and an appreciative judgement. (Lalande, 1992: 1184–1185)

Thus the word 'value' appears as very likely to objectify subjective preferences. Like the definition of 'performance', the local definition of 'value' in firms can be very different according to firms, and 'value' is always highly political and subjectively informed. Hiding the possibly disputable meaning of 'value' decreases the risk of social dispute. Who can argue against 'value'?

Beyond labels one of the most frequent discursive devices used for the promotion of management systems is the construction of oppositions that make old systems appear outdated, ineffective, and even dangerous in comparison with the system under promotion, which is granted relevance, effectiveness and long-lasting success. Such a discourse is generally accompanied with an abundance of two-column tables comparing old and new systems. Various works have deconstructed such oppositions in showing how this dualistic presentation sheds light on differences but does not address similarities in systems, for instance unresolved problems whatever the system. The discourses associated with business process re-engineering (Boje et al., 1997), shareholder value (Froud et al., 2000), competence management and boundary-less careers (Livian, 2002), or new management control (Bourguignon, 2003) have thus been scrutinized. These analyses have shown how oppositions made it possible to ignore some aspects of the comparison, which otherwise could have raised concerns and weakened the demonstration of the superiority and inevitability of the new system. Some of these works have relied on Derrida's (1972) deconstruction method to show the illusory character of the opposition and how the new and the old are not in a relation of opposition but of complementarity. For instance, non-financial performance measures complement the analysis of performance realized by financial measures; although, both types of measures are generally presented in opposition – as the adjective 'non-financial' suggests. It is argued here that the presentation in form of opposition (exemplified by the two-column table) gives an appearance of rigour and objectivity to the discourse. Indeed tables are common presentations in reputedly objective disciplines such as maths and this facade of objectivity is likely to be transferred to the thing described, so that finally debate and dispute are prevented.

To sum up, the objectification of social subjectivities realized through categorization, inscription and frequent quantification results in a reduction of otherwise probable social dispute. Occasionally discursive devices (words used, forms of discourse) can also be used as unobtrusive but active masks of subjectivities or providers of objective-looking representations.

MANAGEMENT SYSTEMS AND REIFICATION AT ETHICAL STAKE

This section presents some elements suggesting that the avoidance of social dispute resulting from the existence and form of management systems (as explained in the third section contributes to maintaining social order and domination, at the detriment to the less powerful constituents of the social group (the fourth and final step of reification, according to the definition above). As a result management systems appear as powerful agents of the reification of the social world. Finally it is shown how the utilitarian perspective on ethics suggests that the negative impacts of management systems can be analysed as unethical, so that management systems are likely to raise ethical concerns.

As in the previous sections, the limited scope of this chapter only makes it possible to give some examples borrowed from recent research in various fields. The works quoted below report consequences of the use of management systems at various levels, namely the macro (society) and micro (firms and their employees) levels.

Regarding the macro level, Froud et al. (1996) have documented the case of the British utility sector regarding the distribution of value between stakeholders. They suggest that the ineluctable conflict between stakeholders has been resolved to the detriment of some stakeholders (namely the suppliers or the employees) for the profit of markets (both financial and commercial ones), which have captured the value created by the former. For instance, Froud et al. (1996) have calculated that at the time of their study, 92 per cent of the employment destroyed in the utility sector in the United Kingdom since its privatization could have been saved if funds distributed to shareholders had been used to pay salaries at the average rate. They conclude that the redistribution is 'near perfect' (Froud et al., 1996: 127–128). Since suppliers and employees can be considered as the less powerful and organized categories of stakeholders, such redistribution reproduces and perpetuates relationships of domination within the economic sphere. Value-based management systems (including highly complex quantified measures of value creation and their inscription in reward schemes) can be considered as powerful assistants of the objectification of the business world leading to this unequal redistribution.

At the firm level, other research has focused on the process through which management systems irresistibly lead to unquestioned downsizing decizion in firms (Beaujolin, 1999; McKinley et al., 2000). Objectification (realized through the translation of human work into cost) is at the core of the lack of debate leading to the reproduction of the local social order and exclusion of the less powerful. Social science has provided abundant evidence of the harmful effects of unemployment on the persons sacked, their families and, further, society. Management systems play a key role in such processes inasmuch as they provide the concepts and instruments supporting detrimental decision-making.

The role of management systems also appears highly problematic with reference to what has been labelled 'the tensions of flexibility' (Périlleux,

2001). In France (but there is no reason why things should be radically different abroad) macro studies undertaken by the French Ministry of Work or professional bodies, and research at the micro level converge to suggest that performance management systems actively contribute to potential severe damage to persons (stress, anxiety, illness, sometimes worse).

On the one hand, for more than 20 years the DARES[7] surveys have scrutinized working conditions in France (1984, 1991, 1998 and 2005). While the first three surveys have exhibited a continuous intensification of work in the form of being 'increasingly obliged in the course of [one's] duties to meet deadlines, respect production norms or consider customers' needs' (Hamon-Cholet and Rougerie, 2000: 243), the most recent one has observed a 'suspension' in this intensification (Bué et al., 2007). For instance the proportion of employees (irrespective of their status) whose working rhythm is imposed by norms or by a short production time (less than one hour) has respectively raised from about 5 (1984 survey) to 16 (1991), 23 (1998) and 25 per cent (2005) (ibid., p. 3). This intensification of pressure on personnel is echoed in qualitative research evidencing its damaging effects on persons. For instance Périlleux (2001) reports the perception of a manager involved in the implementation of a JIT system in the late 1990s. For this participant lean production, described as 'increasingly smaller orders to be met in increasingly tighter lapses of time under increasingly higher quality requirements' (Périlleux, 2001: 161) is associated with a feeling of being permanently controlled and visible, not to mention that of being trapped in insoluble double binds (ibid., p. 163) and a loss of professional identity (ibid., p. 161). A permanent anxiety and fear of failure are the consequences of flexibility, and they turn into feelings of helplessness when failure occurs (ibid., p. 166). The biography studied by Périlleux ends with depression and a suicide attempt. One could not be clearer about the damaging consequences of the management arrangements related to flexibility.

On the other hand, data from recurrent surveys about management control practices collected by a French association of management accountants (ADFCG8) makes it possible to suggest that, at least partly, the damaging pressure is communicated through management control and HRM systems. The survey conducted in 1998 (the fifth since 1969) evidences that line managers are increasingly involved in planning, budgeting and performance follow-up. For instance in 1998 in about 90 per cent of the firms surveyed line managers made corrective action proposals – versus only 32 per cent of the firms surveyed in 1986 (Jordan, 1998: 8). Meetings between line managers and management accountants were also more frequent, so that management accountants perceive their job as decreasingly 'technical'. Of the firms surveyed 77 per cent used performance-based remuneration for line managers – versus only 48 per cent in 1986 (ibid., p. 26). Performance scorecards often included quality and time measures (in 1998, 54 per cent of the firms).[9] All of these evolutions can explain why, during the same period, surveys and organization participants reported a higher pressure by their hierarchy on performance under its various aspects (in particular time and quality) and an increased perception of being visible. The intensification of pressure goes along with an intensification of control that perpetuates relations of domination in organizations. The objectification of social activities embodied in MC systems, through extensive quantified measurement, prevents social dispute and proves ultimately harmful to participants.

Management systems reify the social world. They turn subjective facts into objects that, additionally, they represent in quantified terms, thus emphasizing their facade of objectivity. The overall resulting objectification enhances perceptions of irrefutability, which prevents social dispute, so that relations of domination are finally reproduced and perpetuated, to the detriment of the dominated.

The existence of detrimental consequences raises ethical concerns. Indeed the classical utilitarian conception of ethics[10] can be summed up as follows: 'An action is right if and only if it produces the greatest balance of pleasure over pain for *everyone*' (Boatright, 2003: 36, emphasis added). Consequences are thus key for determining the rightness of an action. An important point in the utilitarian perspective is that the situation of everyone should be taken into consideration for the ethical judgement, and that positive consequences should be maximized. The notions of pleasure (or happiness or good) and pain, mentioned in the seminal work by Jeremy Bentham have been extensively debated, in particular by John Stuart Mill (*Utilitarianism*, 1863). A broad understanding is generally accepted that goodness is human well-being (Boatright, 2003: 32).

Admittedly a strict application of the utilitarian perspective is not easy. What is happiness? How to measure it? How to balance good and evil in large social groups? However such a perspective appears relevant in situations gathering a whole variety of social agents possibly involved in relationships of domination. Indeed such complex and unbalanced (in terms of power) situations make it possible to disregard the interests of some minorities (defined in either quantitative or power terms), so that ultimately these minorities are not ethically treated.

As active contributors to the reification of the social world, which possibly puts the well-being of persons at stake, as shown in the previous examples, management systems cannot be exempted from any risk of being unethical.

DISCUSSION AND CONCLUSION

This concluding section considers the contribution and limitations of the present analysis and suggests some academic perspectives as well as implications for practice.

This chapter has attempted to show how management systems are active agents of the reification of the social world. As such, they play an active part in the associated possible detrimental effects on persons – which can be considered as unethical from the utilitarianism perspective on ethics. Although the demonstration above has carefully gathered a number of elements suggesting that management systems could raise ethical concerns, it is necessary to gauge the limits of this hypothesis.

First, while the notion of consequence is easy to conceptualize on paper, it is always difficult to assess in practice. The idea of 'consequence' implies a relationship of cause and effect, which can never be proved. The social world is so complex that multiple causes may interact to produce a final observable outcome, so that it is impossible to pretend to having inventoried all possible causes and explained their interaction. Moreover when statistics are used they only demonstrate correlation not causality. Thus the notion of consequence is always a tricky one for the researcher because logics often lead to hypothesized relationships of cause and effect, the strict proof of which is impossible. For instance in the analysis above, it is not inconsistent to assume that intensified control practices (in the form of an increased involvement of managers and connection with their remuneration) contribute to the intensification of pressure on employees. However such a causal assumption cannot be proved. Similarly one could question the consequentiality of feelings of anxiety and other negative emotions (as a result of the intensification of pressure) and wonder whether other factors (for instance personality) are not as causal as the one suspected. Quite generally the utilitarian perspective on ethics raises this problem of the assessment of consequences and this is a serious difficulty since consequences are key in this perspective.

A way of addressing this impediment would be to change the epistemological perspective: who is the one who should assess both the existence of a consequence and its possible level of detriment? Is it the researcher (as exemplified in the present demonstration and discussed above), which implicitly assumes a positivist stance, or the person him- or herself, as would be relevant from the interpretive stance? Well-being is a highly personal construct. This writer therefore suggests that further research considering the ethics of management systems from the utilitarian perspective be conducted under the interpretive perspective. More generally such suggestion is valid for any research encompassing the utilitarian perspective on ethics.

Second, although management systems appear as powerful agents of reification, it is likely that the way systems are used may strengthen or, conversely, moderate the reifying effects of systems themselves. As explained in the introduction, the analytical demonstration above has not considered real use. But usage may add to or lessen reification. For instance regarding performance management, if the manager regards and acts towards team members as 'actors' or 'performers', which is a depersonalized view of persons, the effects of the system will certainly be more reifying (and beyond, more damaging for the persons) than if the manager views and manages them as 'subjects', that is, human beings engaged in cognitive and emotional processes. Depersonalization means reification, so that use may strengthen or alleviate the reification realized by the system. In this author's view further research should consider systems in use, not just formal systems as they are described in procedure books or promoted by their designers. Such a focus is consistent with this writer's former proposal of changing epistemological perspective (from the positivist to the interpretive one), since the interpretive perspective implies experience.

Third, the above conclusion – that management systems are likely to be detrimental to persons – conflicts with some common ideas that, conversely, they might be profitable to persons. For instance sophisticated appraisal systems (those using behavioural scales for example) are considered as a comparative progress beyond simple ratings – which are rightly considered as more arbitrary and subjective (since, as noted above, the evaluative judgement is spontaneously produced). Beyond this, quantification in performance appraisal, which is assumed to increase the fairness of its outcome, is generally highly appreciated by all actors involved (HR experts, evaluators and evaluatees). It is also valued because it prevents the risk of possible dispute (Bourguignon and Chiapello, 2005). The avoidance of dispute by the hierarchy or functional experts is easily understandable. But evaluatees also can find a personal interest in avoiding conflict – for instance uncommitted employees who do not wish to do more than the minimum required and consequently perceive quantitative performance measures (which make the minimum threshold much easier to gauge) as more adequate for their evaluation (Bourguignon, 2000). In other words employees, not only upper managers (as assumed in the above analysis), may have an interest in avoiding social dispute. The hypothesis raised thus deserves refinement that could be deepened by further research. The counter-example above suggests that objectivity can be appreciated in business contexts where the degree of subjectivity in decisions leads to experiencing subjectivity as something detrimental. This brings us back to the experiential nature of the detriment and on the influence of both the context and the experiencing person on the perception of the detriment.

Fourth, the author is fully aware that the present analysis does not thoroughly escape the reification trap, which an attempt has been made to deconstruct. The level of generality of this analysis leads to reducing the complexity of 'real' management systems in a way that reifies their unique and always contextual character. To a certain extent it paradoxically develops a reified view on management systems, which should not be surprising if we admit with Berger and Luckmann that '... as soon as an objective social world is established, the possibility of reification is never far away' (1967: 89). Interpretive research is a way of resisting this hardly escapable reification process.

Additional research should then further investigate the hypothesis raised in this exploratory conceptual analysis. This author suggests conducting research under the interpretive perspective while paying attention to the nature of the possible detriment (emotions, cognitive dissonance and so on) and how it makes sense with regard to the persons themselves (their expectations, their values and so on), as well as the context. For instance the social value of objectivity and subjectivity depends on corporate cultures and this is likely to influence the experience of objectivity (and, more, reification) of participants. Understanding such experience should make it possible to refine the analysis and hypothesis presented above.

Further research is also needed not only to develop and deepen knowledge about the question (as is the case with any research question) but also to restore the consciousness of the construction of reality and the dialectical relationship between reality and its creators. As claimed by Berger and Luckmann,

> The analysis of reification is important because it serves as a standing corrective to the reifying propensities of theoretical thought in general and sociological thought in particular. It is particularly important for the sociology of knowledge, because it prevents it from falling into an undialectical conception of the relationship between what men do and what they think. (Berger and Luckmann, 1967: 91)

As well, more research is crucially important because, in the view of this author, it should be part of scholars' social responsibility to unveil possible unethical aspects of their research objects.

Lastly the present analysis has significant implications for practice. It suggests that anyone involved in management system teaching, design or use (that is, teachers, consultants and managers) should be aware that ethics is possibly at stake with management systems. Ethical use of management systems would entail paying attention to – and trying to alleviate – its detrimental (unethical) effects, and an ethical teacher could shed light on the reification realized through management systems – although such an exercise would probably entail generalizations and, perhaps, even paradoxical reification!

NOTES

1. The author gratefully acknowledges helpful comments of Bernard Colasse, Patrick Gilbert and Pascal de la Morinerie on an earlier version of this text. Thanks also to Richard P. Casna for his editorial help.
2. Unless mentioned all emphases (italics, bold, quotes and so on) are original.
3. In this case study the basic criterion for segmenting activities was the value provided by each activity to the customer, as is generally the case.
4. More precisely 'the perceived firm's objectives' and 'the perceived (by team members) subjectivity of upper management'.
5. The equality rule means that two equivalent objects are measured by equal values; according to the additivity rule, if an object is made out of two components, the value of this object is the arithmetical sum of the values of both components. The unit rule means that you can define a unit for measurement of the object (Carnap, 1966: 73).
6. Compare, for example, 'improve X significantly' and 'increase X by 20%.'
7. DARES (Direction de l'Animation de la Recherche, des Etudes et des Statistiques) is the Department of the French Ministry of Work in charge of research, studies and statistics.
8. Association des Directeurs Financiers et des Contrôleurs de Gestion (CFOs and Management Accountants Association).
9. Unfortunately no comparative data are available on this specific theme. One can raise the hypothesis that if previous surveys (1986 and before) have not collected such information, this is perhaps because at one time performance scorecards only included financial measures. Such a hypothesis is not inconsistent with the date of publication of books and articles recommending the use of non-financial indicators in the very late 1980s in France.
10. Alternative perspectives on ethics are those of either a deontological or virtue approach. According to the deontological perspective (Kant), intentions, not consequences, offer a basis for the judgement about ethics. Virtue ethics (Aristotle) refer to the acting person's virtue. See Boatright (2003) for a review.

REFERENCES

Baron, James N. and Kreps, David M., (1999), *Strategic Human Resources*, John Wiley, New York.

Beaujolin, Rachel, (1999), *Les Vertiges de l'Emploi : l'Entreprise Face aux Réductions d'Effectifs*, Grasset, Paris.

Berger, Peter and Luckmann, Thomas (1967), *The Social Construction of Reality*, Anchor Books, New York, (Original edition: 1966, New York: Doubleday Dell Publishing Group).

Boatright, Jeffrey B., (2003), *Ethics and the Conduct of Business*, 4th ed., Prentice Hall, Upper Saddle River, NJ.

Boje, David M., Rosile, Grace A., Dennehy, Robert F. and Donald J. Summers (1997), 'Restorying reengineering. Some deconstructions and post-modern alternatives', *Communication Research*, **24** (6), 631–668.

Bourguignon, Annick (1997), 'Sous les pavés, la plage... ou les multiples fonctions du vocabulaire comptable : l'exemple de la performance', *Comptabilité-Contrôle-Audit*, **3** (1), 89–101.

Bourguignon, Annick (2000), 'The Perception of Performance Evaluation Criteria (2): Determinants of Perception Styles', Working Papers of the ESSEC Research Centre, No. 00008, Cergy-Pontoise, France.

Bourguignon, Annick (2003), '"Il faut bien que quelque chose change pour que l'essentiel demeure": la dimension idéologique du "nouveau" contrôle de gestion', *Comptabilité-Contrôle-Audit*, numéro spécial Innovations Managériales (mai), 27–53.

Bourguignon, Annick (2004), 'Performance management and management control: evaluated managers' point of view', *European Accounting Review*, **13** (4), 659–687.

Bourguignon, Annick (2005), 'Management accounting and value creation: the profit and loss of reification', *Critical Perspectives on Accounting*, **16** (4), 353–389.

Bourguignon, Annick and Chiapello, Eve (2005), 'The role of criticism in the dynamics of performance evaluation systems', *Critical Perspectives on Accounting*, **16** (6), 665–700.

Bourguignon, Annick, Saulpic, Olivier and Zarlowski, Philippe (2005), '"Le coût unitaire, ce n'est pas ma priorité", ou le difficile mariage de la performance économique et sociale dans une entreprise du secteur public', *Revue de Gestion des Ressources Humaines*, **57**, 42–61.

Bruner, Jerome S., (1957), 'On perceptual readiness', *Psychological Review*, **64** (2), 123–152.

Burrell, Gibson and Morgan, Gareth (1979), *Sociological Paradigms and Organizational Analysis*, Heinemann, London.

Bué, Jennifer, Coutrot, Thomas, Hamon-Cholet, Sylvie and Lydie Vinck (2007), 'Conditions de travail : une pause dans l'intensification du travail', *Premières Synthèses* (Dares), 01.2.

Carnap, Rudolf (1966), *An Introduction to the Philosophy of Science*, Basic Books, New York.

Chiapello, Eve (2003), 'Reconciling the two principal meanings of the notion of ideology: the example of the concept of the "spirit of capitalism"', *European Journal of Social Theory*, **6** (2), 155–171.

Cooper, Robin, Kaplan, Robert S., Maisel, Lawrence S., Morrissey, Eileen and Oehm, Ronald M. (1992), *Implementing Activity-based Cost Management: Moving from Analysis to Action*, Institute of Management Accountants, Montvale, NJ.

Derrida, Jacques (1972), *Positions*, Editions de Minuit, Paris.

Froud, Julie, Haslam, Colin, Johal, Sukhdev, Shaoul, Jean and Williams, Karel (1996), 'Stakeholder economy? From utility privatisation to New Labour', *Capital and Class*, **60**, 119–134.

Froud, Julie, Haslam, Colin, Johal, Sukhdev and Karel Williams (2000), 'Shareholder value and financialization: consultancy promises, management moves", *Economy and Society*, **29** (1), 80–110.

Gendron, Yves and Baker, Richard C., (2005), 'On interdisciplinary movements: the development of a network of support around Foucauldian perspectives in accounting research', *European Accounting Review*, **14** (3), 525–559.

Hamon-Cholet, Sylvie and Rougerie, Catherine (2000), 'La charge mentale au travail: des enjeux complexes pour les salariés', *Economie et Statistique*, **339–340**, 243–255.

Jordan, Hughes (1998), Planification et contrôle de gestion en France en 1998, *Cahiers de Recherche du Groupe HEC* (Jouy-en-Josas, France), 644/1998.

Lalande, André (1992), *Vocabulaire Technique et Critique de la Philosophie*, Quadrige/PUF, Paris.

Lavelle, Louis (1991), *Traité des Valeurs*. Vol.1: *Théorie Générale de la Valeur*, 2nd edn., Presses Universitaires de France, Paris.

Le Moigne, Jean-Louis (1995), *Les Epistémologies Constructivistes*, Presses Universitaires de France, Paris.

Livian, Yves- Frédéric (2002), 'La gestion comme récit. Petite introduction à la narratologie de certains thèmes de gestion des ressources humaines', *Gérer et Comprendre*, **70**, 41–47.

Lukács, Georg (1923), *Geschichte und Klassenbewusstsein*, Malik-Verlag, Berlin, (French edition (1959), *Histoire et Conscience de Classe*, Editions de Minuit, Paris; English edition (1971), History and Class Consciousness, Merlin Press, London).

Maitre, Pierre (1984), *Plans d'Entreprise et Contrôle de Gestion*, Dunod, Paris.

Marx, Karl (1867), *Das Kapital, Kritik der Politischen Oekonomie*, Verlag von Otto Meissner, Hamburg (French edition (1993), *Le Capital. Livre premier*, Quadrige/Presses Universitaires de France, Paris; English edition (1967), *Capital, a Critique of Political Economy*, International Publishers, New York).

McKinley, William, Zhao, Jun and Rust, Kathleen Garrett (2000), 'A sociocognitive interpretation of organizational downsizing', *Academy of Management Review*, **25** (1), 227–243.

Otley, David (1999), 'Performance management: a framework for management control systems research', *Management Accounting Research*, **10**, 363–382.

Périlleux, Thomas (2001), *Les Tensions de la Flexibilité. L'Epreuve du Travail Contemporain*, Desclée de Brouwer, Paris.

Pezet, Anne (2000), *La Décision d'Investissement Industriel: le Cas de l'Aluminium*, Economica, Paris.

Wittgenstein, Ludwig (1921), 'Logisch-philosophische Abhandlung', *Annalen der Naturphilosophie*, (French edition (1961), *Tractatus Logico-philosophicus*, Gallimard, Paris; English edition (1975), *Tractatus Logico-philosophicus*, Routledge and Kegan Paul, London).

12. The Paradoxical Situation of Ethics in Business

Gilles van Wijk

INTRODUCTION

Corporate life has probably been plagued by unethical behaviour for as long as it has existed. But, with the increasing impact of such behaviour on human rights, on working life, on environment, and on (small) shareholders, the problem has become a serious issue. The paradox is that the more is being done about ethics, the less (corporate) behaviour seems to be concerned, beyond paying lip service. The more ethics is studied, taught, promoted inside and around the company, the less it is understood. Managers tend to see ethics as a means to control employee behaviour or to develop a good company image. Lawmakers impose training in ethics on managers responsible for major misconduct. Employees have to sign codes of ethics like a contract. All seem to consider ethics as an object of positive knowledge that can be codified, learned and enforced.

In line with the classical Aristotelian vision, we will consider ethics to be based on principles pursued for the good of mankind. Having superior objectives rather than practical significance like a rule or a law, the instrumentalization of principles or moral values does not make sense, unless it were possible to give an operational definition of the good of mankind.

We will argue in this chapter that the confusion results from the conflation of ethics, which is an important aspect of our identity, with the knowledge of ethics that can be pursued through learning. Not only is ethics absolutely not a means to control others, but it is also situated at quite another level in our personal consciousness and it cannot be instrumentalized for any purpose.

The following sections will address the evidence for this confusion and try to demonstrate that the consequences lead to bluring the distinction between sincerity and pretence. We will conclude by arguing that, in terms of effectiveness, a clear separation has to be maintained between formal dispositions aiming at reducing abuses, and ethical behaviour that is an inherently private responsibility towards ourselves.

ETHICS AS POSITIVE KNOWLEDGE

The question of ethics is often addressed by companies in a very direct and pragmatic way, when a case of scandal, fraud, or other abuse is affecting the company directly or indirectly. Rules will be emphasized, new controls will be implemented and, as a result of consequent efforts, moral values will be restored inside the company. It appears to be merely a matter of managerial decision. In doing so, it is implied that ethics, or moral behaviour, can be achieved simply by respecting a set of explicit rules. But ethics is not contained in a set of explicit rules. Ethics is a set of principles of right conduct. Truth, courage, honesty are among these principles. They have a universal meaning, yet they exist only in individual action. They cannot be captured by rules, even if these genuinely aim at generalizing them in business practice. Rules are enforceable; they have a strong instrumental value. Principles can only be enacted, they are not instrumental – they are gratuitous acts. We act on the basis of principles not for any particular outcome, but because it is our way of asserting what we are, our identity. Ethical behaviour makes us free (Arendt, 1993).

Reviewing a number of business situations, it appears that this distorted notion of ethics is used with a variety of purposes. It is consequently instrumentalized in a number of related ways: to control business, to pretend goodness, and on occasion to deceive. First of all, imposing ethics in a company by way of a code or a chart has become fairly common practice: it articulates a number of rules of supposedly good behaviour. 'Good' in this context means in the company's interest, not really the good of humankind. Many companies have their employees study and accept elaborate ethical codes. The attempt to control behaviour is explicit and employees can get training sessions to 'learn' to be 'ethical' and they are in most cases asked to sign the chart, as a sign of commitment. In effect, these documents insist typically on specific behavioural items, making or taking bribes, providing or hiding information, *and* on the need to report them. The company seeks to use the code to control what is going on inside the company, rather than being concerned with proper behaviour.

There is an asymmetry between the honesty required from employees, and the control effected by the company. For the employee, proper conduct is a universal notion, and hence it is more a matter of judgement than a question of training. Rules that can be taught are contrary to the essence of ethics and can lead to abuses on the part of the employer. He may ask employees to report on questionable behaviour, and introduce a hotline. This generates even more confusion between what may be an ethical decision and plain denouncement. People sitting at the other end of the hotline are supposed to know better than the employee who is directly involved in the situation. It is taken for granted that management is alone inside the company capable of defining proper conduct. Drafting ethics charts somehow gives a moral authority of some over many, with chances of distortion to satisfy shareholders' or others' private interests.

Moral obligation to report for those who sincerely believe that this is the right thing to do, and organizational control are intimately mixed. Enron as a case in point is famous for having had an elaborate code of conduct signed by Kenneth Lay. More recently, Siemens AG, member of a prestigious committee to improve business practices, was found guilty of paying bribes extensively to customers and unions. Tobacco companies have claimed and financed research to demonstrate that their products were harmless. Total, a French oil company has had an independent certification wrongly claiming that their products were extracted by workers fairly treated in terms of human rights, and so on.

The question whether it is good practice or not to advertise the morality of a company is often raised. Indeed, if a company is ethical, why not say so and collect some benefits from our morality? Isn't it just asserting the truth? In fact, the claim raises two problems in terms of definition and in terms of finality. First, it implies that a company considered as a single entity can be moral. What does this mean? The company as a whole can very well be composed of individual actors most of whom may faithfully try to act ethically, this does not necessarily sum up, were it alone for the diversity of the actors. Of course, from a statistical point of view, the company could be considered to be moral because a large majority of its agents tend to act ethically. Ethical funds claim that they have 80 per cent of their portfolio invested in perfectly ethical companies: they reinforce the idea that ethics is measurable.

Second, ethics involves interpersonal behaviour as well as concern for the environment as was set out by Jonas (1984) analysing the responsibility of humankind towards nature in the age of technology. Because of the variety it entails, and because of the number of agents acting on account of any organization, the claim for an organization to be ethical is inherently of dubious value. Moreover, by our definition, ethics, and moral behaviour can only exist through individual action.

The value of such advertising is therefore extremely questionable. Finally, there is the additional problem that any company can make such claim, honestly or fully aware that it does not live up to the ethical standards. In the end, the question is not whether the statement is true or not, but whether it is believed. And, the statement will be believed – because of good marketing – for the wrong reason. The persuasiveness in communication has become a technical matter unrelated to the actual content of the message. Of course, an independent certification agency could make sure that the advertising is truthful and the company moral. By the virtue of its supposed independence, it could deliver a certificate. But the certification agency adds a level of control transforming ethics still more into a measurable attribute that can be externally appreciated ... and manipulated. The company would not be more ethical because of the threat of the independent certification. Advertising or publicizing the morality of a company, even with the best of intentions, ultimately disserves ethics and reinforces confusion.

Deception can also be found where strategic moves are motivated by so-called ethical concerns. Factories in the garment industry in South East Asia have been closed because they have supposedly not been complying with the company ethics code. But this radical action has been said to be motivated by the fact that the factory was not profitable. Other plants with similar questionable practices survive without particular problems inside as subcontractors to the same company: they offer continued performance...

CONSEQUENCES OF THE EMPHASIS ON ETHICS

The evidence of the paradoxical outcomes of the emphasis on ethics is multiple. A couple of years ago, a study compared two cohorts of students in terms of their responsiveness to ethical issues (Aspen Institute, 2002). Business students receiving training in ethics were found to have become less sensitive to those issues than the other cohort of engineering students who received no special training. Some argue that, had the business students not received the training, the situation might have been much worse. The fact remains that during their spell in business school, MBA students became more focused on company profitability and less on things like customer service. It remains difficult to appreciate the value of this indication: the research has assessed attitudes more than it has observed behaviour, and even if behaviour were to be observed, it would not easily be interpreted: principles are enacted, and the judgement on which these actions are based cannot be assessed statistically. Still, this study can serve as an indication of the graduates' orientations.

In another remarkable case, a well-known publisher has distributed video lectures on ethics by top managers. One of the more brilliant and convincing lecturers was eventually found guilty of fiscal fraud and sentenced to jail. The video disappeared silently from the shelves. Yet, it might have been an important lesson as to the particular nature of ethics: a notion that can be presented and discussed persuasively though it may be no more than pretence.

The emphasis on ethics does not translate necessarily into more ethical behaviour, on the contrary there frequently appear instead to be great skills involved in making believe that there is a genuine concern for ethical behaviour while there is in fact mostly arrogance with respect to human values. As a result, more and more experts, 'ethicists', are necessary to solve the problems. The knowledge of ethics which is acquired through positive learning replaces the ethical behaviour inspired by principles. As a knowledge, ethical behaviour can be displayed. As a genuine inspiration, ethical behaviour is not publicly visible, at best it can be inferred after the fact (Arendt, 1993).

COUNTER EVIDENCE FOR THE PROGRESS OF ETHICS IN BUSINESS LIFE

Opposing the pessimistic view of a broad misunderstanding regarding ethics, it may be argued that the cases mentioned are much publicized exceptions to an overall improvement of the situation. This point of view can be reinforced by the fact that when ethics works, it will not be talked about and will often be taken for granted. This asymmetric situation is likely to give outsiders an impression of widespread amorality, whereas things may not be so bad in reality.

Business and researchers have therefore criticized the above evidence on multiple counts. Overall they claim that the situation is by far not as dim as it is often presented. Before explaining why this attitude seems ill-founded, it is useful to review the various arguments proposed by this optimistic view of things. Indeed, they are revealing about the very conception of ethics of these advocates, and about the perception of the people who still are concerned by the moral situation in business life.

The first argument is that companies today are much more careful to avoid morally questionable practices. Nike, one of the well-known evildoers, is now widely recognized for being one of the best companies in North America for ensuring that standards are met at its Asian suppliers. It has released, in 2005 a list of more than 7000 suppliers to public/NGO scrutiny. The notion of corporate social responsibility has been spreading, becoming a fact of business life. Public opinion ignores this and prefers scandal: correct behaviour doesn't attract nearly as much attention as corporate delinquency. Furthermore, formal efforts to improve a situation can bear fruits in the longer term, if they are in line with the society's deep values. In a historic perspective, the positive outcomes of companies' efforts might be compared to the situation in Western Europe, towards the end of the nineteenth century: when child labour began to be questioned. Legislation was debated in

England and France, and was eventually introduced. Fifty years later, the fact that children should be protected, educated and not exploited in demeaning jobs has become normal.

The second argument is that there is now a market for 'things to feel angry about'. Action groups and NGOs have a business: they will promote righteous causes, and the public will listen and literally buy into the good causes, probably because it vindicates some of our frustrations with modern life. The resulting discredit that falls onto the companies, said ironically to belong to the 'Cabal of Business Villainy' (Maich, 2006), is however undeserved, in many instances at least. The public is naïve and gullible, and the real culprits of major misdeeds are likely to be left alone. On the other hand, NGOs will prefer to act on causes that will attract them a lot of exposure and endowments, rather than being really significant.

A third argument is how to deal with such aggression: what are the policies for business firms under attack? Basically, three options are explored: fight back, stay put, or cooperate. The general assumption is that companies have suffered from these attacks. Most executives will be happy to avoid being accused by Greenpeace of some major environmental pollution. In effect, after studying the actual impact of NGOs, it is often spectacular but short-lived. The impact on performance turns out to be modest, with weak and passing effects on economic performance indicators like share price. At the time of apartheid, one company withdrawing from South Africa, actually saw its share price decline. Some researchers argue (for example, Spar, 2005) that it still may be interesting to talk to activists, because they can be the source of a competitive advantage. The business logic has gone full circle, and morality is now seen as one of the ways to enhance performance.

The point of these three arguments is that at no time are the actual moral issues underlying the situations at hand addressed. Rather, without going into the causes of behaviour, firms are presented as more socially responsible, NGOs as having outrageous behaviour feeding righteous indignation, and finally strategic analysis suggests simple opportunistic handling: be ethical if must be because of public image and/or if this gives you a competitive advantage.

Firms and a number of researchers are seeing ethical issues as a problem for the public image, as a potential threat to performance. These issues are not seen as problems because there is a deep sense of moral obligation. In addition, it is important to note that the unit of analysis is the firm, not the individual. Yet ethics is a subjective individual problem, and individual ethics do not add up to a collective morality. Most people in business as well as researchers would agree on an individual moral perspective, but things are different at the firm level. Overall, fact and discussion suggest that business life is merely pragmatic: if ethics means good business than we will be ethical, but why would we, as individuals or as a company, sacrifice performance to ethical behaviour? In conclusion, optimism as to the situation of our society with respect to ethics is all too convenient: it validates the collective control conception of ethics and relieves the individual of his moral responsibility.

LEARNING ETHICS?

Ethics is not an object of knowledge. Moral standards are shaped by all sorts of things, direct experience, family life, cultural tradition, and religious upbringing. It cannot be studied and implemented like a technique or a method. There is a vast misconception regarding ethics. If you lack it, you cannot acquire or simply learn it – like a driving lesson. Executives of WorldCom tried under the Sarbanes Oxley law, had to pledge that they would not do it again, and that they would undergo ethical training. What makes this sound funny is that given the extent of book dressing and stock pumping, it seems pointless to demand a solemn commitment from those gentlemen. Ethics is not a knowledge, a technique or a skill that can be learned like finance or marketing.

Ethics is our quest for the good. It is best approached by moral values like truthfulness, honesty, courage, and so on. These are not rules, they cannot be contained in a control system. In effect, they are principles that 'inspire' action: the value is not an attribute, it only exists in the moment it is inspiring action.

We are sincere when we act and express ourselves in that way. Yet we can also act in a way to deceive the observer, and pretend to be sincere. Nobody is likely to find out, we are responsible only to ourselves. If the good of man is our ultimate purpose, it cannot be separated from our social identity. Purposes can generally be subordinated to one another, and have intermediary material ends. They can be separated out, studied, become objects of knowledge, and instrumentalized with rules and procedures. Ethics instead has an ultimate purpose for which there are no other ends. The goodness of an action can only be decided by the individual, and everyone brings somewhat different concepts of ethical behaviour with him. There are, therefore, no standards by which goodness can be defined and implemented. Quite to the contrary, separating out relevant features of ethics and implementing them somehow through training and guidelines, cannot generate ethical behaviour. It may lead instead to the pretence of moral behaviour.

Ethics has an intrinsic quality: the reward is in the ethical action itself, not in its outcome. Truthfulness exists only when the truth is spoken. Control systems do exist, and sanctions will stimulate the tendency to speak the truth, but neither sanctions, nor rewards, will replace the intrinsic worthiness of speaking the truth. This feeling of worth is perceived by the individual, and the reward is found in the act. Because goodness is an end in itself, we have the responsibility to decide how to act, and we have to live with the consequences. Of course, on occasion, we can and do look the other way. This is certainly true of business life where action is fast and responsibility often diluted. It is, hence, not possible to arrive at a direct controlled way of learning ethics.

REDEFINING THE ULTIMATE END

Ethics is an integral part of how we see the world and ourselves as part of it. It is a form of consciousness. We can become aware of it, though it is hard to express. It seems to be the elusive answer to our existential question of why man does exist. In this sense, talking about ethics can only be introspective, not normative. When we separate ethics out as an object of knowledge it loses its very nature, and it acquires a formal character. Similarly, we can study a corpse in minute detail, as an object, but this will give no clues as to the phenomenon of life.

Modern society provides ample opportunities of escaping from ourselves, of 'entertaining' ourselves, freeing us temporally at least, from our moral responsibility. We argue here that this creates a void about the sense of our existence. In modern society this void is filled by the notions of profit and performance. This very simple purpose is at once sufficiently broad to appeal to many, and to be relevant to individual action. Economists have given this belief in profits as the ultimate goal, legitimacy. Milton Friedman is most articulate, contending that emphasis on profitability is *the* legitimate ethical principle:

> In a free economy, there is one and only one social responsibility of business – to use its resources and engage in activities designed to increase its profits, so long as it stays within the rules of the game, which is to say, engages in open and free competition, without deception or fraud. (Friedman, 1970)

Profit without deception conveniently replaces moral goodness. The popular notion of 'ethics is good business' becomes almost a redundancy. Equitable commerce provides an interesting illustration: the objective is to give the original producer a decent price for his products, in order for him to make a living. However, given the popularity of the movement, big retailers have found this to be a fast growing market, and fairly price insensitive. They have therefore increased their prices and been able to collect substantial profits. When some pointed out that this was not the idea, the retailers have responded that they didn't see the harm (Wall Street Journal, 2004).

When performance is the ultimate social responsibility, the moral values that constitute ethics can become instrumentalized. They can be defined on an ad hoc basis, controlled, and studied for their impact on performance. If loyalty is taken as an example, the shift in its practical meaning is illustrative. Being loyal in absolute terms is being true to our personal commitments, a way of acting out solidarity. But loyalty to the firm is different. It is 'good' to be loyal to the firm and defend its interests (enhance performance). As a matter of fact, employees often display strong loyalty to their firms, and those who are critical tend to be isolated, ignored, and eventually excluded. They are not good 'team players'. For instance, refusing to report questionable practices inside the organization may be a matter of principle: one may not want to squeal. Yet, those who do object have been looked upon with contempt if not suspicion. Their arguments about the importance of individual responsibility and their refusal of compliance with the hierarchy reflect the latent conflict between universal values and practical performance objectives.

Setting profit and performance as the ultimate ends in business, manager and employee behaviour become largely coherent. First this explains why reference is frequently made to business ethics, differentiating it from ethics in general. As long as ethics is uniquely defined as the quest for the good of mankind, there is no reason to differentiate domains like business from private ethics. But once 'goodness' in business life is redefined as equivalent to profit, the differentiation becomes obvious. Paradoxically, a good father and husband may turn into a coldly calculating manager, and it makes perfect sense in our economic and social system: the manager will be applauded for his outstanding performance, while the good father will generously provide all that is needed to his family and be an example in his community.

Second, on this basis, business literature, research, teaching, consulting, and managing are logically focused on performance and tacitly accept as 'good' those things that will contribute to the bottom line while not being forbidden by law. The impact on practice is significant. Indeed, it has frequently been observed that laws, and contracts, cannot specify all contingencies, and that there will therefore always be some loopholes. As a result, economic actors acting rationally will take advantage of the loopholes, regardless of what moral values may suggest. Without going to these extremes, the change in the ultimate end generates another substitution. With profit as the ultimate social responsibility, moral values are displaced and become instrumental.

We owe the truth to the shareholder, we must work hard to ensure performance for the company, and our loyalty is for the company rather than for our co-workers. These 'guidelines' are enforced by management systems, and imposed with little discussion. Information systems in the company silently reinforce the orientation. Those who do not adhere to this value system are soon declared unfit or completely outlawed. Company performance values are a matter of principle. A student pointed out once that we all have moral values but that it is not our responsibility, in the company, to apply them. To the question whose responsibility it could be, the answer was 'the government', suggesting that the lawmakers are in charge of defining the broad moral operating frame.

The redefinition of the ultimate end has given full coherence to what can be observed to happen in the company: an emphasis on profit as an end in itself, and a formalization of moral values: truthfulness, honesty, solidarity, courage acquire a rule like status, and can be controlled and implemented to further the firm's social responsibility. As a consequence we can observe a number of ad hoc uses of the rules, and the public can be shocked by a number of extreme cases of business ruthlessness. The paradox between an emphasis on ethics and ruthless practices is there.

However, at this point, a difficult question remains: how has the sense of business profit and performance come to dominate so thoroughly our aspirations towards the good of man? We will recognize quite easily that business life, in the end does not count that much in our existence. In the following section, we will discuss two factors that may have contributed to this situation: a renunciation of responsibility at the individual level, and the institutionalization of our environment to the effect that the social system is replaced by an encompassing organizational system.

THE BALANCE IN THE BUSINESS SYSTEM

Social life and organizational life are usually not seen as contexts where the rules of the game can be defined on an ad hoc basis. Quite the contrary, many attempts seem to have had little impact whether it is the idea that commerce is good because it will lead mankind to more peaceful relations (Paine 1951: 215), or the Marxist vision that the labour/management antagonism would lead to class conflict and eventually to a socially minded world (Marx, 1963). The current ambiguity with respect to the status of ethics is therefore problematic. Milton Friedman has expressed with authority a situation that has been evolving. He has given it some more visibility and legitimacy. However, explaining how fundamental moral values have been displaced requires other insights.

Very tentatively, we propose here two factors that may have contributed to the change, providing the business world with its own balance. The first factor has to do with the actor's responsibility. Unlike the situation at home or as man in the street, the individual in the organization is faced with a system within which he is supposed to operate. In order to be effective and efficient, this organizational system is made up of many layers and units that have specific responsibilities attributed formally. Moreover, the system is woven together by an information system that reports in detail everyone's actions and achievements. In this closely controlled system, the so-called social fabric is not required. Political allegiance and coalitions inside the firm exist but are regarded as dysfunctional. They entail at any rate more material interests than moral values. In this environment, the actor has every reason to operate in response to the system's demands, in a highly contingent fashion. Lofty concerns about moral behaviour are not the issue. Whistleblowers trouble smooth operations. Action is fairly challenging, as performance is not easy to achieve and this is enough responsibility. From a career perspective, from a recognition perspective, from an organizational perspective it is best to play along in this game. The moral responsibility just seems a luxury that most of us do not think we can to afford.

The second factor is complementary to the individual perspective above. The organization constitutes a system with its own intrinsic logic. The actors in this system learn the rules and soon identify themselves with them. The system provides everything from a challenging performance objective to health care and security. Entering an organization, an individual accepts it as a whole. If he doesn't, he will be sanctioned or excluded, threatening his 'quality of life'. Acting in the name of the company, or upon the company, it is OK to be pragmatic if not outright cynical. The local environment will reward him. But this does also lead to a conflict.

Acting in our personal name, we perceive the difficulty of being responsible for our acts. Somehow the company seems to shield the actor, and he escapes his moral obligations. The opposite thesis, that the division of labour fosters solidarity has been held by Durkheim (1902). However, despite his remarkable analysis, it appears that morality in companies, if it exists, is brought in by the actors and is not the result of the development of a social network during the ongoing exchanges. The discontinuity is imposed on the actor by our current system. By education and culture, we may have the required perspective on our actions, but we accept the status quo of business ethics and man in the street ethics. That way, we stand a better chance of being successful and we will not be looked down upon as friendly fools. Being cynical has definitely acquired a better image than being moral.

The man in the street seems progressively to evolve towards the same situation. The commercial systems, the various administrations, consumer fashions, television and information systems continuously reduce our need for a social system. The free market and the liberal vision of the world render everybody individually responsible for his fate. This is what we learn and the world we experience. If, as it is acknowledged, solidarity is necessary, such actions will be the responsibility of 'the government' and integrated one way or another into the overall social system. Only at the family level does there remain a natural environment for gratuitous assistance, truthfulness, solidarity and the like.

CONCLUSION

From the perspective of a classical definition of ethics, a substantial shift is observed in the notions of moral behaviour and social responsibility. In effect this shift is attributed to a redefinition of the ultimate end of manhood: it has become performance and profit, instead of a general notion of goodness. This redefinition leads to a paradoxical situation: goodness is no longer an end in itself, but is operationalized to achieve performance. But rules of good behaviour inside the organization do not mesh with principles of goodness in general, hence the paradox.

If the paradox stands up despite the radical departure from traditional conceptions of ethics, it is because the individual is educated in the business system, and this relieves him from individual responsibility. He prefers his 'system responsibility' that can be easily vindicated through the prevailing (organizational) control system. Also, the institutional environment creates a system in which social responsibility *à la* Milton Friedman is reinforced, while ethical behaviour is ignored or even sanctioned.

The only context where ethics may still prevail is the personal relation sphere, family and friends, where no-nonsense can be spoken. There we see the blossoming of 'things to get angry about' that make scandals interesting: they appeal to our sense of what ought to be. The question is to what extent this opportunity for maintaining moral values can be missed, by lack of education or culture. In any case the impact on the level of society is that we have become highly exposed to manipulation, and naïve. After all, it may be the lawmaker with his formal approach to problems, who may be in the best position to revalidate some fundamental moral values.

REFERENCES

Arendt, H., (1993), *Between Past and Future*, New York: Penguin Classics.
Aspen Institute, (2002), 'Longitudinal survey of MBA student attitudes on the relationship of business to society; are business schools influencing

students to consider how business affects society?', Initiative for Social Innovation through Business, Aspen Institute.

Durkheim, E., (1922), *De la Division du Travail Social*, Paris: Félix Alcan.

Friedman, M., (1970), *The New York Times Magazine*, 13 September, 1970.

Jonas, H., (1984), *The Imperative of Responsibility – In Search of an Ethics for the Technological Age*, Chicago, Il.: The University of Chicago Press.

Maich, St., (2006), 'French fries and sneakers: pure evil', http://www.macleans.ca.

Marx, K., (1963), *Le Capital*, Paris : Gallimard - Bibliothèque de La Pléiade.

Paine, T., (1951), *The Rights of Man*, New York: E. P. Dutton

Spar, D. L. and La Mure, L. T., (2003), 'The power of activism: assessing the impact of NGOs on global business', *California Management Review*, **45** (3), Spring.

Wall Street Journal, (2004), 'Consumers are paying a premium to embrace 'fair trade' campaign', by Steve Stecklow and Erin White, 8 June, 2004.

13. Ethics and Management Education: The MBA under Attack

Richard Déry, Chantale Mailhot and Véronique Schaeffer

INTRODUCTION

If we were to listen to the ever persistent university rumours the clamour could be deafening. Apparently business schools are besieged from all sides and the enemy is within their walls. Certain professors of these schools are even prophesying joyfully the end of the MBA, the mythical programme which nonetheless made them famous. In this context several authors have presented ethics as the final shield, the ultimate path to salvation and the way to redemption which will bring about the rebirth of the programme whose death was announced prematurely. This chapter intentionally takes a methodological distance from this solution and instead as a subject of study places the entire debate on the relevance of the MBA. By studying 293 articles on the MBA published since 2000, it argues that ethics is only one political solution among many others and that the MBA is truly the subject of a war of political worlds where the definition of the common good is at stake.

In the spring of 1908 in Germantown, a Philadelphia suburb, a meeting between two professors and a famous engineer would change the course of history, at least that of the university system. Frederic Winslow Taylor who had peacefully withdrawn to his estate, far from the fury that his ideas and interventions had generated in businesses, received a visit from Wallace C. Sabine, the Dean of Harvard Graduate School and the economics professor Edwin F. Gay (Pouget, 1998). Like many others before them these two professors had gone seeking the advice of the master in an atmosphere that would take on a Vatican-like quality. However, unlike the usual conversations on labour organization in workshops, the meeting rather concerned the pertinence of implementing a university management programme based on Taylor's works. Taylor thought that management could only be learned in concrete work settings but despite his reluctance the Dean of Harvard decided to establish a school dedicated specifically to management education. The famous Harvard Business School came into being and the MBA progressively took shape. With the creation of business schools, the Britannic Royal Society of Science programme was finally concretized and in an era of budding modernity the sciences, vocational education and trade were developed as the ideal of modern thinking. Sustained by this ideal, business schools now became well established alongside universities and polytechnics.

Initiated under the sceptical regard of the one who had inspired its creation, the MBA spread rapidly all over the world. It became the subject of as much praise as criticism, envy as contempt and hope as disenchantment. Even in its native country where Protestant ethics seemed to be the social glue and where everything had to be earned through the emancipating virtues of free enterprise, fundamental questioning of the MBA was intense. In the 1950s reports were even done by Carnegie and by the Ford Foundation which questioned the legitimacy and relevance of university education in management. To lessen the severity of their criticisms these reports suggested the incorporation of a technical and essentially empirical and experiential knowledge-based discipline. Certain disciplines such as economics, statistics and psychology therefore made their entrance in the business school universe.

Of course with historical hindsight and the help of economic anthropology (Polanyi and Arensberg, 1975) we are able to understand these historical criticisms and put them in perspective in relation to the fact that the economic sphere has always been held suspect and that its noble representatives, the bourgeois, have always been the target of contempt. Moreover, wasn't Hermes the god of trade, son of Zeus and May, also the god of thieves? It is not surprising therefore that the MBA which many consider to be the royal path towards the gates of economic power, has from the beginning been the subject of questioning, doubts, sarcasm and even severe criticisms.

Up until quite recently this was understandable. For some the MBA was only a programme of study which having gained credibility as a discipline through recommendations aimed at providing knowledge, had nothing much to reproach itself for, while for others by definition the MBA could only be at best an imitation of university studies and at the worse a perverse approbation of the excesses of an unbridled economic liberalism. Therefore, those who were working in business schools and the others, looked like characters of an old Western movie where the good guys were on one side and the bad guys on the other, This rift reassured the business school professors who interpreted it as a sign of social distinction and of the obvious universal success of their pioneering programme which couldn't but generate human jealousy.

But with the new millennium the situation has become more complicated since more and more Business School academics are criticizing teaching, especially those of the MBA programmes. For some of them the MBA programmes condense teaching which leaves the door open to instrumental rationality and in the name of efficiency encourages unethical behaviours (Gaujelac, 2005). Others think that the MBA is not really useful (Pfeffer and Fong, 2004) and that it could even be harmful to the performance of businesses which are careless enough to rely on the analytical capabilities of holders of MBA diplomas (Mintzberg, 2004). Besides, as luck would have it, the economic news is punctuated with an unprecedented number of financial scandals. It is only human nature to think that where there is smoke there is fire. There is therefore a great temptation to establish a cause and effect link between the increasing numbers of business school graduates and the increase in financial scandals.

For many the answer to all the criticism and misfortune inevitably lies in ethics. Consequently, reviews dedicated to business ethics are being written, conferences are being organized, books are appearing in bookstores, accreditation organizations such as the Association to Advance Collegiate Schools of Business (AACSB), the Association of MBA (AMBA) and the European Quality Improvement System (EQUIS) recommend that courses on ethics be integrated in MBA programmes and in certain business schools new business ethics chairs are being created.

In a way, this appeal to ethics as an antidote to the inherent troubles that business schools are facing is not new. In fact, it is a kind of repetition of the 1950s debate which, as was mentioned before, was settled with the introduction of certain scientific disciplines to the MBA programmes. This time it would appear that the introduction of disciplines such as philosophy, and especially ethics will restore order, improve the education of students and preserve the credibility of business schools.

Even though at first glance the ethical solution appears to be a generally accepted solution it is not a certainty that everyone thinks it provides a satisfactory answer to their questions. To a certain extent ethics is only the tip of the iceberg, the side that is publicized by the media of the war between different concepts of the MBA, the different ways of seeing its relevance and therefore the common good that it could offer. So instead of focusing solely on the ethical question, it might be more useful to establish a discourse on the MBA as a subject of study and explain the logics on which it is based. In this way we will show that by reducing the debate on the MBA to only the question of ethics is equivalent to being locked into a vision of the world which is founded precisely on ethics. Other visions of the world are shown and in each of them it is possible to find a definition of common good which does not consider ethics to be the basis of community action nor the key to the happiness of the majority.

The diversity of the criticisms and logics concerning the common good that result from the discourses on the MBA in fact brings to bear its significance when it is put back in the context of the diversity of ideal worlds, each of which offers a solution to the problem of the relevance of the MBA. Therefore we need to clarify theoretically and empirically this diversity of the worlds in which the MBA still remains the subject of comments, justifications and even criticisms.

THE ANALYTICAL FRAMEWORK: THE PEDAGOGICAL WORLD WHICH SERVES CONCEPTUAL CITIES

In order to fully consider the question concerning the MBA, without getting entangled in the ethical debate or the question of the theoretical rectitude of the relativism of the truth concerning all the points of view, we have decided to use the theoretical framework of Boltanski and Thévenot (1991). In *Les Economies de la Grandeur*, Boltanski and Thévenot suggest a theoretical framework which enables the interpretation of the various agreements and disagreements of daily life, which can also offer an explanation to the discursive conflict inherent in the debate concerning the MBA.

According to Boltanski and Thévenot, social life is filled with agreements and disagreements which indicate the coexistence of a variety of logics of action used by individuals in their interactions. In fact as everybody knows, communal life is never simple; there is always a social game of coordination and mutual adaptation involved based on political organization principles. Social life always has a political dimension and is the result of potentially antagonistic encounters. Since human beings are creatures of habit who conform to norms, the interactions which shape these encounters constantly shape political projects, the way of thinking for the common good and the welfare of the community. Consequently, whether or not interacting is conscious, it gives life to political principles which results in different views on the common good, living together in harmony, good and evil, and so on.

Therefore through their social interactions human beings practice major political philosophies without necessarily being conscious of doing so. Since the beginning of time humans have sometimes unconsciously employed the principles of political philosophy according to Hobbes, Smith, Rousseau and so on, to shape the world. These political worlds are therefore neither theoretical constructs nor utopias but through the inevitable circularity of habit which is the principle of action, they are embodied and enriched by day to day social life. Boltanski and Thévenot have identified and characterized these worlds which are at the same time ideal, normative and material.

Each of the major political philosophies suggests an ideal social life and creates some kind of ideal city. According to Boltanski and Thévenot, humans activate and build six types of cities: Inspired, Domestic, Civic,

Opinion, Industrial and Merchant. They are based respectively on the political philosophies of Saint Augustin, Bossuet, Rousseau, Hobbes, Saint Simon and Smith. By placing themselves in the ideal framework of one of these cities humans activate their principles and as a result make them concrete. Therefore, this means that by drawing on the theoretical imaginings of political philosophy which constitutes the framework of the cities, humans give sense to their social interactions and can justify them. It is also through these imaginings that they formulate criticisms and recognize good and bad which is necessary for the common good. Therefore each city has its own manner of judging individuals, things and situations as good or bad, desirable or not, in the words of Boltanski and Thévenot, great or small.

The anchoring of the cities in the concrete world is brought about through the activation of various objects or entities which serve as bases as well as mediators during human interaction, and through habits justify the actions of humans, and give them sense, a sense which is inevitably political, since this has always been the case with social life. Merchandise, for example, therefore plays a double role as lever and mediator in the building of trade in the world and technical tools such as the chronograph or the pocket calculator participate in the building of the industrial world by serving as a concrete basis for the justification of the action which activates them. So a city is not just an ideal and normative political world, because through the reflexive action which embodies it and inscribes it into a concrete reality it shifts from the philosophical sphere where it came into being into ontological space where it can freely extend and as a result change into a world of people comprised of an infinite variety of individuals, like the principles expressed in words, objects, relations between people, between people and beings and between beings and other beings, and so on.

Each city is sovereign, coherent and self-sufficient and constitutes a world in itself. Even though relations between the cities are possible none of them really needs the other to feel complete and to offer its citizens rich and stable ontological security. Therefore each city offers its citizens a complete social system, a universe made of shared equivalencies, principles that are coherent with regards to people, objects, illustrations and relational figures. Table 13.1 summarizes some characteristics of the six cities.

Even though all the cities are fundamentally autonomous and omnipotent they cannot be measured against each other. They can build bridges between each other and open exchange and transaction paths. Debates can emerge from these meetings which can reinforce the differences in identities and the axiology of each city. If for example, a meeting between the 'city of industry' and the 'city of inspiration' can open debate on the subject of efficiently bringing a profoundly original idea into play, it can also give rise to criticism where 'inspiration' blames 'industry' of being only concerned with usefulness and efficiency to the detriment of true creativity, while the industry city will only see in the projects of the inspired city waves of unrealistic and unpredictable or even dangerous utopias.

	Common superior principle	*Greatness*	*List of subjects*	*Smallness*
Inspired city	Escapes measurement, inspiration	Spontaneous, escapes reason	Creator, artist	Frozen, habit, routine
Domestic city	Personal relationships, tradition, hierarchy	Benevolent, honest, faithful, shrewd	Artisan, superior, inferior	Impolite, vulgar, flatterer, traitor
Opinion city	The others, the public	Renowned, recognized	Personality, leader of opinion, star	Unknown, hidden, ordinary, indifference
Civic city	Pre-eminence of communities, general will	Representative, legal	Citizen, representative community	Divided, special, minority, arbitrary
Merchant city	Competition	Winner, desirable, value	Competitors customers, wealth	Detested, loser
Industrial city	Performance, efficiency, future	Functional, viable, operational	Technocrats, professionals	Inefficient, non-productive

Table 13. 1 The cities (adapted from Boltanski and Thévenot, 1991: 177–182 and Amblard et al., 1996: 88)

For the citizens of the city of industry the citizens of the city of inspiration are only dreamers with disturbed minds while for the city of inspiration the citizens of the city of industry will be considered to be soulless technocrats without ideals. Of course, the relationships between the different cities are not necessarily characterized by contempt or open conflict, but the strength of each city added to the ideal to be achieved gives rise to a situation that is favourable to this kind of conflict.

With regards to the current debate concerning the relevance of the MBA in our society, by relying on the framework of interpretation which Boltanski and Thévenot suggest we can build six pedagogical worlds which are also a way for the MBA to contribute to building 'conceptual cities' and in so doing promote a certain concept of common good. Therefore theoretically we have the following six pedagogical worlds:

- **The inspired pedagogical world**: The MBA would train imaginative, creative and spontaneous managers and in this way offer society originality, solutions that are free of all attachments to a routine past where rules and habits serve only as a hindrance to the building of a society that is truly free and new. In this world the common good can be found alongside creativity which only liberty that is fully assumed can generate.

- **The domestic pedagogical world**: The MBA would train benevolent, honest, faithful managers who respect habits and customs as well as authority and who make the respect of tradition the basis of all success. In this world tradition constitutes the common good.

- **The civic pedagogical world**: The MBA would train managers who put the community first and who are able to assume their role of community representative and in so doing stimulate the democratic debate with utmost respect for everyone. In this world legally executing the will of the community through a rich social ethic represents the common good.

- **The opinion pedagogical world**: The MBA would train persuasive managers who are acknowledged leaders of opinion. In this world, renown and prestige represent the common good.

- **The industrial pedagogical world**: The MBA would train professional, performant, efficient managers who are functional, reliable and operational. Through their analytical abilities these managers would establish efficiency which is the common good in this world.

- **The merchant pedagogical world**: The MBA would train managers who excel in competitive environments and who esteem what they do and manage. In this world the common good comes naturally from healthy competition.

Theoretically the debate over the relevance of the MBA would result from the meeting of these ideal pedagogical worlds and at the MBA level would materialise the tensions which are at the heart of the political building of the society. The debate over the relevance of the MBA is therefore political since it is a part of society whether it legitimizes it or not. When management researchers and practitioners write articles on the MBA and by doing so become involved in the public debate, they participate consciously or unconsciously in the promotion of a pedagogical world and its ideal of the common good. Writing about the MBA necessarily leads to the implicit or explicit expression of a position which contributes to the realization of a specific conception of the common good. It also leads to the disregard of other forms of common good and to the inevitable political debate which also concerns the expression of inalienable human freedom.

Even if the interpretative framework founded on the Boltanski and Thévenot theory allows a theoretical explanation of a particular concept of common good and clarification of the question on ethics which would only be the chosen political option of one of the pedagogical worlds, namely the civic world, this framework still remains to be tested through confrontation with the empirical reality of the debate as it may be understood from the articles on the MBA.

SUBJECT AND METHOD

In order to show the variety of options available concerning the relevance of the MBA we have put together a corpus of articles taken from the ProQuest data base. By using the key words 'MBA programs and graduates' and 'Business schools' and limiting the research to only articles published since 2000, we made an index of 293 articles, 219 of which were published in scientific reviews and 74 in business magazines.[1] We limited our research to articles published since 2000 in order to look at the debate in its current stage as this is the precise subject of our research. Moreover, the choice of a corpus consisting of as many scientific articles as articles published in the major business magazines comes from our desire to respect the fundamental disagreement which is the principle on which business schools are based, that is the disagreement between the scientific side and the professional side.

We have chosen to focus on the summary of the articles where the rhetorical core of the authors' argumentation can be found. Each article was then classified according to its contribution to a pedagogical world which is also the means of building the political cities.

Depending on the viewpoint on the MBA we classified the articles according to different pedagogical worlds and consequently the political cities for which they become the spokespersons through their rhetoric. In this way all the articles according to which the MBA trains original, singular and creative individuals were classified in the 'inspired pedagogical world'. The MBA prepares these graduates to change their usual ways of thinking in order to create new ways of doing things and finding original solutions to the time-consuming problem of organized action. Articles which paint a picture of managers with an MBA as exceptional individuals or free-thinkers fall into this pedagogical world.

All articles in which the MBA programme is seen as respectful of tradition, authority, the hierarchy and business culture, were classified in the Domestic world. In these articles the 'manager with an MBA' appears as an artisan who by relying on business history and culture ensures its healthy and harmonious development.

Articles which point out the necessity to educate managers who are ethical and act responsibly for the common well-being are placed in the Civic pedagogical world. In these articles the 'manager with an MBA' appears as a representative of the organized community. He respects its will and ensures the responsible anchorage of the society in its natural environment.

Articles in which the MBA is considered to be a programme which educates leaders of opinion who favour the recognition and renown of business are classified in the 'opinion world'.

Articles which see the MBA as educating competent managers who work to improve the efficiency of businesses are classified in the 'industrial world'. Therefore all the articles which argue that the MBA is not able to educate competent, efficient managers who are sensitive to the technical needs of the business are classified in the 'industrial world'. The logic that characterises the industrial world is also given preference in articles where the authors suggest a change in the way of teaching especially to increase the contact with practitioners in order to facilitate the transmission of practical knowledge.

Finally, all the articles which highlight the necessity of ensuring businesses that they will have managers who are performant and who are capable of implementing competitive strategies that are adapted to the current economic imperatives are classified in the 'merchant world'.

During the classification of the articles we were faced with significant difficulty. Some of the articles presented the MBA as a world in itself and not as a political instrument of the greater world, that is as 'conceptual cities'. Many articles question the pedagogical dynamic and favour learning in the classroom without any consideration of any societal relationship with any of the conceptual cities. Of course this type of article might employ the rhetoric of the cities but this does not make the MBA an instrument that serves them. This only serves to demonstrate the fact that the cities are not limited to a methodological level and that they can be used at different levels of social life, including the level of the MBA programmes which are seen as closed and autonomous environments.

The presence in the corpus of articles of a vision of the MBA as a closed and autonomous environment led us to build a third order of reality alongside the cities and pedagogical worlds, 'worlds per se' which are described as follows:

- **The inspired world per se**: The MBA is a social space that is free of all constraints, a territory where creativity dominates practice.
- **The domestic world per se**: The MBA is a hierarchical social space where everyone, administrators, professors, and students, occupies a space and respects that of the others.

- **The civic world per se**: The MBA is a social, democratic space founded on the social contract which recognizes the primacy of the general will of the community over that of its individuals.
- **The opinion world per se**: The MBA is a social space that is dominated by debate where everyone tries to enforce his leadership and to gain the respect of the others so as to acquire symbolic recognition.
- **The industrial world per se**: The MBA is an efficient social space as much in its management and its teachings as in the interpersonal relationships which extend from it.
- **The merchant world per se**: The MBA is a social space in the form of a market. On the one hand, MBAs are in competition with each other; on the other hand, the MBA is seen as product fabric which must be put on the market.

Moreover, another set of articles also posed a problem; those in which the MBA was a truly instrumental territory without serving as a more or less explicit political ideal but rather as an experimental laboratory for formal, scientific reflection. In this set of articles the MBA has no reality in itself and is not studied for what it is or what it might be. It is only a reservoir of guinea pigs from which the researcher can take a sample of humans who are not considered as MBA students, to study what interests him otherwise, given that this 'otherwise' has nothing to do with the MBA.

Considering the large number of articles, the wisest methodological action would have been to exclude them since they do not contribute to the problematic of the study, notably the debate on the relevance of the MBA. In a way they were non-relevant, outside of the field. Nonetheless, these articles soon became significant to us in relation to the debate. In fact it is at least significant that at a time when the rumour which was still vernacular and persistent was making the MBA out to be a territory under siege which would require reflection and debate, numerous authors had not taken note of it, did not mention it and continued as if it were 'business as usual', giving reflections on pedagogical school management or using samples of MBA students to study something completely different. Such behaviour seemed to us to be a way, certainly unplanned for in our theoretical framework, but nonetheless a way of participating in the debate. In a fundamentally political world there is no way of escaping it, and refusing to acknowledge the debate or lack of concern about it is also a way of participating in it. Therefore we have kept these articles and chosen to interpret them in the same manner as the articles which fit into one of the other pedagogical worlds. In order to properly translate the reality while remaining within the framework of this research, this set of articles remained to be described. We used the category 'no man's land', a country which as its name suggests, is neither urban nor human in that it has no societal projects, does not have any particular political philosophy and develops on the outskirts of pedagogical worlds which are on the other hand, one way or the other, secured to the ideal of the conceptual cities.

DESCRIPTION OF THE RESULTS

As is shown in Table 13.2 the corpus studied included 293 articles, 219 of which were published in scientific reviews and 74 in business magazines. These two sources are distinguishable as much by their authors as by their target audiences. While scientific reviews subscribe mainly to an academic logic and are largely the work of academics addressing their peers, the business magazine articles subscribe to a professional logic and are written by journalists who are trying to reach a vast audience which is essentially comprised of managers.

	Scientific reviews		*Business magazines*		*Total*	
	no.	%	no.	%	no.	%
Pedagogical worlds	65	29.7	15	20.3	80	27.3
No man's land	154	70.3	59	79.7	213	72.7
Total	219	100	74	100	293	100

Table 13.2 Distribution of the articles of the corpus

Moreover it is clearly shown in Table 13. 2 that the 'no man's land' is the joint labour of academics and journalists and in equivalent proportions. In addition, it is interesting to note that at the same time that the MBA is the subject of lively criticism and could demand the taking of a stand at the political level through dialogue between the cities, the vast majority of the articles shut themselves into the 'no man's land', a shelter from the shock of the cities.

Table 13.3 demonstrates that the majority of the articles in this 'no man's land' present the MBA as a 'world per se'. Moreover it is notable that utilisation of the MBA as an experimental and sampling territory is not surprisingly, done only by the academics.

	Scientific reviews		Business magazines		Total	
	no.	%	no.	%	no.	%
Experimenting field	53	34.4	-	-	53	24.9
World in itself	101	65.6	59	100	160	75.1
Total	154	100	59	100	213	100

Table 13. 3 Distribution of the articles of 'no man's land'

Although the authors in the corpus do not connect their arguments to the political debate of the cities, neither do they escape the rhetorical register that they have at their disposal. So the authors may very well remain distant from the political debates in order to build themselves a little world quite by itself, but they are a part of it nonetheless, even indirectly, and activate the logic which is the principle of each of the cities. Table 13.4 shows the distribution of the worlds per se according to a discursive logic that is used for their construction.

	Scientific reviews		Business magazines		Total	
World in itself	no.	%	no.	%	no.	%
Inspired	-	-	-	-	-	-
Domestic	-	-	1	1.7	1	0.6
Civic	-	-	-	-	-	-
Opinion	1	1	9	15.3	10	6.3
Industrial	71	70.3	-	-	71	44.4
Merchant	29	28.7	49	83	78	48.8
Total	101	100	59	100	160	100

Table 13.4 Distribution of the worlds per se of 'no man's land'

This table demonstrates that the MBA seen in terms of a *world per se* is, for the academics, mainly an industrial world marked by the search for efficiency, and for the journalists, above all a merchant space in which MBAs are in competition with each other in addition to producing like a business, diplomas for a market which in this way fills its needs for workers. It is also interesting to note that opinion has a certain weight in the construction of the *worlds per se*. In fact the articles, which are almost all journalistic and which help to build them, highlight the prestige of the MBAs and their search for recognition in the rankings which takes inventory of them.

If we push the description of the worlds per se a bit further, Table 13.5 demonstrates that while the MBA is conceived as an 'industrial world per se', the academics in the corpus, who are the only ones to see the MBA as such, portray it either in terms of its pedagogical efficiency, that is its teaching methods, the relationships between the students and between them and the professors, or from the angle of the programme management and its connection with the business school universe.

Themes	Scientific reviews		Business magazines		Total	
	no.	%	no.	%	no.	%
Pedagogical efficiency	54	76.1	-	-	54	76.1
Management of the establishment	17	23.9	-	-	17	23.9
Total	71	100	-	-	71	100

Table 13.5 Distribution of the themes of the' industrial world per se'

As is illustrated in Table 13.6, when the MBA is constructed according to the terms of the 'merchant world' it is for the updating of the career prospects of their graduates (42.3 per cent), information concerning the MBA and the courses they offer (17.9 per cent), the market on which the MBA programmes are in competition with each other (24.4 per cent), and finally, 15.4 per cent of the articles of the 'merchant world per se' is addressed to students and highlight advantages/costs economic analyses, analyses which should be first choice in an MBA level education.

Themes	Scientific reviews		Business magazines		Total	
	no.	%	no.	%	no.	%
Career prospects for the MBA	16	55.2	17	34.7	33	42.3
Information on courses offered	-	-	14	28.6	14	17.9
The MBA market	7	24.1	12	24.5	19	24.4
MBA advantages/costs	6	20.7	6	12.2	12	15.4
Total	29	100	49	100	78	100

Table 13.6 Distribution of the themes of the 'merchant world per se'

The Pedagogical Worlds

If we now dissect the subset of articles which subscribe to the logic of the pedagogical worlds which would serve the political ideal of the 'conceptual cities', it can be noted as Table 13.7 illustrates, that in 63.8 per cent of all the articles it is quite clearly the 'industrial world' which dominates the discursive space, as much in the university community (63.1 per cent) as in the journalistic fraternity (66.7 per cent). With regards to these articles, in a way the MBA is first and foremost if not essentially a service tool for the common good in the industrial arena, that is efficiency. This is the keyword, the ideal life favoured by the majority of authors of the articles studied. The common good is therefore the inevitable consequence of the efficiency which adherence to the 'industrial city' procures and if the MBA truly intends to subscribe to the pursuit of this ideal it must construct through osmosis or mimesis an Industrial pedagogical world.

Pedagogical world	Scientific reviews		Business magazines		Total	
	no	%	no.	%	no.	%
Inspired	-	-	-	-	-	-
Domestic	-	-	-	-	-	-
Civic	24	36.9	5	33.3	29	36.2
Opinion	-	-	-	-	-	-
Industrial	41	63.1	10	66.7	51	63.8
Merchant	-	-	-	-	-	-
Total	65	100	15	100	80	100

Table 13.7 Distribution of the articles according to the pedagogical worlds

In the construction of the 'industrial pedagogical world' the authors join forces around a single important theme which is obviously unifying, that is the improvement of study programmes in order to train even more efficient managers and in this way respond to the needs of businesses in terms of expertise.

In second place but very far behind the industrial space is the 'civic pedagogical world' in 36.3 per cent of the articles and based on three major themes as Table 13.8 illustrates. At first the authors reflected on the relevance of the teaching of ethics as an antidote to the fraudulent behaviours which more and more frequently punctuate the business news. Then they reflect on the necessity of education concerning the social responsibility of businesses with regards to the natural environment. Finally they note the consequences of the implantation of the MBA programmes in a variety of countries and suggest an adaptation of the contents of the courses to national cultures.

Themes	Scientific reviews		Business magazines		Total	
	no.	%	no.	%	no.	%
Education in ethics	5	20.8	5	100.0	10	34.5
Environmental responsibility	3	12.5	-	-	3	10.3
Adaptation of the education to the cultures	16	66.7	-	-	16	55.2
Total	24	100	5	100	29	100

Table 13.8 Distribution of the articles according to the 'civic pedagogical world'

Finally it was noted that the 'opinion', 'inspiration', 'domestic' and 'merchant' worlds were absent from the corpus of articles on the 'pedagogical' worlds. Can we conclude that management only has to have the logic of creativity, tradition, and recognition and that it keeps commercial reflection in isolation? Do the specific views of these pedagogical worlds have nothing to contribute to the debate on the relevance of the MBA? Will the debate be limited to a single encounter between two worlds, the 'civic' and 'industrial' worlds? In light of the results the answer seems to lean towards the affirmative. But before judging and coming to a too hasty conclusion concerning the reduction of the debate to a confrontation of only two worlds, it is advisable to regroup the 'worlds per se' and the 'pedagogical worlds' according to discursive logics.

The Rhetorical Influence of the Cities

If we combine the discursive logics used in the construction of the worlds per se and the pedagogical worlds in order to clarify the rhetorical influence of the Cities on the imagination of the authors of the entire corpus of study, as Table 13.9 illustrates only the rhetoric of the 'city of inspiration' does not participate in the debate.

It is also shown that by combining the worlds per se with the pedagogical worlds the rhetorical registers of the 'industrial' and 'merchant' cities totally dominate the dialogue space. With 12.1 per cent of the total articles, the civic register takes place way behind these two cities and as a result of this seems to be rather marginal in relation to the constitution of the corpus.

The cities	Scientific reviews		Business magazines		Total	
	no.	%	no.	%	no.	%
Inspired	-	-	-	-	-	-
Domestic	-	-	1	1.4	1	0.4
Civic	24	14.5	5	6.8	29	12.1
Of opinion	1	0.6	9	12.2	10	4.2
Industrial	112	67.5	10	13.5	122	50.8
Merchant	29	17.5	49	66.2	78	32.5
Total	166	100	74	100	240	100

Table 13.9 Distribution of the articles according to their discursive register

In terms of the description of the results, the war of the worlds therefore displays a confrontation between the ideal of efficiency of the 'industrial city', and the market as the common good. The ethic of the 'civic city' is therefore at the periphery of the debate.

INTERPRETATION OF THE DATA: THE WAR OF THE WORLDS

Enthusiasts of strong sensations, whose unbridled imagination is largely fed by Hollywood cinema through American television series, video games or gothic literature which cradles adolescents who dream of becoming Gandalf or Harry Potter, run the risk of being cruelly deceived. The announced war between the dark force which embodies soulless, master-less management, and the purity of the irreproachable, noble ideal of certain ethical discourses, obviously did not take place. At the very least this research seems to show that those who, since the beginning of the new millennium have been using the MBA as a subject of study, are very few in wanting to commit themselves to this path. Nonetheless, the WorldComs, Tycos, Enrons and so on of this world are not the poisonous fruit of a psychotic imagination battling against outbreaks of delirious fever which can no longer be stopped. These scandals are quite real and all those who work in business schools, if not affected by them, must have heard about them and been confronted with the consequent ethical discourse. Even the big pedagogical accreditation organizations – which no one would dare to place next to the critics – didn't they unanimously recommend that business schools introduce ethics in the MBA degree course? Finally, management gurus such as Mintzberg and Pfeffer – the demi-gods of administration's fine words – don't they recommend an inside out revision of the MBA and even to end it? Did we dream all of this? Could we be the victims of the *small university world*, that universe which is so quick to make of the slightest criticism a fox in the henhouse?

The distance between experimental life and the content of our corpus therefore truly has what it takes to surprise the most indifferent and objective researchers. Could it be possible that we have missed the debate? Could the subject have been so poorly constructed that hidden under the pile of our studies was what is essential and therefore obviously remained invisible to our eyes? Of course, the results demand this type of questioning but locking oneself in to the questioning and reducing the deception that they might arouse to something essentially methodological seems somewhat shallow in terms of argumentation, especially since this seems to do a disservice to the current debate. In fact, stating that when they make the MBA an object of study academics and business journalists don't make much of the ethical question, is taking an ethical stand and is a way of participating in the debate. This is not a negation or a lack of concern but simply the consequence of a universe, that of business schools which obviously see the common good in other terms besides those utilized by the tenants of the 'civic city'.

In light of the results of the research, we are forced to admit that if there is a war of the worlds it is certainly not the one we expected or banked on finding in the current literature. Ethics does not confront technique in the new edition of the mythical and singular combat between David and Goliath. No, it is not the 'civic' and 'industrial' cities which give in to combat but rather the 'merchant' and 'industrial' cities. This must be surprising enough to all those who far too often get them mixed up and merge the two. And yet, as compatible as they might be they couldn't have more distinct political projects and ideals of what constitutes the common good. Efficient technique, the fruit of a reason that is endlessly more instrumental and productive, is not the equivalent of the market mechanism which, like the law of universal gravity, demands that everything submit to the irresistible and ever invincible force of attraction. On the one hand there is the player and his freely expressed sovereignty in terms of technique, and on the other hand, an occult force, the market, which leaves no other choice to individuals but the mechanical adjustment in the great economic dance of supply and demand in the perpetual search for an improbable stable equilibrium.

In this war that must come to an end, the 'industrial city' is in command and dominates the pretenders to the central operator post of the MBA. Should we be surprised by this? From its beginning, as was alluded to in the opening anecdote of this text, wasn't the MBA a pure product of the 'industrial city'? Overflowing with the words of Frederick Winslow Taylor then with those of those other education engineers, such as Fayol and Mintzberg, legendary business school figures, can the MBA escape its condition of social engineering? Of course in a modern world which makes liberty the main foundation on which it builds, other choices and other cities may have been possible. The MBA could have and still can take other paths and serve other political ideals. Moreover, the mermaids of the 'merchant city' for which business magazine journalists largely take over the relay, sing their sweet song and more than one member of the business schools allow themselves to be seduced by it, to change direction and hoist the great sails towards this new Eden, rich with promises and a brilliant future. Nonetheless, in light of the corpus studied, the MBA is obviously not turning its back on its past and does not run the risk of running aground on the reefs of the merchant world. In the beginning it was industrial, it then acquired a place in the sun of the university system by developing its industrial logic, and remains faithful to its origins, come hell or high water. Still mainly founded on the technical efficiency of the Saint Simon ideal which is supposed to be the bearer of social progress, the MBA remains resolutely won over by the supposedly emancipating virtues of this political project. In fact the articles in the corpus show that the MBA is still the property of the 'industrial city'. On one hand it has a dominating percentage of the volume of articles produced, and on the other hand the other cities do not question its legitimacy and are content to demand adjustments, that is to say, a place in the shade of its walls. They demand consideration of ethics in the education of tomorrow's experts, then they highlight the relevance of reinforcing the reputation of the MBA by rankings which are aimed at purifying the educational scenery of programmes which are not brilliant in terms of serving the industrial cause, and later on they emphasize the necessity to develop greater merchant vigilance. So everything takes place as if the 'industrial city' could not be overthrown and that in order to survive the others only have to submit to its logic and therefore play the role of suburbs that are as disciplined as they are won over to the ideal of the efficiency of the unassailable metropolis. This is how the 'merchant city', while reducing the MBA to a worker reservoir, subscribes to the efficiency of the 'industrial city' which contributes to the added value of the diplomas which are therefore more easily placed on the market. In the same way, the corpus studied shows that in picking up on the idea of the relevance of teaching ethics the 'civic city' does not suggest a revision of the education and the logic of the MBA, at most it suggests an addendum, a necessary addition that is as useful as it is efficient. Finally, the 'opinion city' also speaks out but not in order to confront the dominant discourse but rather to double its symbolic force and thereby procure the ranking of the MBA.

Having said this, in the very heart of the imperial industrial city there is a diversity of views. There is significant difference especially between the scientific articles and reviews and those of the business magazines. In the latter, a lot of authors consider the MBA to be the royal path to management education and articles are written in a very descriptive style which consists of witnessing the benefits of the training especially by describing the MBA degree courses, providing information on the innovations or presenting the professional records of former graduates. The scientific reviews rather reflect on the contents of the programmes which is in keeping with the search for technical improvement of the education in relation to the competencies supplied to the future graduates.

There are also some ripples of rebellion within the 'industrial city'. Authors such as Mintzberg, Pfeffer and Fong question the MBA's capacity to fulfil their contract with the head institution of the 'industrial city', businesses. The critics don't spare the 'merchant city' which is accused of wanting to move away from the common good by reducing the MBA to the rank of a product designed to generate profits for business schools to the detriment of the quality of the contents. Neither do these critics spare the followers of the 'no man's land' world who are accused of a teaching that is unsuited to the demands of true efficacy, especially since they do research that is not related to the concerns of businesses, which they don't know sufficiently well, and as a result of this cannot adequately serve the one who in this regard should be their unique reason for existing and the pivotal foundation of their actions.

In the midst of this fratricidal debate between partisans of the 'industrial city' but also in that which reunites them and puts them against the apologists of the 'merchant city', the 'civic city' has made its bed and formed an alliance which some might see as abnormal, perverse and fundamentally sterile, with the 'industrial city'. In fact, while lifting the veil on the fraudulent behaviour of certain management practitioners and raising the subject of the risks inherent in an education that is strictly instrumental and technical, it allied itself to the 'industrial city' to harshly denounce the excesses of the market and suggested the integration of ethics in the classical MBA education system, an education which would not question the instrumental logic of the MBA anyway.

Even if the alliance with the 'civic city' in this way procures a certain moral support for the 'industrial city' in the war which puts it against the 'merchant city', the power of the 'civic city' is nonetheless very minor as is demonstrated by the fact that only 29 of the articles in the corpus are devoted to it, only 13 of which touch on the question of ethics and social responsibility. That only 4.4 per cent of the articles in the corpus highlight the moral aspect of the education and practice of management is enough to cause surprise if one should trust the rumours in the media that the economic frauds have generated in the whole society. This weak echo of the ethical questions can certainly not be explained by the lack of general interest in the content of the MBA education since the 'industrial city' uses it as one of its main defences as is demonstrated by all the articles for which improvement of the contents is the only saving creed. A weak explanation by the 'civic city' may be due to a certain internal perplexity of the city itself concerning the efficiency of such an education in making administrative behaviours the stamp of ethical considerations. This perplexity is expressed on different levels in three of the articles of the corpus of 293 which we classified. Lam (2004) asks the following question: 'Do business courses have any influence on the workplace environment?' In *Business Week*, Garten (2005) suggests that business schools should place more emphasis during selection interviews on the appreciation of ethical qualities that individuals demonstrate in their current life. In *Fast Company*, Deutschman (2005) promotes the use of a test perfected by a criminal psychology professor, during the recruitment of managerial staff since their MBA is not enough to guarantee moral values. Might we understand that while forming an alliance the 'civic city' keeps its guard up and actually does not place too much hope in the possible fruits that its collaboration might bring, even if it is only to counter the advances of the Merchant City which is in competition with the 'industrial city' for territorial supremacy? In the context of the corpus studied we can only make conjectures, but what is clear is that the civic city's alliance with its potential rival is only profitable to the latter.

Finally, in this latent war between the political cities it is at least notable that the 'inspiration city' is completely absent as if its discourse couldn't contribute to the debate. Unless the trait that is artistic and ferociously rebellious which characterises the 'inspiration city' is fundamentally incompatible with industrial urbanism which is one of the main concepts of the MBA, and that because of this it is unable to convince the members of business schools to be its spokespersons.

In terms of this resolutely and intentionally provocative discursive research, we can attempt to make a prediction on the way this war of the worlds will end. Of course, no one in this world is divine and pretending to have the prophetic powers of a modern Merlin would be, to say the least, socially very risky and epistemologically condemnable. Nonetheless, if all the same we cross the epistemological Rubicon and pass outside of the social taboos, you may bet that based on the long history of management sciences, the circumstantial alliance between the 'civic' and 'industrial' cities will only end with one winner, the 'industrial city'. The latter has always been able to assimilate the criticisms which throughout time have held it siege. In a way it has fed on and built itself directly on these criticisms which however, wanted to make it collapse into decline and oblivion. Like a technocratic Midas, everything it touches transforms into efficient techniques that still serve social engineering which raises instrumental efficiency to an ideal of life, an irresistible common good. Therefore the day when all the MBAs on earth offer technical courses in business ethics and when finally it is *business as usual* in the best of all worlds, is not far off.

NOTE

1. The list of articles is available on www.hec.ca/ recherche/ publications/ cahiers/ 2006/ 06-09.pdf.

BIBLIOGRAPHY

Amblard, Henri, Bernoux, Philippe, Herreros, Gilles and Livian, Yves-Frédéric (1996), *Les Nouvelles Approches Sociologiques des Organisations*, Éditions du Seuil, Paris.

Bennis, Warren J. and O'Toole, James (2005), 'How business schools lost their way', *Harvard Business Review*, **83** (5), 96.

Baechler, Jean (1971), *Les Origines du Capitalisme*, Gallimard, Paris.

Boltanski, Luc and Chiapello, Eve (1999), *Le Nouvel Esprit du Capitalisme*, Gallimard, Paris.

Boltanski, Luc and Thévenot, Laurent (1991), *De la Justification. Les Economies de Grandeur*, Éditions Gallimard, Paris.

Chiapello, Eve (1997), 'Les organisations et le travail artistique sont-ils contrôlables?', *Réseaux*, **86**, 77–113.

Deutschman, Alan (2005), 'Is your boss a psychopath?', *Fast Company,* **96**, 44–51.

Dupuy, Jean-Pierre, Eymard-Duvernay, François, Favereau, Olivier, Orléan, André, Salais, Robert and Thévenot, Laurent (1989), 'Introduction', *Revue Economique*, **40** (2), 141–145.

Ellul, Jacques ([1967], 1998), *Métamorphose du Bourgeois*, La table ronde, Paris.

Garten, Jeffrey E., (2005), 'B-Schools: only a C+ in ethics', *Business Week*, **3949**, 110.

Gaulejac, Vincent de (2005), *La Société Malade de la Gestion*, Editions du Seuil, Paris.

Lam, Che-fai. (2004). Understanding the Ethical Decisions and Behaviours of Hong Kong Business Managers: An Implication for Business Ethics Education. *Management Research News*, **27** (10), 69–77.

Mailhot, Chantal (2004), *La Gestion de la Recherche : le Cas d'un Partenariat Entreprise-Université*, Thèse de doctorat, HEC Montréal.

Mintzberg, Henry (2004), *Managers Not MBAs. A Hard Look at the Soft Practice of Managing and Management Development*, Berrett-Koehler, San Francisco, 464.

Pfeffer, Jeffrey and Fong, Christina T., (2004), 'The business school "business": some lessons from the US experience', *Journal of Management Studies*, **41**, 1501–1520.

Pfeffer, Jeffrey and Fong, Christina T., (2002), 'The end of business schools? Less success than meets the eyes', *Academy of Management Learning and Education Journal*, **1** (1), 78–95.

Polanyi, Karl and Arensberg, Conrad (1975), *Les Systèmes Economiques dans l'Histoire et dans la Théorie*, Larousse, Paris.

Pouget, Michel (1998), *Taylor et le Taylorisme*, PUF, Paris.

Thévenot, Luc (1989), 'Équilibre et rationalité dans un univers complexe', *Revue Economique,* **40** (2), 147–197.

Index